4446428200

D1758101

A Priori

WITHDRAWN
from
STIRLING UNIVERSITY LIBRARY

Central Problems of Philosophy
Series Editor: John Shand

This series of books presents concise, clear, and rigorous analyses of the core problems that preoccupy philosophers across all approaches to the discipline. Each book encapsulates the essential arguments and debates, providing an authoritative guide to the subject while also introducing original perspectives. This series of books by an international team of authors aims to cover those fundamental topics that, taken together, constitute the full breadth of philosophy.

AP
10
MAR

POP

A Priori

Edwin Mares

WITHDRAWN
from
STIRLING UNIVERSITY LIBRARY

Library
University of Stirling
STIRLING   FK9 4LA

McGill-Queen's University Press
Montreal & Kingston • Ithaca

01 0618557.

02.118

© Edwin Mares, 2011

ISBN 978-0-7735-3940-2 (cloth)
ISBN 978-0-7735-3941-9 (paper)

Legal deposit fourth quarter 2011
Bibliothèque nationale du Québec

This book is copyright under the Berne Convention.
No reproduction without permission.
All rights reserved.

Published simultaneously outside North America
by Acumen Publishing Limited

McGill-Queen's University Press acknowledges the financial support
of the Government of Canada through the Canada Book Fund for its
activities.

Library and Archives Canada Cataloguing in Publication

Mares, Edwin David
    A priori / Edwin Mares.

(Central problems of philosophy)
Includes bibliographical references and index.
ISBN 978-0-7735-3940-2 (bound).--ISBN 978-0-7735-3941-9
(pbk.)

    1. A priori. 2. Knowledge, Theory of. I. Title. II. Series:
Central problems of philosophy

BD181.3.M37 2011   121'.3   C2011-905272-5

Printed and bound in the UK by MPG Books Group.

For Sue

Contents

Preface

I had the idea for writing a book on a priori knowledge from giving a few lectures in a colleague's course on epistemology. I found the available books on a priori knowledge out of date or too difficult for undergraduates. I hope this book is more accessible.

I think the topic of a priori knowledge is a good one to teach to undergraduates. It helps to tie epistemology in with the other subjects that they are taught. It overlaps with ethics (especially with metaethics), logic, philosophy of science and metaphysics. I have tried, especially in the later chapters of this book, to make clear the connections between a priori knowledge and these other fields. Anyone who wishes to follow the radical empiricists and reject a priori knowledge should realize the repercussions for these other fields.

I did not write this book only for students. In it, I try to defend the idea that there is a priori knowledge. Often professional philosophers treat a priori justification as if it were something rather spooky. They associate it with Plato's doctrine of recollection or some sort of extra-sensory perception. My chapter on Aristotelian theories of a priori justification is supposed to help alleviate their fears. Many philosophers also remain suspicious of the analytic–synthetic distinction. There are, however, some good recent defences of analyticity. I try to present them in a manner that is accessible to working philosophers (who may not be epistemologists) as well as to students.

Chapters 9–12 are about applications of a priori knowledge. The purpose of these chapters, in addition to showing the importance of a priori knowledge, is to give a means for evaluating the various theories of a priori knowledge (or the rejection of it). The last chapter is a scorecard of how well all the theories do for their various applications. What I think it demonstrates is that it is unwise to accept a single theory of a priori justification. Different theories seem to work better in different fields of knowledge. It is one of my theses that we should (and can) adopt more than one theory of a priori knowledge.

I could have written much more on the subject. The role of the a priori in science, although discussed in the context of mathematical knowledge, deserves much more attention. I could have had a chapter on the use of thought experiments in science. Are these really a priori? What can they show us about *empirical* laws or theories? Similarly, there is a current interest in the methods used by philosophy itself, especially in metaphysics. Traditionally, it was thought that conceptual analysis is a priori, but Timothy Williamson has recently argued that it is not. I could have written another chapter on this topic. But one cannot include everything in one book, nor even every topic that has to do with a priori knowledge.

Acknowledgements

In writing this book, I have benefited from discussions with many other philosophers and several people have read the manuscript, either in sections or in its entirety. My greatest debts of this sort are to Stuart Brock and Carrie Jenkins, who both read and commented on the whole manuscript. I am also grateful to Nick Agar, Ismay Barwell, Max Cresswell, David Eng, Simon Keller, Francesco Orillia, Francesco Paoli and Adriane Rini, to the participants at the Conference on Continuity and Discreteness in Urbino, Italy, and to the philosophers of the universities of Macerata and Cagliari in 2009, where I presented parts of this book.

At Acumen, Steven Gerrard's editorial assistance was invaluable, as was Kate Williams's copy-editing. I am also grateful to Sue, Jesse, Tui and, of course, Zermela and Lola.

1 Introduction

1.1 What is a priori knowledge?

Consider the statement "Every coloured thing is extended in space". This seems obviously true. If we think about some things that have no length or breadth or depth, we see that they have no colours. Examples of such things are individual points in space and, at least according to traditional philosophy, thoughts. A point cannot have any colour and neither can a thought (although, of course, we can think about colours). But surveying such objects seems unnecessary. We do not have to check everything that has a colour to discover whether it is extended in space. It seems that we can just know this by thinking about it. Traditionally, philosophers have said that this is something that we can know a priori, that is, we can know it independently of experience. Thus, some philosophers say that we can know a priori that every coloured thing is extended. Our knowledge in this case is supposedly independent of experience.

Let us look at another example. Think of a geometrical figure with three straight sides. Let it also be closed: do not allow any gaps in it. How many angles does this figure have? You know the answer: it has three angles. You do not need to check real three-sided figures to make sure they have three angles. From a consideration of the nature of three-sided figures alone, you can know that they all have three angles. This is a priori reasoning.

Here is a partial list of the sorts of things that philosophers have held that we can know a priori:

- Analytic sentences: for example, "All bachelors are unmarried", "all vixens are foxes".
- Mathematical truths: for example, "$2 + 2 = 4$"; "for any natural number x greater than or equal to 3 there are no numbers w, y and z such that $w^x + y^x = z^x$".
- Moral principles: for example, "it is wrong to harm innocent people".
- Conceptual analyses: for example, "red is a colour and not a shape"; "nothing can be both red and green all over at the same time"; "every coloured thing is extended in space".
- Logical principles: for example, "S or not-S"; "not-(S and not-S)".

In this book we shall look at the issue of how we know these sorts of things. In Chapters 3–8 we shall examine theories of a priori knowledge and the view that there is no a priori knowledge. In Chapters 9–12 we shall look at various topics that are supposedly the object of a priori knowledge – morality, logic, mathematics, modality and philosophy itself – and apply the theories from the first half of the book to see how well these theories work.

1.2 What is so important about a priori knowledge?

Some philosophers deny that we can know anything a priori. In this book, I call these philosophers "radical empiricists" because they think that all knowledge is at least in some way empirical. But it is difficult to explain how we know some sorts of propositions empirically. Two categories of propositions stand out in this regard:

- Propositions that state necessary truths: for example, the proposition that it is necessary that $2 + 2 = 4$.
- Propositions that state norms of certain sorts: for example, the proposition that it is morally wrong to harm innocent people.

With regard to the first sort of proposition, my claim is not that it is difficult to explain how we can know empirically that $2 + 2 = 4$ is true, but rather that it is difficult to understand how we could know empirically that it is necessarily true. According to many philosophers, our experience of the world tells us what happens to be true; experience does not tell us what is necessary. These philosophers hold that there must be an a priori element in our knowing what is necessarily true. I discuss the topic of our knowing what is necessary or possible in Chapters 2, 10, 11 and 12, in my discussions of logical, mathematical and modal knowledge.

Similarly, many philosophers hold that we can know empirically what is the case; but experience alone does not tell us what should be the case. With regard to moral norms, it is difficult to see how they could be purely empirical. Perhaps, as J. S. Mill tells us, we all desire to be happy. But should we want to be happy? How could we find this out empirically?

Epistemology too has norms. It tells us what sorts of propositions we should accept and what sorts of justifications we should use. Clearly, empirical evidence can be relevant to epistemology, but what sort of empirical evidence can be used to determine whether (as reliabilists claim) we should only have beliefs that are produced by reliable processes or (as coherentists claim) we should only have beliefs that are supported by and support other beliefs? Empirical evidence may help us find out which beliefs are produced reliably and empirical investigation may help us find support for our beliefs, but the norms that tell us to find this evidence are not themselves purely empirical. And epistemological theories that we shall discuss contain norms such as these.

Of course there are other norms – legal norms, the rules of games and so on – that are accessible to us empirically. But to many philosophers morality and epistemology seem to be different. I discuss these topics in detail in Chapters 6 and 9.

Radical empiricists have not given in to this appeal to modal, moral and logical knowledge, although they have heard it many times. Often they deny that there are necessary truths or facts about what we should do. Sometimes they argue, with regard to both ethics and epistemology, that norms are facts about social *institutions*. An institution is something that people create, like a government or a club. These philosophers think of morality as a social institution, one that we perhaps do not consciously create, but a human creation nonetheless. On this view, moral norms can be discovered empirically by examining society and epistemological norms can be discovered by examining science. Thus they reject the jobs that a priori reasoning traditionally has been given. In Chapter 6, I look at radical empiricism and the attempt to do epistemology without the a priori. In Chapter 9 I look at radical empiricist views about ethics.

1.3 A note on "knowledge"

One problem with the topic of a priori knowledge is that it seems to require us to talk about *knowledge*. But the very definition of "knowledge" is one of the most controversial topics in epistemology, and it would be nice to avoid getting embroiled in this debate. Some philosophers talk about a priori "justification" instead of a priori knowledge. I talk a great deal in this book about justification, but we cannot just replace the notion of knowledge with that of justification. As we shall see in §1.4, there are two distinct notions of a priori knowledge and only one of them has to do with a priori justification. I use the term "knowledge" quite often in this book, but only in an intuitive sense. When there is reason to be more careful, I use "a priori belief" to indicate a belief that has a priori status.

As we shall see, a claim that a belief is a priori can mean one of two things. First, it may mean that its *justification* is in some way independent of experience. In other words, there is support for the claim that does not contain any data taken from experience. Second, the claim that a belief is a priori may mean that the belief cannot be refuted empirically. In such cases, we cannot use empirical data to prove that the belief is false.[1]

Note that these two notions of apriority are not exclusive. We could maintain that a belief is a priori if and only if it is justified independently of experience and cannot be falsified by experience. But I discuss the two basic notions independently of one another. In what follows, when I examine various conceptions of apriority I ask which sense of apriority is meant.

Both of these conceptions need further exploration, so let us look at them in more depth.

1.4 A priori justification

The first conception of the a priori holds that an a priori belief is one that is justified or at least capable of being justified independently of empirical evidence. But what sort of independence is this? We rarely, if ever, know anything completely independently of sense experience. Consider, for example, the analytic sentence "Every bachelor is unmarried". This is one of our paradigm examples of something that can be known a priori (if anything can be). But one cannot know that this sentence is true without knowing the meanings of the words contained in it. We learn the meanings of words by experience: we read them in a dictionary or we are told them by others, or by some similar experience.

Still, many philosophers hold that we can know the truth of this sentence a priori. One way of understanding this position is to make a distinction between the *enabling* and *justificatory* roles of experience. Having experience of a certain sort enables us to have the belief that this sentence is true and to justify this belief. This is the experience in which we learn the meanings of the words in the sentence. But, on this view, the justification of the belief that this sentence is true depends only on our understanding of the sentence.[2]

Any epistemology that allows for a priori knowledge, apart from strong forms of nativism (see Chapter 4), needs to distinguish between enabling and justifying. Otherwise, any claim about a belief being a priori might be undermined by the claim that we learn the concepts involved empirically.

There are two approaches that one can take to defining "a priori justification". First, one can give a general definition of what it is for a justification to be a priori, and then examine various theories of a priori justification to see whether they are adequate and, in particular, whether their form of justification satisfies the definition. Second, one can examine various theories of a priori justification and then extract from them particular definitions of what it means for a justification to be a priori. I take the second route.

The reason that I do not want to give a general definition is that it is very difficult to give a definition that is adequately general. Contrast, for example, a belief that the analytic sentence "All bachelors are unmarried" is true with an innate belief. The innate belief is independent of experience because it is unlearned.[3] The analytic judgement is independent of experience because grasping the meaning of the sentence is enough to see that it is true; we do not need to check any bachelors to confirm what it says. But its meaning is learned. In these two examples, we see two very different rationales for claiming that a belief is a priori. Now, I am not claiming that it is impossible to find a definition of a priori justification that adequately covers both of these cases, but I am saying that I do not think it is necessary to do so. If we decide that we want to take the term "a priori justification" as expressing several closely related concepts, it seems to do no serious harm to my project. So I leave it open as to whether there is a single definition of "a priori justification".

In this book, I look at specific theories of apriority. According to each of these (except radical empiricism), there are a priori beliefs. But the reasons why each of these theories claims that certain beliefs are a priori differ from one another. In each chapter I comment on these reasons and I consider whether they are adequate warrant to call a belief a priori.

1.5 Theories of justification

In this book I discuss various theories of a priori justification, such as Aristotelianism, analytic justification and self-evidence. Epistemologists usually think not just in terms of what an a priori justification needs to be like, but rather what a justification of any sort needs to be like. There are many general theories of justification, but the three that I discuss are *foundationalism*, *coherentism* and *reliabilism*.

According to foundationalism, there are basic beliefs. These are beliefs that either cannot or need not be justified. They are epistemologically basic in the sense that they are the foundation for the justification of other beliefs.

Coherentism incorporates a much less linear view of justification. Our beliefs form a mutually supporting whole. There are interconnections between beliefs that make each belief (and the system as a whole) justified. Coherentists define "justification" as follows: a belief is justified if it "fits into" a system of beliefs. In what is perhaps the most popular version of coherentism, a system of beliefs is a set of beliefs that explain one another. A belief fits into a system if it is explained by or explains other elements of the system.

In discussions of a priori justification, the notion of explanation used is often a generalization of our usual notion of explanation. Our normal notions of justification often include physical concepts such as causation. But, as we shall see in Chapter 11, coherence arguments are used to justify the claim that there are abstract mathematical objects: things that do not exist in time or space and so do not cause events in the normal sense.[4] What these abstract objects do is explain the nature of other propositions that one believes and help to create conceptual links for the agent. For example, in Chapter 11 I look at the use of the notion of a set (a special sort of collection) in mathematics. Many contemporary mathematicians and philosophers think that different objects discussed in mathematics – numbers, functions and so on – are sets. Having this belief justifies the use of properties that mathematicians know hold of sets to understand things about functions, numbers and other mathematical objects. I discuss coherence methods in a priori justification (and a priori falsification) often in this book.

One might think there is a serious tension between coherentism and the claim that there is a priori justification. If at least some of the beliefs in a belief set are empirical, and justification for the person who holds these beliefs amounts to fitting into this set, then it would seem that this justification is not independent of experience.[5] How serious this tension is depends on the exact view of coherence one accepts. But if one adopts a suitably subtle version of coherentism, one can avoid this difficulty. Consider, for example, our belief that $2 + 2 = 4$. This belief can predict and explain certain empirical beliefs. It can help to explain why you received the change you did when making a particular purchase. But such explanations might be *asymmetrical*. That is, the belief that $2 + 2 = 4$ might explain empirical beliefs, but not be explained by any empirical beliefs. In this case, the asymmetry might be used to account for why we can claim that the belief counts as a priori despite the fact that it coheres with a system of beliefs, some of which are empirical.

Reliabilists define "justification" in terms of how we come to have a belief. A belief is justified for reliabilists if it is produced by a reliable belief-forming process. Although we sometimes make errors because of what we perceive, our perceptual mechanisms are generally reliable (if we are not ill, or on drugs, and so on). Thus, our perceptual beliefs ("there is a chair over there", "this jersey is red" and so on) are justified.

We should, however, be careful to distinguish between reliabilism and the view that it is important to determine whether our belief-forming processes are reliable. Reliabilism entails the latter, but other epistemologies can hold that whether a means of justification is reliable is important. Coherentists, for example, sometimes hold that we try to accept only beliefs that are formed in reliable ways. Most of us have the belief that we should accept only beliefs that are formed in such ways. If we get into disputes with one another, we often question the reliability of the sources of their information. This sort of move in a debate has force because we believe that reliability is important. Coherentists claim that if we have such beliefs we should try to make our other beliefs cohere with them, that is, we should try to adopt only beliefs that we believe to be reliably supported.[6]

Similarly, reliabilists make use of coherence methods. If a coherence method is a reliable guide to the truth, then a reliabilist has to accept it as an appropriate method for justifying beliefs. Many reliabilists claim that some coherence methods provide good justifications.[7]

1.6 Immunity from empirical refutation

One property that is often connected with a priori beliefs is that they are immune from empirical refutation. This means that if we have an a priori belief then there is no empirical evidence that can show it to be false. Consider the definition of the word "bachelor" as "unmarried man". If you accept "a bachelor is an unmarried man" as a definition, then you take up the commitment to believe that every bachelor is unmarried and a man. If you come to believe that anyone is a married bachelor, say, you will not really reject the belief that all bachelors are unmarried; rather, you will have changed what you mean by "bachelor". Of course, we can decide to change how we define words, but no empirical evidence can prove that our definitions are incorrect.

Hartry Field takes immunity from empirical falsification to be the defining characteristic of an a priori belief. He says that if a proposition cannot be empirically refuted, we are (all other things being equal) entitled to believe it. His view is called the *entitlement theory of apriority*. Field adopts this view because he does not think there is any reasonable way of defining a priori justification. I think Field is wrong about a priori justification, but his view also seems to me to be viable.[8]

Other philosophers, such as W. V. Quine, have held that immunity from empirical refutation is central to a belief's being a priori. As we shall see in Chapters 5 and 6, Quine thinks that all our beliefs are vulnerable to empirical refutation. Here, let us look briefly at an argument due to Philip Kitcher for the same view. Consider, for example, a mathematical belief. Kitcher points out that if a large group of experts – in this case mathematicians – disagree with the belief, most of us would rationally take this as evidence against it. Clearly, the evidence that a large number of mathematicians disagree with a belief is empirical evidence. Thus, this belief is not immune to empirical refutation.

Clearly we can think up possible experiences like those in Kitcher's argument for any case of supposed a priori belief. We need to rule out such cases if we want to hold that the empirical immunity conception is reasonable. Field (2005) says that we should demand that in judging empirical immunity we need only consider "direct" evidence against the belief, rather than evidence about what people think of the belief. Field only claims that this is a "rough stab" at a response, but I think it is along the right lines.

Let us consider two short arguments. These arguments are for the rejection of my mathematical belief, but we can call them "justificatory arguments" since they justify the rejection of this belief.[9]

Let us use p to designate my belief that I am considering rejecting. Here is a more precise version of the first justificatory argument:

1. A large group of mathematicians believe not-p.
2. A large group of mathematicians believing not-p is good evidence for the belief that not-p.
3. I should believe whatever I have good evidence to believe (all things being equal).
4. Therefore, I should believe not-p.

The first premise is empirical. The second may be as well. It might even be supported by induction: in the past, perhaps, when a large group of mathematicians have believed something it has turned out to be right. Thus, we can say that the conclusion is supported by empirical premises. Consider, on the other hand, the following argument. Here q represent the proposition that the mathematicians have proved that contradicts p.

1. q
2. q implies not-p
3. Therefore, not-p

This argument represents the mathematicians' own reasoning for the rejection of p.[10] The premises of this argument are both a priori. Thus, the conclusion is justified completely a priori.

The first point to notice is that the conclusions are different. The conclusion of the first argument is about what my attitude should be with regard to p and the conclusion of the second tells me that p is false. We can apply Field's point here. The second argument provides us with direct evidence against p. The first argument gives us reason to reject p, but it is only indirect evidence against the truth of p.

By itself, the existence of the first argument does not undermine the claim that p cannot be refuted by empirical evidence. It is not p itself that is refuted by empirical evidence; it is the claim that I should believe that p that is falsified by empirical evidence. But the difference in conclusions can be made relatively unimportant by changing the way the first argument is presented. We can turn it from a deductive argument into an inductive argument:

1. A large group of mathematicians believe not-p.
2. In the past, when a large group of mathematicians have believed a mathematical proposition, it has usually been true.
3. Therefore, not-p.

This is not a deductively valid argument, but an inductively strong argument. Rewriting the argument as explicitly inductive in this way shows how the empirical evidence is supposed to bear on p itself, not just propositions about what one should believe.

The use of an inductive argument against p, however, is beside the point. The immunity conception does not say that we can have no empirical evidence against a priori beliefs. Rather, it says that a priori beliefs are consistent with any empirical evidence. Premises 1 and 2 of the above argument are logically consistent with the truth of p, even if they give us good reason to abandon the belief in p. For the large group of mathematicians may be wrong in this particular case.

Note that we can combine the immunity conception with the jus-tificational conception and hold that a belief is a priori if and only if it is justified by a priori means and immune from empirical refu-tation. Although this view is common in the history of philosophy, I do not think it is a good idea to combine the two conceptions. It makes a priori knowledge extremely hard to obtain.[11]

1.7 Plan of the book

My aim in the book is to give a survey of views concerning a priori knowledge, but also to convince the reader that we do know some things a priori. In the twentieth century the a priori was looked on with suspicion. There was a revolt against the speculative phi-losophy of the nineteenth century and there was a movement back to empiricism. Even though the empiricists of the early twentieth century did not completely eschew a priori knowledge, they mar-ginalized it. In the middle of the century, Quine attacked the idea that there is anything that we know a priori and his criticisms were taken by many to have been conclusive. Now, however, we see a re-emergence of the idea of a priori knowledge. My aim, in part, is to support this resurgence.

I also wish to make available and support certain theories of the a priori. In particular, my classification of certain positions as "Aristotelian" is non-standard, but I think edifying. I think these positions, which include Aristotle's, Locke's, Hume's, Russell's and Husserl's views, as well as those of certain contemporary philoso-phers such as Laurence BonJour, can be seen to have very important similarities. I think that Aristotelianism, moreover, can be used as an epistemology of mathematics, of modality, and of the a priori elements of natural science.

I am not, however, an advocate of only one theory of the a priori. We may have beliefs that are a priori in ways different from one another and we may need more than one theory of the a priori to explain them all.

The book is divided into three parts. Part I consists of this chap-ter and the next. These introduce the reader to the central issues involved in the debate about a priori knowledge. Part II consists of Chapters 3–8. In these, I discuss various theories of a priori know-ledge: rationalism, nativism, analyticity, radical empiricism (the rejection of a priori knowledge), Kantianism and Aristotelianism. In Part III, I apply these theories to a range of types of knowledge that have traditionally been considered to be a priori: moral knowledge, logical knowledge, mathematical knowledge and modal knowledge.

Further reading

Albert Casullo's *A Priori Justification* (2003) is a very good, although rather technical, survey of contemporary views about a priori justification. Laurence BonJour's *In Defense of Pure Reason* (1998) also contains a good survey of views concerning the a priori.

Hartry Field's entitlement view is presented in his articles "Recent Debates about the A Priori" (2005) and "Epistemological Nonfactualism and the A Prioricity of Logic" (1998).

Philip Kitcher's rejection of the a priori is in the first two chapters of his *The Nature of Mathematical Knowledge* (1985).

A good survey of contemporary theories of knowledge is BonJour's *Epistemology* (2002). For a good book on the debate between internalists and externalists, see BonJour and Ernest Sosa, *Epistemic Justification* (2003).

2 Necessity and certainty

2.1 Taking care of business

This chapter has two purposes. First, it is a housekeeping chapter. In Chapter 1, I asserted that there is a close tie between necessity and apriority: it seems that all our knowledge of necessities is a priori. In this chapter I set out a framework for talking about necessity: possible-world semantics. I also discuss theories of propositions. I do so because in later chapters we appeal to the notion of a proposition quite often.

The second purpose of this chapter is to discuss further the relationship between necessity and the a priori, and I introduce another property that a priori beliefs are supposed to have: certainty. I present and discuss two famous arguments due to Saul Kripke that attempt to complicate the connection between apriority and necessity. One shows that there are necessities that we know a posteriori (i.e. empirically) and the other shows that there are contingent propositions that we know a priori. Neither of these arguments, I suggest, endanger the claim that a priori knowledge is intimately involved in all our knowledge of necessities. But both arguments are interesting and important, and force us to be careful about the link between apriority and necessity.

I then look at the link between the a priori and certainty. Traditionally, and according to some contemporary philosophers, since a priori justification does not require any input from "outside", it must be certain. But most contemporary philosophers want to deny this. Some, like BonJour, claim that it is empirically defeasible. We will look at this view in later chapters. What we shall examine here is the claim that certain of our a priori beliefs are a priori defeasible, that is, they can be undermined by other a priori beliefs.

The chapter ends with a discussion of Hilary Putnam's contextualism about the a priori. He claims that certain beliefs can be contingently a priori, that is, a priori in one context and empirically defeasible in another context. This view might be right, although it is not clear that his argument for it shows that it is.

2.2 The framework: possible worlds

I discuss problems concerning necessity throughout this book. In order to do so, it will be convenient to have a theory of necessity to frame these problems and proposed solutions to them. The standard theory of necessity is currently *possible-world semantics*, and we adopt that as a framework.

According to possible-world semantics, there is a set of possible worlds. A possible world is a way the universe might have been. In different possible worlds, different propositions are true. For example, in some possible worlds there are tap-dancing dogs, in others Newton's physics is true and so on.

Given a set of possible worlds, we can define many different sorts of necessity. There are restricted and unrestricted necessities. As an example of a restricted form of necessity, consider the laws of nature. These are supposed to be necessarily true. For example, it is necessarily true that the speed of light in a vacuum is 299,792,458 metres per second. This is a statement not just about what is the case, but about what must be. It is about what is necessary. In order to deal with this sort of necessity – physical or "nomic" necessity – we need a set of possible worlds and an *accessibility relation*. We say that a world w_2 is nomically accessible from another world w_1 if and only if the laws of nature of w_1 are true in w_2. We then give the following truth condition for statements about physical necessity:

> In w, "it is physically necessary that S" is true if and only if S is true in every world nomically accessible from w.

From the point of view of our own world, only certain other worlds are physically possible. These are worlds that obey the laws of nature that are in our world. But there can be other possible worlds that have laws of nature different from our own.

Consider the worlds described by some science-fiction story, such as *Star Trek* or *Star Wars*. In both of these stories it is possible to travel faster than the speed of light. In *Star Trek* spaceships are able to warp space–time, in effect to bring things closer to them, and in *Star Wars* there are other dimensions, known as hyperspace, in which one can move faster than the speed of light. It is likely that neither hyperspace nor faster-than-light motion is possible in our own universe. So the worlds described by *Star Trek* and the worlds described by *Star Wars* are not physically possible relative to our world. Yet they are metaphysically possible.

There is a form of necessity, however, that does describe what is true in all possible worlds. Philosophers call this *metaphysical necessity*. Thus, we have the following truth condition for metaphysical necessity:

> In *w*, "it is metaphysically necessary that *S*" is true if and only if *S* is true in every possible world.

Here are some examples of propositions that are supposed to be metaphysically necessary:

- Red is a colour.
- Red is not a shape.
- Every coloured thing is extended.
- Two is a larger number than one.
- If it exists, the planet Venus is identical to itself.

These metaphysically necessary propositions are the sorts of propositions we shall be concerned with when we talk about a priori knowledge of necessary truths. We shall not be concerned with, say, the laws of physics. We shall, however, discuss the role of a priori knowledge in science in Chapters 8 and 11, but not in relation to the necessity of laws of nature.[1]

Possible-world semantics also gives us a nice treatment of statements about what is possible. For a restricted form of necessity we have:

In w, "it is possible that S" is true if and only if in some world accessible from w, S is true.

In the unrestricted form of necessity we have:

In w, "it is possible that S" is true if and only if in some world S is true.

Possible-world semantics is appealing because it gives a *compositional* analysis of the truth conditions of statements about necessity and possibility. A theory of truth is compositional if and only if in it the truth or falsity of complex sentences is determined by the truth or falsity of the sentences that make them up. Consider the sentence "The moon is made of green cheese and mice want to eat the moon". This sentence is made up of the two sentences "The moon is made of green cheese" and "Mice want to eat the moon", so it is a complex sentence. Moreover, its truth or falsity is determined by the truth or falsity of these two sentences and the meaning of the word "and". Our theory of truth has the rule:

In w, "S_1 and S_2" is true if and only if S_1 is true in w and S_2 is true in w.

If we know this rule, then we can conjoin any two sentences, the truth-values of which we know, and be able to determine the truth-value of the complex sentence. This explains how we learn how to evaluate the truth or falsity of complex statements that we have never heard before. Turning to statements about necessity, although we may not know for a given sentence S whether it is true in all possible worlds, we can understand what it would mean for it to be so. Understanding what it would mean for a statement to be true is at least one part of what it is to understand the statement. Thus, a compositional theory of truth can play an important part in a theory of how we understand statements.

We now have a framework for talking about necessity: possible-world semantics. But what are possible worlds? I have said that they are ways the world might have been, but this leaves much room for interpretation. Philosophers have held a very wide range of views about the nature of possible worlds. Concrete realists, such as David

Lewis, hold that possible worlds are parallel universes. They contain real things such as you, me and the planets. They have space and time, too. There are moderate realists who hold that possible worlds are abstract objects, like properties. They are ways the world could have been, but they are not really physical universes like our own. There are also anti-realists, who hold that possible worlds are mental constructs or fictions of some sort. I do not try to decide in this book. In another book my colleague Stuart Brock and I (Brock & Mares 2007) discuss the metaphysics of possible worlds in some depth, and I discuss this topic again in Chapter 12. My current concern is the use of possible worlds in epistemology.

2.3 Propositions

Now that we know what possible-world semantics is, we can also introduce the notion of a *proposition*. One of the difficulties in understanding the debates about a priori knowledge is in understanding what the objects of this sort of knowledge are. Sometimes, it would seem that what we know is that a particular sentence is true, but sentences often do not fit as objects of knowledge.

Consider the sentence "I am Ed". When I say it, this sentence is true. Unless you are an Ed, if you say it, it is false. But you might know that what I am saying when I say it is true. If I say "I am Ed" and you agree with me, it would seem that there is something that we both believe. It is not the sentence. It is what the sentence expresses. This is called a *proposition*.

In the philosophical literature there are various theories of propositions. There are theories of structured propositions and theories of unstructured propositions. An unstructured proposition is a set of possible worlds. For example, the unstructured proposition expressed by the sentence "Dogs bark" is the set of worlds in which dogs bark. The theory of unstructured propositions is extremely useful for logic. We can use it, for instance, to define the relationship of entailment between propositions: one proposition entails another if the first is included within (i.e. is a "subset of") the second.

The theory of structured propositions is a bit more complicated. According to the theory of structured propositions, a proposition contains entities that correspond to various parts of the sentences or thoughts that express them. For example, the statement "Zermela barks" represents a proposition that contains *Zermela* and *the property of barking* as constituents. We can represent this structured proposition as <Barking, Zermela>.

Some philosophers think that structured propositions are preferable to unstructured propositions to represent the objects of belief because they are finer grained. Two statements that are logically equivalent represent the same unstructured proposition. For example, a statement of the form "Not both *A* and *B*" is logically equivalent to a statement of the form "Not-*A* or not-*B*".

Two such statements are true in all of the same possible worlds. Hence they represent the same unstructured propositions. But they represent different structured propositions. Where α is the structured proposition represented by *A* and β is the structured proposition represented by *B*, "not both *A* and *B*" expresses the proposition <Not, <And, <α, β>>>, and "not-*A* or not-*B*" expresses <Or, <<Not, α>, <Not, β>>>. Thus, it is easier to explain, using structured propositions, how a person can believe that it is not both the case that *A* and *B* without believing that not-*A* or not-*B*.

Now consider the sentence "If I exist, I am Ed". Clearly, if I say this, it is true and if you say it (and are not an Ed) then it is false. Suppose that I say it. Then on the occasion in which I say it, it expresses the same proposition as the sentence "If Ed exists, Ed is Ed". This proposition is necessarily true, and (I contend) it can be known a priori. But the sentence "If I exist, I am Ed" sometimes expresses a true proposition and sometimes expresses a false proposition. It depends on who says it. We shall return to this topic in the next section.

It might seem that the theory of structured propositions has an advantage over the theory of unstructured propositions when it comes to explaining the objects of belief. The theory of structured propositions can distinguish between beliefs that are logically equivalent in terms of their contents. But this advantage may not be quite so clear. People who hold the theory of unstructured propositions may distinguish between these beliefs not in terms of their contents, but in terms of the way in which they are believed.

For example, consider someone's belief that the square root of 4 is 2. In the theory of structured propositions, we can distinguish between the proposition <Identity, <2, 2>> (which is just the belief that 2 is identical to itself) and the proposition <Identity, <<square root, 4>, 2>>, which includes the function of square root as an element in the proposition. The proponent of unstructured propositions can say that the difference between these two beliefs is not in their content but rather in how the person comes to believe them. If she just knows by rote that the square root of 4 is 2, then we might represent her belief as being the belief that 2 is identical to itself. On the other hand, if she understands what "square root" means and she comes to believe that the square root of 4 is 2 because she computes it, then we can say that her belief is about the square-root function as well as being about 4 and 2. But the real difference for the unstructured proposition theory is the way in which the proposition is believed rather than in the proposition that is believed. The proposition is just the set of all possible worlds in both cases.

In this book, I use structured propositions since they are more convenient. But this does not indicate a real commitment on my part to the view that there are structured propositions. Rather, I think that the theory of unstructured propositions together with a view about how we think about them can do just as well.

In the next section we look at another element of semantic theory that I employ in this book.

2.4 Double indexing

One semantic technique that I use (especially in Chapter 5) is double indexing. In §2.3 above, we already saw this technique in use.

Consider the sentence "It is now 1:12am". When I wrote that sentence, it was true. The time at which I wrote that sentence makes up part of the *context of utterance* of that sentence. An utterance of a sentence is the saying, writing or signing (etc.) of that sentence. A single sentence (or, more precisely, a sentence *type*) can be uttered many times. Various elements go into making up a context of utterance. For example, the person uttering the sentence is an element in the context, and so is the time and place at which it is uttered. In order to interpret words like "I", we need to know who utters the sentence. To interpret words like "now", "yesterday" and so on, we need to know the time of utterance. And to interpret words like "here", "there", "ten kilometres away" and so on, we need the place of utterance. The place of utterance is also useful in interpreting the sentence given above, since it determines what is meant by "1:12am": the place determines the time zone of the utterance.

The context of utterance, together with the sentence itself, determines the proposition that is expressed. In order to determine whether that proposition is true, we need a *context of evaluation*. A context of evaluation is a possible world at which a proposition is true or false. For example, consider the sentence "If I exist, I am Ed". As stated by me it expresses the proposition that is also represented by "if Ed exists, Ed is Ed". This proposition is true in all possible worlds.

2.5 Necessary a posteriori propositions

I said in Chapter 1 that it is difficult to understand how our knowledge that certain propositions are necessarily true could be empirical. It is, however, currently commonplace to claim that there is empirical knowledge of this sort. The central argument for this claim is due to Kripke.

Note that no one has ever claimed that any proposition that is necessarily true can only be known a priori. It is uncontroversial that some propositions that are necessarily true can be known empirically. As we shall see in Chapters 5 and 10, most philosophers hold that all sentences of the form "either S or not-S" are necessarily true. But we can know empirically, for example, that either it is raining or it is not raining. Right now, by looking out of my window I can see that it is not raining. So I know, using a little logic, that either it is raining or it is not raining. Thus I can know some proposition S empirically and, moreover, S is necessarily true. But I do not know empirically *that S* is necessarily true.

In order to understand Kripke's argument, we first need some theoretical background. The argument concerns a type of linguistic expression called a "natural-kind term". The terms "gold", "wood", "dog" and "musk ox" are all natural-kind terms. They are supposed to cut nature at its joints. They are supposed to pick out real divisions in nature. For contrast, think of the phrase "comfortable chair". I think my favourite chair is comfortable, but my partner thinks it is too soft. What counts as a comfortable chair depends on who is talking about it and in what context. It does not pick out a real distinction in nature.

Kripke's example concerns the sentence "It is necessarily true that water is H_2O". Both "water" and "H_2O" are natural-kind terms. According to Kripke, what makes water a natural kind is that every bit of water has the same internal structure. This internal structure is that of being made up of molecules that are two atoms of hydrogen bonded to one of oxygen. This is the *essence* of water. To be water is to have this internal structure, in any possible world. Thus, Kripke claims that "Water is H_2O" is necessarily true.

Moreover, he claims that we know this empirically. Here is a reconstruction of his argument:

1. Water is H_2O.   (empirical fact)
2. "Water" and "H_2O" are natural-kind terms.
3. Any identity that holds between two natural-kind terms is necessarily true.
4. Therefore, "Water is H_2O" is necessarily true.   (by 1,2,3)
5. Therefore, we know empirically that "Water is H_2O" is necessarily true.   (by 1–4)

I think that this argument is sound, but I do not think it undermines the claim that without a priori knowledge it is difficult (or even impossible) to understand how we know necessities. The issue concerns lines 2 and 3 of this argument.

First let us look at line 2. How do we know that "water" and "H_2O" are natural-kind terms? I think we know this a priori. This might seem strange, since we learn the meanings of phrases, including these phrases, empirically. These phrases, however, are natural-kind terms by the stipulation of the English-speaking community. That we stipulate rather than discover something to be true makes it in that sense a priori.

Now let us turn to line 3. How can we know that identities between natural-kind terms must be necessary? If we know it at all, we know it a priori. Natural-kind terms, according to Kripke, refer to the inner structure of things, regardless of how we subjectively understand them. The word "water" refers to the real inner chemical structure of water, regardless of whether people are ignorant of that inner structure. Kripke claims that natural-kind terms are rigid designators: they refer to the same inner structure in all worlds. This idea captures the idea that they refer to that inner structure regardless of what we know about particular natural kinds. So, "water" and "H_2O" both refer to the same thing in all possible worlds, so the sentence "Water is H_2O" is necessarily true. The reasoning that arrived at this conclusion is entirely a priori. It is difficult to see how it could be otherwise. So, both lines 2 and 3 of the inference, if they are known at all, are known a priori.

This means that Kripke's argument does not show that there are any necessities that are known completely empirically: a priori knowledge is involved in some way.

2.6 Contingent a priori propositions

Kripke also claims that certain propositions that we know a priori are merely contingently true. A proposition is contingently true if it is possible but not necessary. That there are a priori contingencies is not a threat to the view that we need a priori reasoning to know necessary truths. Although this argument does not pose a threat to any views that I hold, it is an interesting argument, and it is important in the debate over the relationship between necessity and apriority.

In order to understand the argument, we need to remember the distinction between the meaning and reference of an expression. The meaning of an expression is what we understand when we interpret what is said. The meaning of an expression is something that determines the referent of the expression in every possible world. The meaning of a name, for example, is a just a mapping from each world to the thing that the name refers to in that world. What the name refers to in each world is a thing, person, place or some other sort of entity.

Let us call the first person born in 2020, if there is one, by the name "Tui" (I pick a unisex name because we do not know whether it will be a boy or girl).[2] So we know that:

> If there is a unique first person born in 2020, then Tui will be born in 2020.

We know this a priori because we have stipulated that we shall call that person Tui. But it is not a necessary truth that the first person born in 2020 will be Tui (or even that whoever is born first in 2020 will be called "Tui").

What is going on here is that the phrase "first person born in 2020" *fixes the reference* of the name "Tui". Because of our stipulation that we are using this name in this way, our use of "Tui" refers to the person who happens to be born first in 2020. Once the referent of the name "Tui" is determined, our statements that include this name express particular propositions. For example, the sentence "Tui will be born in 2020" expresses the proposition <is born in, <Tui, 2020>>.

In this representation of the proposition, "Tui" represents not the word, but the person. It is a contingent fact that this person is (or will be) born in 2020. This statement is true if and only if the person named by "Tui" is the first person born in 2020. The fact that the name refers to a person if and only if that person is the first person born in 2020 is a feature of how the name refers. The connection between the name "Tui" and 2020 does not enter into all the facts about the person who is (or will be) called "Tui".

This argument is interesting for us, not only because it shows that being known a priori does not entail that a proposition is necessarily true, but also because it shows that some statements made true by our stipulations are not necessarily true. We shall return to this topic in Chapter 5.

2.7 Certainty and the a priori

Now we turn to the other traditional property of a priori beliefs: certainty. There are three notions of certainty that are important in epistemology. The first is the notion of a belief that is given a very *high degree of credence*. That is, we feel very sure of some of our beliefs. Right now, I am certain that I am in a room and writing my book. But we should distinguish this notion from the concept of infallibility and the concept of a belief that it is not rational to revise. A belief that is infallible is one that cannot be false. For example, it may be that it makes no sense for us to hold that an analytic sentence is false. But although I feel certain now that I am in a room writing a book, it might make sense for me in a minute to come to believe that I was wrong. Suppose that I suddenly think I see an elephant in the room. Then it would make sense to think that I am dreaming and not writing this book. So we might attribute a very high degree of credence to a belief without claiming that it is infallible.

The notion of a belief that it does not make sense to revise is one that I shall discuss later in this chapter. In this section, I discuss the claim that a priori justification is infallible.

Before we talk about the truth of this claim, we should distinguish between two versions of the opposing view. One might hold that no a priori beliefs are infallible or merely that not all a priori beliefs are infallible. To say that all a priori beliefs are fallible is to hold that for each a priori belief, we could imagine some evidence (empirical or a priori) that would show us that it is false. I am not sure that anyone holds this view. But many philosophers hold the view that it is possible to refute at least some beliefs with a priori justification.

Descartes held that what we come to believe through a process of a priori justification is infallible. He held that if we apply his method correctly, we are guaranteed to produce true beliefs. We shall discuss Descartes' view at length later. Some contemporary philosophers also hold that whatever a priori knowledge we have must be infallible. Kitcher writes: "If a person is entitled to ignore empirical information about the type of world she inhabits, then that must be because she has at her disposal a method that guarantees true belief" (1985: 30).

It is not clear, however, that the use of a priori justification entitles us to ignore empirical information if any were to arise. It might be that there is no possible empirical information in a particular case, but although we might still have some method for justifying beliefs of the relevant kind, it may not be conclusive. Moreover, in some cases there might be non-empirical reasons to reject a belief that was originally adopted for a priori reasons. For example, if we adopt a theory – say, a foundation for mathematics – because it is the best one we have thought up, and then later a simpler or more powerful foundation is devised by a mathematician, we would be entitled to adopt the latter for a priori reasons.

In contemporary theories of apriority, it is common to hold that a priori beliefs are fallible. Many of those who hold versions of the justificational conception of the a priori take a priori justification to be defeasible. As we shall see in Chapter 3, BonJour holds that some of our a priori beliefs are empirically defeasible. Even some of those philosophers who hold empirical immunity conceptions of the a priori allow a priori beliefs to be fallible (although not empirically falsifiable). But some traditional theories, such as Descartes' view, claim that at least some of our a priori beliefs are certain (see e.g. Chapter 3).

Certainty is difficult to come by. If we insist that a priori justification provide us with certainty, we are going to have to admit that we rarely have a priori justification. This will marginalize its role in epistemology. Moreover, in many paradigm cases of a priori justification, it seems that we can go wrong. One of the more common examples is that of a long proof in mathematics. We might think that we have followed all the steps and seen that the proof is correct. It would seem, then, that we are justified in believing the conclusion of the proof. But suppose that there is a slip at one step and the proof is wrong. This has happened to me and to everyone else who works in mathematics or logic.

One might reply that an incorrect proof is not a justification of its conclusion. It might appear to be a justification, but it is not a real justification. Although I think this move makes justification too difficult, let us grant it for the moment and change the example. Many proofs begin with some assumptions about the mathematical structures that the proof is about. These assumptions might have been reached by an a priori insight into the nature of the structures, but been wrong. Let us look at an example due to Alvin Plantinga.

A function on the real numbers is a mapping from real numbers (the decimal numbers) to real numbers. For example, the function x^2 takes a number r and returns the result of multiplying r by itself. Recall graphing functions from school mathematics classes. We call a function "continuous" if its graph does not have any breaks in it. The function x^2 is continuous, but a function $f(x)$ defined by "if x is less than 3, then $f(x) = 0$, and if x is 3 or greater than 3, then $f(x) = 1$" is not continuous. At 3, the value of the function jumps from 0 to 1. This function is continuous over numbers less than 3 and numbers greater than 3. It is only discontinuous at 3. Someone might think that a function that is defined on all the numbers must be continuous over some interval. In the nineteenth century, however, functions were discovered that are defined everywhere on the real numbers but are not continuous anywhere. For example, this is true of the function that gives the value 1 to any rational number (a number that can be defined by the ratio of two natural numbers) and the value 0 to any irrational numbers (decimal numbers that cannot be defined by any such ratio). Between any two rational numbers there is an irrational number and between any two irrational numbers there is a rational number. So this function jumps from 0 to 1 or 1 to 0 at every point.

This example is supposed to show that our a priori insight is fallible. Once again we may reject this example on the basis that we do not have real insight when we are incorrect. Kitcher's definition of a priori justification that we examined in Chapter 1 says that we can only be a priori justified when we believe true propositions. If we have an epistemology that claims in general that we are justified only when we believe truths, then it seems reasonable to hold this about a priori justification. But Kitcher thinks this is a unique feature of a priori justification and does not hold of empirical justification. If we can avoid making this distinction, we should. Justification is supposed to confer something important on beliefs. If fallible processes can do so for empirical beliefs, why not for a priori beliefs?

2.8 A priori defeasibility

As we saw in Chapter 1, some philosophers hold that a belief is a priori in virtue of its being empirically indefeasible. But some of these philosophers, such as Field, also believe that a priori beliefs are defeasible. This combination of views is possible; one can hold that some beliefs can be undercut by *a priori reasoning*.

The clearest cases of a priori undercutting occur when a theory is shown to be internally inconsistent. As we shall see in Chapter 10, not every philosopher thinks that this is a reason to abandon a theory, but the vast majority of philosophers and mathematicians do think that it is conclusive. Theories that have turned out to be inconsistent have been proposed several times in the history of mathematics. We shall look at one such example in Chapter 11.

Another sort of a priori undercutting comes about when a theory is proposed and then a theory with stronger *theoretical virtues* comes about as a replacement. This happened with regard to calculus. Before the advent of calculus, speed was calculated by dividing the distance a thing has moved over a time period by the duration of that time period. The notion of speed at an instant in time made no sense. Isaac Newton introduced calculus because his physics required there to be speeds (and especially accelerations) at instances in time. He did so by using *infinitesimals*. An infinitesimal is an infinitely small quantity. He calculated the speed of a thing at an instant of time by determining the distance that it travels over an infinitesimal duration of time around that instant. The notion of an infinitesimal does the theoretical job that it is supposed to do. We also know now that the theory of infinitesimals is consistent.[3] But the notion of an infinitely small quantity is unintuitive. In the late nineteenth century, mathematicians came up with an alternative version of the calculus, which uses only real numbers (the decimal numbers) and rejects the idea of there being infinitely small quantities. This theory is much more intuitive than the theory of infinitesimals and is preferred by the vast majority of mathematicians today.

Among the virtues theories can have are intuitiveness, strength (they can explain more than rival theories) and simplicity. We often rank theories on the basis of how much of these virtues they have.

The epistemological status of the use of theoretical virtues to determine what to believe is controversial. Many coherentists think their use is integral to the notion of justification. As we saw in Chapter 1, many coherentists think that justificatory relationships between beliefs are explanatory relationships. A belief coheres with other beliefs, on this view, if it explains and is explained by these other beliefs. For them, a good explanation may appeal to the theoretical virtues of the beliefs doing the explaining. The status of theoretical virtues in foundationalism and reliabilism, however, is much more tenuous.

2.9 Contextualism

In his "Philosophy of Physics" (1979), Hilary Putnam argues that some beliefs can be considered at certain times to be a priori and considered at other times to be empirical. Putnam uses the empirical immunity notion of apriority that I discussed in Chapter 1. His claim is that in some historical contexts a belief can be refuted empirically, but in other contexts it cannot be. This is why Putnam's view is known as "contextualism".[4]

His argument appeals to an example that I shall discuss in various places in this book, so I go into it in some depth here.

A geometrical theory – or "a geometry", as it is more commonly called – is a set of postulates about things such as lines and points. Before 1916, Euclidean geometry was used by physicists to represent the nature of space. After 1916, with Einstein's discovery of the general theory of relativity, Euclidean geometry was no longer used to describe space. Instead, another geometrical theory – Riemannian geometry – was taken to be an accurate description of space.

The problem with Euclidean geometry concerns its fifth postulate, also known as the "parallel postulate". I shall not state the parallel postulate in its original form, but rather in the form of Playfair's axiom, which is simpler. It says that if we have a plane (a two-dimensional space) and a line in this plane, then through any point in the plane that is not on that line there is one and only one line that we can draw parallel to that first line (see Fig. 2.1).

According to general relativity, gravity works by bodies curving space. Consider again a two-dimensional space, but this time think of it as being like a rubber sheet. Heavy things (such as planets) sink into this sheet. When other things roll past the heavy bodies they tend to roll down the curve in the sheet towards them. This is just a rough analogy, but I hope you get the idea.

The key feature of this view for us is that space itself can be curved. Parallel lines work very differently on curved surfaces than they do on flat ones. Think of a straight line as the shortest distance between two points. In modern geometry we call a straight line in this sense a "geodesic", but I shall use the more colloquial phrase "straight line". Now consider a simple curved surface: the surface

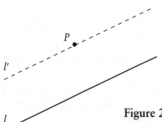

Figure 2.1 Through the point P there is one and only one line that is parallel to l, that is, l'.

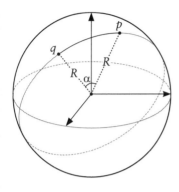

Figure 2.2 The shortest distance between points p and q on the surface of the sphere is a segment of the great circle passing through p and q.

of a sphere. The shortest distance between two points is always a segment of a *great circle*.

The line from q to p in Figure 2.2 is a segment of a great circle. But consider a point on this sphere not on this line, such as the north pole of the sphere. How many great circles can be drawn through that point that are parallel to the line through q and p? None. All great circles intersect with one another. Reimannian geometry, although more complicated than spherical geometry, is somewhat like this. When used in the theory of relativity, in the parts of space that are curved by heavy bodies such as the sun, there may be no parallel lines. Thus, according to relativity theory, the parallel postulate is not true of actual space.

The claim that Euclidean geometry is an accurate description of physical space was supposedly empirically falsified during an eclipse in 1919. As we shall see in Chapter 7, Michael Friedman claims that the data from that eclipse does not in fact contradict Euclidean geometry as a description of space. But we shall set Friedman's view aside for now. Figure 2.3 is a diagram of what occurred. The star behind the sun appears to have moved from its original position because the light from it is bent by the curving of space, which is caused by the mass of the sun. It is the apparent movement of the star that is observed and that supposedly confirms relativity theory.

What Putnam is interested in is whether the postulates of geometry are empirical. Here we have the question: is Euclid's parallel postulate empirically refuted by this data? Putnam's answer is that it depends on the context in which we consider the data. Let us contrast two different sorts of circumstances: (i) a context in

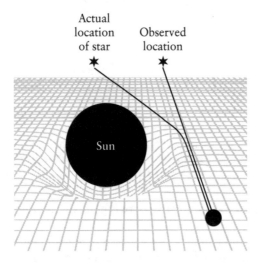

Figure 2.3 Light from a distant star being bent by the curvature of space caused by the mass of the sun.

which Euclidean geometry is the only available geometrical theory; (ii) a context in which scientists have alternative geometrical theories (such as Euclidean and Riemannian geometries) from which to choose.

In circumstance (i), Putnam claims that it is "good methodology" to treat the parallel postulate as being "immune from revision" (1979: 92). Like many other philosophers of science, Putnam holds that we cannot confirm or refute theories unless we test them against alternative explanations. The idea is this: science is looking for the best explanation of the empirical data. Any explanation is better than no explanation. So if the only geometrical theory we have is Euclidean, then we have to accept physical theories based on Euclidean geometry. In circumstance (ii), in contrast, it makes sense to abandon Euclidean geometry.

Putnam thus claims that Euclidean geometry, including its fifth postulate, was, but is no longer, a priori. It was immune to empirical refutation only as long as there was no viable alternative geometrical theory. But the issue is slightly more complicated than this. If we were to retain Euclidean geometry as a theory of space even after the data from the eclipse, however, we would have to abandon other beliefs. One belief that it would be plausible to reject is that light travels in straight lines.

Scientists take the data from the eclipse to show that massive objects curve space in part because scientists hold that light rays move in straight lines. But what is the status of the sentence "Light rays move in straight lines"? The proposition that this expresses is not necessarily true. As Putnam points out, we can easily imagine universes in which light moves in spirals or zigzags. But the proposition is not empirical either, because light rays are our means for measuring how straight a path is in space. We have no independent means for determining that light travels in straight lines.

From a semantic and epistemological point of view, light rays are like the metre rod in Paris: they are the standard by which other things are measured. But like the metre rod, they could have failed to "measure up"; light could have failed to move in straight lines. Thus, it seems natural to claim that the proposition that light rays move in straight lines is contingent but a priori. Scientists stipulate that they are the standard by which we measure straightness, but the fact that they are appropriate for this task is a contingent feature of this world.

The use of light rays as a standard is a way of making empirical the notion of a straight line. In the 1920s, Percy Bridgman developed the theory of operational definitions. The central claim of that theory is that definitions of certain scientific concepts are given by the ways that we have to measure them. For example, for Bridgman, "the path of a light ray is a straight line" is a definition of "straight line". But operational definitions are odd sorts of definitions. As we have seen, they are only contingently appropriate for certain concepts. We usually think of a definition as giving us the meaning of a concept and, for most philosophers, the meaning of a concept remains true in every possible world. If in some worlds light rays do not move in straight lines, then "the path of a light ray is a straight line" cannot be a definition of "straight line" in the normal sense of "definition".

Even though operational definitions are only contingent, it would seem difficult to abandon them. If we reject the belief that light rays travel in straight lines, then we need an alternative operational definition of "straight lines". If we do not have an alternative operational definition, then we have no empirical way of telling whether things are travelling in straight lines. It is often important in science that we do so.

There is a trade-off between maintaining Euclidean geometry and abandoning the operational definition of "straight line". On the one hand Euclidean geometry is intuitive, and on the other having a means for determining straight lines is useful. Would it have been better to retain Euclidean geometry and abandon the use of light rays in this regard? This is an extremely difficult question to answer. For Putnam, Einstein's theory, with its rejection of Euclidean geometry, is a better overall theory than Newton's theory, given the empirical data. Thus, he claims that Newton's theory, including its use of Euclidean geometry, can now be considered to have been empirically refuted. Friedman argues, against Putnam, that we can still regard the use of Euclidean geometry in Newton's theory (and the use of Riemannian geometry in Einstein's theory) as a priori, but I shall leave that topic until Chapter 8.

2.10 Summary

In this chapter I set out a framework for discussing modality (possibility and necessity). This framework is the standard one now used for that task: possible-world semantics. I also discussed theories of propositions, since we shall appeal to propositions throughout this book.

I discuss Kripke's arguments that show that we know empirically some propositions to be necessarily true and some contingent propositions we know a priori. I argue that neither of these arguments endangers the importance of a priori belief as our route to knowing about what is necessarily true. For, even in cases in which we know empirically that a proposition is necessarily true, a priori knowledge seems to be involved in an essential way.

I also look at an example of a priori beliefs being undermined by other a priori beliefs. This shows that a priori beliefs are not necessarily certain. This fact gives us a criterion to use when evaluating theories of a priori justification. We can ask whether they allow for uncertain a priori beliefs.

The chapter ends with a discussion of whether the notion of apriority is absolute. I look at an argument due to Putnam to establish that some beliefs are a priori in some circumstances but not in others. I suggest that this argument is inconclusive.

Further reading

On structured and unstructured propositions and how they fit into semantic theory, see Max Cresswell's *Structured Meanings* (1985).

The classic source on double indexing is David Kaplan's "Demonstratives" (1989). For a textbook presentation of double indexing, see Ted Sider's *Logic for Philosophy* (2010).

Kripke's arguments are in *Naming and Necessity* (1980). There is an enormous literature on the contingent a priori and the necessary a posteriori.

On reliabilism and theoretical virtues, Peter Lipton's *Inference to the Best Explanation* (2004) is a clear and readable book almost entirely dedicated to the subject.

3 Rationalism and self-evidence

3.1 Rationalism

"Rationalism" is defined in various ways in the philosophical literature. In the canon of English-speaking philosophy departments, rationalism is associated with three philosophers: Descartes, Spinoza and Leibniz. With these philosophers in mind, Charlie Huenemann (2008: 7–8) characterizes rationalist epistemology in terms of the following four theses:

(i) There is a priori knowledge.
(ii) We have innate ideas or beliefs.
(iii) We have a "privileged cognitive machinery which allows for the distinction between the intellect and imagination".
(iv) Pure reason is more reliable than empirical justification.

Chapter 4 of this book is devoted entirely to discussing innate ideas and beliefs, so we shall not discuss thesis (ii) at any length in this chapter. Thesis (i), of course, is the topic of this entire book, and all the theories that we discuss, except radical empiricism, accept it. In this chapter we shall concentrate on theses (iii) and (iv).

Thesis (iii) is particularly interesting. Empiricist critiques of rationalism often accuse rationalists of confusing the limits of their imaginations with real insight into what is necessarily true. For example, some rationalists claim that we can know that nothing can be both red and green all over at the same time. A radical empiricist, such as Mill, would reply that we cannot imagine such an object, but that may just be a fact about what we can imagine at the moment rather than a fact about things. Rationalists think that what we can conceive goes beyond what we can imagine and that our conceptual abilities are reliable indicators of what is necessarily true. We shall return to this link between conceivability and necessity in Chapter 12.

With regard to thesis (iv), historically most rationalists have claimed that the intellect is more reliable then sensation. And they allow the intellect to contradict and overrule what the senses tell them. But recently there have been some philosophers who call themselves "rationalists" but think that the findings of our intellect are empirically defeasible. BonJour is perhaps the best example of this sort of philosopher. His favourite example is the one concerning our belief that nothing can be both red and green all over at the same time. It seems obvious that this is true. But what if we had experience of something that is both red and green all over at the same time? Would we not then relinquish our previous belief that nothing could be both these colours? Whether this is a real counter-example depends on what one thinks the scope of rationalist justification is. I shall discuss this problem in this chapter.

Rationalism, as I treat it in this book, is the view that, all things being equal, we should accept what pure reason tells us to accept. Thus, rationalism gives us a theory of a priori justification. It tells us that certain beliefs that we have are justified without our having any empirical evidence for them. We have a faculty – pure reason – that produces such justified beliefs. This characterization of rationalism does not force rationalists to hold that beliefs produced by pure reason are immune from empirical refutation. It only says that, *in the absence of other factors*, we should accept whatever pure reason dictates.

Among rationalists, I distinguish between *strong rationalists*, who hold that pure reason – the intellect alone – can reliably deliver truths about things that are independent of our minds, and *weak rationalists*, who think that pure reason can only tell us about things that are mind dependent. For example, Kant is a rationalist, but he claims that everything we know a priori is really about our own minds. Thus, I call him a "weak rationalist". Descartes, on the other hand, thinks that we can know a priori that God exists and so he is a strong rationalist.

Pure rationalism is the view that appeals to pure reason should be given a lot of weight even when they are not supported with further evidence of their reliability. Pure rationalism is currently not in fashion in philosophy. But unpopularity is no reason to disregard it. There is, however, a good reason for its unpopularity. Without further theory it is unclear how rational insight is supposed to fit into our best current theories of how the mind works.

We can, however, avoid this need to explain how rational insight fits into the workings of the mind by adopting a rationalist foundationalism. On this view, among our basic beliefs are those that are produced by rational insight. We do not need to justify these beliefs. It may be that one goal of a rationalist foundationalism is to produce a coherent theory of the mind, but rationalist foundationalists do not make it a prerequisite of appealing to rational insight that we have such a theory.

In this chapter, we briefly discuss rationalist coherentism and reliabilism, both of which seem to me to be tenable views, but we concentrate on rationalist foundationalism. This view, largely through the influence of Descartes, is historically important. At the end of the chapter, we examine Descartes' own views and a particular difficulty for rationalist foundationalism: the *Cartesian circle*.

3.2 History of rationalism

The first systematic rationalist in Western philosophy is Plato (*c*.424–347 BCE). Plato distinguishes between two sorts of knowledge: knowledge of sensible objects and knowledge of the "Forms". Forms are abstract objects; they are nowhere in space or time. The Forms are ideals in the sense that they are somehow perfect and that sensible things never quite measure up to the Forms. If we want to know about what good or justice, for example, really are, then we are asking about the nature of the Forms or good or justice, not about actual people or actions.

On Plato's view, our knowledge of the Forms is a priori. It is not learned through our sense experience. When we experience things we often classify them in terms of the Forms, but in doing so we project our knowledge of the Forms onto the things; we do not exact this knowledge from our experience. We shall go further into Plato's view about how to gain knowledge of the Forms in Chapter 4.

Some medieval philosophers held that God gives us insight into the nature of things. This view is called the theory of "divine illumination". Augustine (354–430) is perhaps the creator of this view. According to Augustine, all our knowledge comes about with the help of God, even our perceptual knowledge. Augustine's view is an interesting form of non-foundationalist rationalism. God is needed to guarantee what our intellect tells us. Thus, we do not need the intellect to conjure up basic beliefs. We can construct a coherentist rationalism based on the theory of divine illumination. The belief that God is telling us what to believe (and that he is reliable in this regard) gives us a reason to accept what our intellects tell us.

Descartes (1596–1650) was the paradigm rationalist. He was a scientist (he worked in both physics and biology) and mathematician (he was the inventor of Cartesian coordinates), as well as a philosopher. As a physicist, he postulated a physical world that is very different from that which common sense and sense perception seem to depict. Physical things do not really have colours, tastes or smells. Moreover, Descartes is a follower of Copernicus. He thinks that the earth moves around the sun, contrary to the way in which things appear to us. Descartes is willing in his scientific thought to allow reason to override our common-sense view of the world. This, as we have seen, is a rationalist tendency.

In his *Meditations*, Descartes attempts to reconstruct philosophy largely using a priori reasoning. This attempt is usually thought to be a foundationalist project, but as we shall see later in this chapter he does at times act like a coherentist. At any rate, his central methods are aprioristic and he appeals often to "clear and distinct ideas", which is a form of rational insight. I discuss this view further at the end of this chapter.

Spinoza (1632–77) and Leibniz (1646–1716) are known more for their metaphysical views than their epistemologies, but both are clearly proponents of a priori justification. Like Descartes, they both appeal to a class of self-evident thoughts, which, like Descartes, they call "clear and distinct ideas". Spinoza's great metaphysical work, the *Ethics*, begins with a set of definitions and supposedly self-evident axioms. He derives all of the principles of his metaphysical system from these axioms. Thus, it would seem that Spinoza is very clearly a rationalist foundationalist, at least concerning philosophical knowledge.[1] Leibniz's epistemology is less obvious, although it is clearly aprioristic. In presenting his metaphysics he rarely, if ever, appeals to experience.

Kant (1724–1804) is a weak rationalist. He thinks that we have some a priori insight into the structure of space, time and physical objects, but he thinks that the spatiotemporal world and the properties of things in it are largely constructed by our minds. What we have knowledge about, according to Kant, is the way in which we must understand the world. This tells us how the empirical world is, in the sense that it tells us how our minds shape that world. I discuss this view in depth in Chapter 7.

In some ways the most extreme rationalist is Hegel (1770–1831). His view is that by reason alone we can come to know an enormous amount about the nature of the physical world, God and history. But he is also a weak rationalist, in the sense that he thinks that we cannot know anything about mind-independent reality. What makes his view so extreme is that he believes that all of reality is mind dependent. He criticizes strong rationalists, on the one hand for holding that there are mind-independent entities, and on the other for making claims about the natures of these entities on the basis of how we think about them.[2] Hegel agrees with Kant that we can only know about the way in which we must understand things, but he rejects Kant's view that there also must be something that is independent of consciousness. Such a thing would be unintelligible and it makes no sense, on Hegel's view, to postulate it.

Hegel thinks, like Kant, that we can use a priori methods to discover how we must understand things, but for him this means that we can come to know a priori about the general structure of the world itself.

Hegel's extreme ambition for rational insight brought about a revolt against rationalism in the nineteenth and twentieth centuries. We shall examine some of the products of this backlash in Chapters 5 and 6. But note that the revolt is only partial. There are rationalist philosophers throughout this period and there are some rationalists among us today.

3.3 Rationalism and contemporary epistemology

Rationalism can be combined with coherentism, reliabilism or foundationalism. I have briefly mentioned rationalist coherentism and foundationalism already, but here we shall examine them in more depth.

Coherentists think that we should accept beliefs only if we can incorporate them into a system of beliefs in which they are explained by other beliefs and/or explain other beliefs. We saw in our brief discussion of the theory of divine illumination a particular version of rationalist coherentism. On this view, the reliability of our intellects is explained by the activity of God. But a non-theist rationalist coherentism is also possible. On one such view, the reliability of the intellect is justified by an argument that appeals to evolution. This argument could perhaps show that natural selection gave us a reliable faculty of a priori judgement as a tool that helped humanity survive and expand.

The use of evolutionary arguments is interesting because we employ empirical arguments to justify the acceptance of a priori beliefs. This is not a contradiction. In order to integrate a priori justification into their theories, coherentists need to make a distinction between two sorts of justification. A belief is *acceptable* with regard to a system of beliefs if and only if that belief coheres with the system. But the immediate justification of a belief is provided by those beliefs that give us immediate reasons to adopt the belief. So, if I have a belief that is produced by a non-empirical source, such as rational insight, then other beliefs that are justified by it (and it alone) are a priori. Let us say that I believe I have the rational insight that p, and I deduce q from p by logical means alone. Then both p and q are a priori, even if I have empirical reasons to believe that rational insight is reliable. If we do not make a distinction between acceptability and immediate justification, then we cannot have a coherentist theory that accepts a priori justification. For if we integrate a belief into a system of beliefs that has even one empirical belief, then all beliefs within that system would be empirically justified.[3] I examine the use of evolutionary arguments further in Chapters 4 and 9.

If our intellects are, in fact, generally reliable in producing correct a priori judgements, then such judgements are justified in the reliabilist's sense. Reliabilists do not require that we believe (let alone have evidence that) our beliefs are justified in order for them to be so. Thus, a rationalist reliabilism is even more straightforwardly possible than a rationalist coherentism.

Foundationalism is perhaps the view that we most closely associate with rationalism, but, as we can see, being a rationalist is compatible with rejecting foundationalism. A rationalist foundationalist holds that some of the beliefs we obtain by pure reason are self-evident or cannot be doubted. Let us call such beliefs those obtained by "rational insight". Later we shall make a distinction between self-evidence and undeniability. Beliefs produced by rational insight are basic beliefs: they need no further justification but justify other beliefs. In the rest of this chapter we investigate the epistemological status of rational insight.

3.4 Rational insight

Rational insight is the key notion in rationalism and the most controversial. Because of the controversy about whether we actually have rational insight, it is crucial for rationalists to provide us with a theory of what it is. In order to defend the claim that we have rational insight, it may be best to try to show that it fits in with the rest of the picture that we have of the world. In the next two sections, I look at one historical and two contemporary theories of rational insight – due to Descartes, BonJour and Robert Audi, respectively – and examine what they say about the nature and scope of this faculty that we are supposed to have.

3.5 Descartes' clear and distinct ideas

The best-known theory of rational insight is Descartes' theory of clear and distinct ideas. The view is expressed nicely in the following passage from one of his earlier works, *Rules for the Direction of the Mind*:

> By "intuition" I do not mean the fluctuating testimony of the senses or the deceptive judgment of the imagination as it botches things together, but the conception of a clear and attentive mind, which is so easy and distinct that there can be no room for doubt about what we are understanding.
>
> (AT: X, 368, rule 3)[4]

Here Descartes says that the ideas of sense perception and imagination are not clear and distinct. He postulates a faculty of pure reason, which he calls the "clear light of reason", and claims that in order to operate properly it should not be hindered by the other faculties of the mind, such as imagination and sense perception.

In a much later work – *The Principles of Philosophy* – Descartes tells us that an idea is clear when it is "present and accessible to an attentive mind". A clear idea is also "strong" or vivid (1984: pt I, ¶45). This characterization seems to fit sensations, which are very vivid and present to an attentive mind, but, as I said, sensations are not clear and distinct ideas for Descartes. What he has in mind here, I think, are concepts or beliefs about relationships between concepts or between properties. Consider, for example, the concept of an octave in music. I am a musical ignoramus so I can only say that an octave is a range of notes. It is not a concept that I really have. It is a concept I only vaguely have.

A distinct idea is an idea that is clear and is such that if it contains other ideas, those other ideas are also clear. Consider, for instance, Australian rules football (the sport played by the Australian Football League [AFL]). I have never been a great fan of that game, and my grasp of the rules is rather tenuous. I know that some points are awarded for actions other than goals, but I do not know what. I have a concept "rules of AFL", but it is not distinct because the ideas (i.e. the propositions) that make up the rules are not clear to me.

Descartes claims that the use of clear and distinct ideas allows us to know facts about things that are independent of our minds. Most famously, Descartes says that we can prove the existence of God by analysis of the idea of God. Here is a brief rendition of the "proof". The idea of God in him is clear and distinct, and it contains in it the idea of an infinite and perfect being. He also uses the idea (the belief, in this case) that every idea requires a cause, and that the cause of the idea of an infinite and perfect being could not have created by him. It must have been created by an infinite and perfect being, that is, God.

3.6 The Cartesian circle

In the *Meditations*, Descartes uses his "method of doubt" to set aside all those beliefs of which he is not certain. He wants to find those beliefs that are completely trustworthy on which to base his metaphysics. He comes to a point at which he is certain only of his own existence and the contents of his present thoughts. In the Third Meditation, he tries to justify beliefs about things outside his own mind and the present moment by proving the existence of God. He does so by appeal to his idea of God. This idea is the idea of an infinite being. He claims that such an idea could not be created by a finite being, and so there must be an infinite being who created it. Having established the existence of God, he can appeal to God's other features (in particular his goodness) to establish that the beliefs that God has given him must be accurate, and using this he attempts to prove the existence of a world outside his own mind and the present moment.

It looks as though Descartes, in the Third Meditation, is using his clear and distinct ideas – in particular, the idea of God – to guarantee the truth of his clear and distinct ideas in general. Pierre Gassendi (1592–1655) accuses him of just this:

> I note that a circular argument appears to have its beginning at this point, according to which you are certain that there must be a God and that he is not a deceiver on the ground that you have a clear and distinct idea of him, and you are certain that a clear and distinct idea must be true on the ground that there is a God who cannot be a deceiver.
>
> (Quoted in Williams 1978: 189)

In his *Discourse on Method*, Descartes seems to agree that God is needed to justify our acceptance of the content of clear and distinct ideas: "[W]hat I just now took as a rule, namely that everything I perceive clearly and distinctly is true, is assured only for the reasons that God is or exists, that he is a perfect being, and that everything in us comes from him" (AT: VI, 38). And, a little later, he writes: "But if we did not know that everything real and true in us comes from a perfect and infinite being then, however clear and distinct our ideas were, we would have no reason to be sure that they had the perfection of being true" (AT: VI, 39).

If Descartes needs to prove God's existence to show that clear and distinct ideas are reliable, then he is stuck in a circular argument. Of course this circularity may not be a real problem, depending on Descartes' other views. If he is a coherentist, for example, then circularity is not an issue. Coherentists think that propositions in a belief system should provide one another with mutual support. But Descartes wants to show that all his beliefs can be placed on a firm foundation. As such, this circle might appear to be an important problem for him.

If Descartes really is a foundationalist, however, then there is no problem either.[5] Clear and distinct beliefs are basic, and so need no further justification. In his "Replies to Objections" to the *Meditations*, Descartes seems to be taking this line. There he says that the only reason he needs God is to assure him that what he *remembers* having proved a short time ago is true (AT: VI, 140). When we are proving things, in philosophy as well as mathematics, we typically prove other propositions before we prove our main proposition. This takes time. Our recollection of what we have already proved can be crucial to the process of proof. To assure us that what we remember has been proved, Descartes says, we need to be sure that God exists. Thus, he claims that if we have a proof of God that we can keep in mind at an instant (so no memory is needed), there is no viciously circular argument.

The problem of the role of memory in justificatory processes is not confined to Descartes' philosophy. Any foundationalist must admit that some of our derivations from basic beliefs are long. In performing a long proof, we cannot recall every basic belief (and perceive it to be self-evident) and recall every self-evident step in reasoning. We must remember only that we had some such beliefs and performed some such steps in reasoning. If certainty is our goal, as it is for Descartes, then this becomes a problem. Memory is not perfectly reliable. Even great mathematicians make mistakes in doing long derivations, because they misremember what they have previously proved. This happens all the time. Most contemporary foundationalists admit that certainty is unobtainable in part because of this problem.

Some commentators have argued that Descartes thinks that certain beliefs arrived at by the analysis of clear and distinct ideas are defeasible (see e.g. Newman 2010: §4.2). This means that some such beliefs can be undermined by further evidence. I think the arguments for this claim are wrong, and that Descartes' clear and distinct perceptions are not defeasible. I also think that the foregoing discussion of the Cartesian circle can shed light on this debate.

The chief evidence for the claim that certain clear and distinct judgements are defeasible is a passage in Descartes' replies to objections to the *Meditations* in which he discusses an atheist geometer. Descartes says that a geometer who is also an atheist can know, via clear and distinct conceptual analysis, that the angles of a triangle add up to 180°. But he also says that she cannot prove that she cannot be wrong. She cannot appeal to a belief that God exists and use God to guarantee her beliefs.

If Descartes were to choose an example that is arrived at directly by intuition (in his sense), then there would be an extremely strong case that he thinks that some intuitive judgements are defeasible. But his example is of a proposition that needs to be proved from the postulates of Euclidean geometry. Descartes is very careful to distinguish between intuition and the deduction of truths from intuitions, and deduction of this sort is what is needed to prove that the angles of a triangle add up to 180° (rule III, in AT: X, 369). Deductions take time and use memory, and this use of memory may be what requires God's guarantee, not the use of clear and distinct judgements.

3.7 BonJour's theory

According to BonJour (1998: 15), rational insight is an "intuitive grasping" of a proposition. He often talks of rational insight as immediate, but he also admits that we can sometimes come to have insight into the truth of a proposition after a process of inference. It would seem that mathematical discoveries are often like this. We come to know a proposition in mathematics through a process of calculation or proof, but after this process we view the resulting proposition as something that is now obviously true.

Rational insight constitutes a form of justification. One is justified in believing what rational insight tells one to believe. But, according to BonJour, rational insight is fallible. As BonJour (*ibid*.: 111) points out, there have been many instances of people claiming that they know a particular proposition by rational insight, but then later that proposition is known to be false.

BonJour's view is particularly interesting because he claims that rational insight is empirically defeasible. This means that he thinks empirical evidence can, in part, show that what someone thought he knew through rational insight is actually false. I say "in part" here because, according to BonJour, in many (perhaps every) case in which empirical evidence seems to come into conflict with a priori beliefs, there are other a priori beliefs in place that help to create the conflict. One might look at the rejection of Euclidean geometry as a case like this. The data collected at the 1919 eclipse conflicts with the thesis that space is Euclidean only if we assume certain other a priori beliefs, such as the belief that light travels in straight lines. As we shall see, however, some other philosophers, such as Friedman, dispute the claim that this sort of refutation is really empirical.[6]

BonJour also claims that we can sometimes correct cases in which we are mistaken regarding rational insights by using coherence techniques. There are two sorts of cases that we should consider. First, there are cases in which we think we have rational insight but are wrong. Such a case might occur when we think we have done a calculation but made a mistake (forgot to carry a 1, say), but then think the answer is obvious when it is actually incorrect. In such cases our other beliefs may help to correct us. If we get silly figures when trying to use that answer in determining our taxes, we might be able to find it as the source of our mistake and then correct it. Second, there are cases in which we do have rational insight but it leads us to believe a falsehood. Clashes with our other a priori beliefs may still allow us to reject that belief.[7]

In rational insight, according to BonJour, we often have *direct access* to the objects of our beliefs. Consider, for example, one's rational insight that nothing can be both red and green all over at the same time. In the grasping of this proposition, BonJour (1998: §6.3) avers, we have the colours red and green directly before our minds, and intuit that they cannot be present in a thing in the same way at the same time.[8] As BonJour points out, this view makes his theory incompatible with theories of the mind that treat the mind as a manipulator of symbols. According to the symbolic or "representational" theory of mind, there are only representations of things before the mind rather than the things themselves. So, in particular, on this theory of mind, we do not have red and green before our minds, but rather representations of them. The direct access view of BonJour's is in conflict with this theory. Whether that is a real disadvantage for BonJour's theory depends on what the fate of the representational theory of mind will be.

3.8 Audi's theory

Audi puts forth a less ambitious theory of rational insight. According to Audi, rational insight is closely connected to our ability to understand propositions. On his view (1996: 114) a proposition is self-evident if it satisfies the following two conditions:[9]

(i) understanding the proposition is sufficient for being justified in believing it;
(ii) if one believes that proposition on the basis of understanding it, then one knows the proposition.[10]

In order to comprehend condition (i), we need to know what it is to understand a proposition. Consider a sentence that expresses a proposition that is commonly treated as self-evident:

If John is a bachelor, then he is unmarried.

If the person who is saying this sentence (or thinking it) takes "bachelor" to represent the property of being an unmarried man, then the proposition that it represents is:

<If, <And, <Not, <Married, John>>, <Man, John>>, <Not, <Married, John>>>

(That is, "*If John is not married and a man, then he is not married*"). This proposition seems obvious. If the person considering it has even the most basic grasp of the concept of conjunction (the concept of *and*) and the concept of a conditional (the concept of *if*) then she can see that this proposition is true.

Note that, contrary to BonJour's view, Audi holds that self-evidence is not defeasible. It cannot be overturned either by empirical or a priori evidence. This is entailed by condition (ii). We cannot know anything that is false. Suppose that one comes to believe that red is a colour merely on the basis of understanding that proposition. Then one knows it. One does not need to seek further justification for one's belief, nor can this belief be undermined by any further evidence. Audi's view of self-evidence is very appropriate for foundationalism. Self-evident propositions that fit Audi's definition are good candidates for basic beliefs.

3.9 Self-evidence and inference

Audi (1996: 115) claims that not all cases of self-evidence are immediate. Sometimes we need to reflect on a proposition before we find it self-evident. This reminds me of the joke about a mathematics lecturer who is explaining something to her class and says, "It is obvious. No, wait; maybe not." She paces and thinks for a while and then says, "Yes, it is obvious." Audi's point is that when we are presented with some concepts it sometimes takes a while to "unpack" them and see how they fit together. Let us consider another example. Suppose that you are told that $1234 \times 789 = 973{,}626$. If you take the speaker at her word and fail to check the equation, then you will not believe this as a self-evident proposition. But if you work through the multiplication, then you will come to realize that the proposition is self-evident.

We can understand our thinking about propositions in cases of a priori justification in terms of *conceptual analysis*. Consider the simple proposition

<If <And, <Not, <Married, John>, <Male, John>>,
<Male, John>>>

("If John is not married and male, he is male.") We think about this proposition in terms of concepts – such as *married*, *male*, *and* – and our concept of the conditional (if … then). Sometimes philosophers like to say that our understanding of these concepts itself allows us to realize that the proposition is true.

But what is it to understand a concept? Consider the concept *and*. We conjoin (place *and* between) two representations of two propositions in order to indicate that both of the propositions represented are true. Clearly, if both propositions are true, then each of those propositions is true. This might sound as though I am repeating myself, but what I mean is that we use the following rule to understand *and*:[11]

P and Q

Therefore, Q

Now, is this rule part of the concept of *and*? As we shall see in Chapter 5, Paul Boghossian thinks that logical rules like this are built into our concepts and Tim Williamson thinks that they are not. In either case, our a priori justifications require that we have the ability to apply rules of reasoning like this.

We can say that a proposition is self-evident often only by assuming certain logical abilities. Perhaps none of us has perfect reasoning abilities. We could say that there may be self-evident propositions that no actual person can find self-evident because the links in reasoning between the concepts used to represent them are too complicated for any actual person.

BonJour, however, defines "self-evidence" in terms of a completely non-inferential form of cognition. We know something self-evidently, according to BonJour, only if we can immediately grasp that the proposition is true. The grasping of a proposition as self-evident must be irreducible, according to BonJour, if we are to avoid an infinite regress. Consider again the inferences behind our recognition of the truth of the proposition that if John is not married and male, he is male. We represented the reasoning process in terms of a rule of logic. This rule has other propositions as premises. If we have to use further inferences to find the premises self-evident, we shall need more propositions to act as premises to justify them. And so on to infinity. BonJour (1998: 108) suggests that our grasping of propositions is non-inferential. The regress has to come to an end at some point, and so we must just be able to "see" that certain propositions are true.[12]

The problem with BonJour's argument is that it presents us with a false dichotomy. The dichotomy that he cites is between either having an infinite regress or taking self-evidence to be irreducible. BonJour is right that we cannot require that our grasping of propositions as self-evident includes the use of other *beliefs*. This will get us into his regress. But this regress is not the only other alternative. Our logical abilities need not be understood always in terms of inferring beliefs from other beliefs. We do sometimes see that certain concepts have certain logical relations to one another and this does not require further propositional thoughts. It may just require an ability (that is innate or learned) to see certain logical connections.

When we see these links, we can often later turn them into explicit logical arguments. Suppose that you are asked to justify your belief that if John is unmarried and male, he is male. Suppose also that you have taken an elementary logic course. As a justification, then, you can give the following inference:

1. John is unmarried and male.   (hypothesis)
2. John is male.   (1, by the rule given above)
3. If John is unmarried and male, he is male.

(1–2, conditional proof)

We shall discuss conditional proof again in Chapter 7. The idea is that if you can prove Y on the hypothesis that X, you can then "discharge" the hypothesis that X and infer "If X, then Y". Of course you do not have to have had a course in logic to know that if John is unmarried and male, then he is male. But one thing that we logic lecturers try to teach students in a course is how to make explicit the rules of reasoning that most of us already use. This justification is to show others that you understand the connections between the parts of the proposition that if John is unmarried and male, he is male. But it seems that we also have the capacity to recognize that these connections exist without making them explicit in our minds. Our grasp of the truth of the proposition seems non-inferential, but it is our inferential abilities that make it possible to have such a grasp.

3.10 What can rational insight tell us?

We have already seen that BonJour thinks that rational insight is defeasible and Audi thinks that it is not defeasible at all. But there may be other differences as well. According to Audi's view, what we can know by rational insight is whatever we can tell is true by virtue of the *contents* (or meanings) of concepts alone. What range of propositions this covers depends on the theory of content that we connect with this view of rational insight.

On one view of concepts – known as the "classical theory" – a concept includes in it those concepts that define it. So, for example, the concept of bachelor includes in it the concept of being unmarried and the concept of being male. It would seem that the following propositions could not be known by means of rational insight:

- Nothing is both red and green all over at the same time.
- Every coloured object is extended in space.

It is not part of the definition of "red" that nothing red can be green in the same way at the same time. Moreover, it is not part of the definition of "colour" that if an object is coloured it has length, height or depth. So, it would seem that these propositions are not known by means of rational insight, according to Audi's theory, when it is combined with the classical view of concepts.[13]

On another view of concepts – called the "theory theory" – the content of a concept is determined by its relationships to other concepts. This view of concepts gets its name from the idea that the terms of a scientific theory are implicitly defined. This means that they are defined by their relation to the other terms in the theory. (I discuss implicit definition in some detail in Chapter 5.) On this view, we each have our own theory of colour, say. It may be that, according to this theory, being red is incompatible with being green and that only things extended in space can be coloured. If so, our two propositions might be known by means of rational insight.

Thus, Audi's view may allow rational insight to cover a set of cases very similar to those covered by BonJour's theory. It depends in an important way on the theory of concepts that we employ.

3.11 Rational insight and fallibility

As I have already pointed out, BonJour thinks that self-evidence is defeasible, and Audi and Descartes do not. Clearly, we are often wrong about things that we *take* to be self-evident. As we saw in Chapter 2, scientists were wrong in thinking that space is Euclidean. They thought this was self-evident. Descartes thought it self-evident that our minds are "thinking substances" and cannot be identical to our bodies. It seems likely that this is false too.

With regard to paradigm cases of self-evidence, it seems difficult to understand how one could go wrong. Consider again the proposition that red is a colour. How could I be wrong about that? There seem to be two ways in which I could go wrong:

- I could fail to understand the proposition fully and so fail to be justified in the way that I think I am justified.
- The proposition could be false and I could be mistaken about its being the sort of proposition that can be self-evident.

In misunderstanding a proposition fully, one can fail completely to understand the properties involved. Consider the proposition that if my desk is brown, then it is extended in space. One might have the concept *brown* to some extent but fail to grasp that anything that has it must have some surface area. He might know, say, that to be brown is to reflect light in a certain range of wavelengths, but not realize that in order to do this a thing must have some area. In this case he would have only a partial understanding of the property of being brown.

Let us consider an example of from the history of philosophy. Descartes claims that our minds are individual substances. His argument, roughly, goes like this:[14]

1. I know that there is thinking going on.
2. If there is thinking, there must be some substance doing the thinking.
3. Therefore, there is a substance (i.e. my mind) that is thinking.

The first premise is justified by introspection. The second premise is a priori and is what interests us here. Descartes was trained by Jesuits in the philosophy of Thomas Aquinas. Aquinas adopted much of Aristotle's metaphysics. According to Aristotle and Aquinas, thinking is an activity that needs to be grounded in a substance, a thing in which properties (such as the property of thinking) inhere. Now let us consider David Hume's view. He thinks that thoughts do not need to inhere in any substance; they may in fact subsist on their own. Descartes thinks that the proposition expressed by "if there is thinking, then there is a substance doing the thinking" is self-evident. Hume thinks it is false.

It seems that we have two choices about how to interpret what is going on here. First, Hume and Descartes may express two different propositions with "if there is thinking, then there is a substance doing the thinking". There is some plausibility to this position. Descartes and Hume certainly have different concepts of "thinking". One treats it as an activity and the other as a name for a thing (or event) of sorts. Let us say that when Descartes uses the word, "thinking" (or, rather, "*pensée*") refers to an activity and when Hume uses the word, "thinking" refers to a thing or event. The proposition Descartes is thinking of is this:

$<$If, $<$There is x, $<$Thinking, $x>>$, $<$There is x, $<$Thinking, $x>>>$

("If something is thinking, then something is thinking.") This is self-evident. What Hume is disputing is Descartes' assumption that when we introspect, we detect the presence of this activity, rather than something else (such as an object or an event).

The second choice is to say that both Descartes and Hume are talking about the same proposition, but at most one of them is right about the properties and objects involved in it. In this case, if Descartes is wrong about the nature of our thinking, then the proposition will only seem self-evident to him, but he will be incorrect about this.

If we take either choice, we can still claim that our *judgements* about what is self-evident are fallible. The theories of Audi and BonJour both allow this.[15]

Consider first the case in which Hume and Descartes are thinking about the same proposition, but the former thinks that it is not self-evident and the latter that it is. On Audi's view, if a proposition is self-evident, then it is true. But we may not always know whether we are talking or thinking about a self-evident proposition. We may not have understood the proposition, and so we are not justified in Audi's sense, even though we might think that we are. On BonJour's view, the issue is even easier. For, according to BonJour, we can actually have rational justification, but this may not guarantee the truth of the proposition.

Now consider the case in which Hume and Descartes are thinking about different propositions. Then Descartes' proposition might be self-evident and Hume's not. But although it might be self-evident that if something is thinking, then something is thinking, it may still be the case that there is nothing that is thinking. And this is compatible with what Hume believes.

3.12 Summary

In this chapter we have discussed rationalist versions of coherentism, reliabilism and, especially, foundationalism. Rationalism is the view that there are justified (perhaps self-justified) beliefs produced in us by pure reason. Rationalist foundationalism, in particular, relies on there being self-evident or undeniable propositions. Whether there are any such propositions is not something that can be easily proved. But many philosophers, I think, have rejected rationalism because they worry that the mechanism of rational insight is somehow spooky. They cannot believe that we have a capacity to discover truths by rational insight. But most of us do think that we can grasp propositions by understanding meanings (as in Audi's theory of self-evidence), so perhaps most philosophers in fact do accept that we have some degree of rational insight. But the important questions are how much rational insight we have and whether it can give us knowledge about matters that are independent of our minds. In Chapters 9–12 I explore these issues further.

As we have also seen, it makes sense to claim that our judgements about what is self-evident and what we cannot doubt are fallible. Thus, although some rationalist foundationalists, such as Descartes, think that self-evidence provides us with certainty, this seems wrong. Just because rationalism does not provide us with certainty does not mean that it should abandoned as an epistemology. It does not seem that there is any more reason, apart from the fact that certain of its proponents wanted it to provide certainty, to hold rationalism up to this standard and not do the same to other epistemologies.

Further reading

A very readable introduction to the classical rationalists – Descartes, Spinoza and Leibniz – is Charlie Huenemann's *Understanding Rationalism* (2008). On Descartes, one excellent (although dated) source is Bernard Williams's *Descartes* (1978).

An accessible version of Audi's views on self-evidence is in his book, *Belief, Justification, and Knowledge* (1986).

4 Nativism

4.1 What is nativism?

Nativism – sometimes called "psychological nativism" – is the doctrine that we have innate capacities, ideas or beliefs. Historically, nativism has been closely related to rationalism. Many rationalists have also been nativists. Plato thinks that our understanding of the forms is, to a large extent, innate; Descartes thinks that we have a great many innate ideas, as do Spinoza and Leibniz. These philosophers all use innateness to help explain how we have a priori knowledge. The sense in which innate ideas or beliefs are independent of experience is quite clear. We do not need to learn them either from experience or from anything else. But, as we shall see, the epistemological status of innate beliefs is rather complicated.

One problem with nativism is that, on some characterizations, every philosopher would seem to be a nativist. Almost every philosopher thinks that we have innate capacities of some kind or other. Hume, who is usually thought to be an enemy of nativism, thinks that we have the innate tendency to form beliefs by the association of ideas. We expect, for example, that a thing will fall if we see its being released because we have formed a habit after seeing this combination many times in the past.

One way of narrowing the class of nativists is to characterize them as holding that we not only have innate general reasoning abilities, such as the disposition to do induction, but we also have *domain-specific* innate ideas, beliefs or capacities. This means that we have ideas, beliefs or capacities that have to do with a smaller range of things that we might think about. For example, the linguist

Noam Chomsky has advanced a view about the innateness of our linguistic abilities. This is domain specific because it concerns only our understanding of our own language and the linguistic behaviour of people. It does not concern everything that we may experience or think about. This domain-specificity requirement, however, will not do for our purposes. One of the forms of nativism that we shall be interested in (in Chapter 10) is the view that our knowledge of deductive logic is innate. Deductive logic is something that we can apply to everything we consider.

Another way of characterizing nativism is to claim that we have innate representations of some kind. Our ability to do induction is not a representation. Restricting nativism in this way is not a good idea in the context of this book. I do not want to commit myself to claiming that our ideas or beliefs are mental representations in any strong sense. They may be dispositions. A disposition is a tendency to act in certain ways. The difference between a capacity and a disposition is very fine (if it exists at all).

Thus I treat being a nativist as a matter of degree. Perhaps all philosophers are nativists to some extent or other, but some – such as Plato and Descartes – are fairly extreme nativists. Hume and Locke, on the other hand, are extremely weak nativists.

4.2 History of nativism

We begin our history with Plato. The version of Plato's theory that we shall examine here is found in his middle period, especially in his dialogues *Meno*, *Phaedrus*, *Republic* and *Theaetetus*. Later in the chapter, we shall look at an argument from one of his earlier dialogues (the *Meno*). Plato's epistemology is very closely connected with his metaphysics. As we saw in Chapter 3, Plato holds that there is a realm of abstract objects: the Forms. As abstract objects, these Forms are not in space or time; thus we do not have sense perception of them. Plato thinks that we have an innate understanding of the Forms. The explanation that he gives of our innate ideas is that we experience the Forms before we are born, and he treats our knowledge of the Forms as a sort of memory of them. This is his *theory of recollection*. How seriously he takes the theory of recollection is not clear. It may be a mere fable or it may be that he really believes it. It is difficult to tell from his writings.

In his later works Descartes claims that most of our ideas are innate. Even those concepts that we usually take to be empirical, such as colour concepts, shape concepts and so on, are innate, according to Descartes. These concepts are dispositional. They are caused to occur in our minds when we have the right sort of experiences, but they exist in our minds as dispositions before we have such experiences (Huenemann 2008: 28). As we saw in §3.6, Descartes also, infamously, holds that we have an innate idea of God, which he uses to prove that his ideas about the world are accurate.

In seventeenth- and eighteenth-century philosophy, both innate beliefs and innate concepts tend to be called "innate ideas". This leads to some confusion. In his *Essay Concerning Human Understanding*, John Locke (1632–1704) says that he rejects innate ideas. Locke thinks that a necessary condition for claiming that a belief is innate is that everyone has it. He calls this "universal consent" (*Essay* bk I, chs 1–2). He takes as examples the beliefs that "whatever is, is" and "it is impossible for the same thing to be and not to be". He points out that children and mentally disabled people do not have these beliefs, and moreover, people do not have these beliefs unless they think about them. Locke says that if we claim that a belief is innate just because anyone who thinks about them who has sufficient ability can realize that they have it, we would not be able to distinguish between innate beliefs and other a priori beliefs. He says that we would not be able to claim that mathematicians discover truths when they prove things, but rather just uncover beliefs that we all have (*Essay* bk I, ch. 1, §8).[1]

In reply to Locke, Leibniz gives two arguments. First, he claims that experience alone cannot provide us with reliable rules of inference. Second, he claims that certain ideas, such as those of being, unity, substance and duration, cannot come from experience (Leibniz 1981: 51). Consider, for example, the idea of substance. Substance is a notion that Leibniz inherits from Aristotle. Things are substances in which properties inhere. We perceive properties, according to Leibniz, but not substance itself. The idea of substance itself, therefore, must have another source: it is innate. We can see that, in his second argument, Leibniz is not really addressing Locke's point. Leibniz is arguing that certain concepts are innate, whereas Locke is attacking the view that we have innate beliefs.

The next great proponent of innate ideas is Kant. We shall not discuss Kant's nativism here, since we will look at it in depth in Chapter 7.

In the twentieth century, perhaps the most important advocate of nativism is Chomsky. As we shall see later in this chapter, Chomsky thinks that the only way we can explain how easily children learn language and why all human languages are of certain forms is to claim that we have an innate grammar. This innate grammar is called *universal grammar*. The grammars of particular human languages implement universal grammar in different ways. In written English, for example, adjectives usually precede the nouns they modify, whereas in French they usually follow them. But, according to Chomsky, underlying both languages is the same universal grammar.

4.3 Innateness and epistemology

The first issue we should deal with is the relationship between innateness and epistemology. The debate about a priori knowledge is a debate about justification, or about whether our beliefs are empirically defeasible. Whether a belief is innate may have something to do with its justification or whether it is empirically defeasible, but the exact relationship between innateness and these epistemological concerns needs to be spelt out clearly.

Reliabilism gives us a straightforward way of giving innate belief epistemological significance. If an innate belief comes about in a fashion that reliably connects it with the fact that it is about, then, according to the reliabilist, we can say that the belief is justified. One way of connecting innate beliefs to a priori knowledge is to claim that these beliefs are the products of an evolutionary process. The general outline of such an explanation is that we have evolved to have such-and-such beliefs and that this evolutionary process produces mostly accurate beliefs.

An evolutionary argument of the sort I have in mind uses the process of *natural selection* to support the accuracy of a belief. A trait of an organism can be said to be naturally selected if it is partially responsible for that organism's being able to survive and reproduce. For example, our having vision is the product of natural selection because organisms that can see are better able to find food, protect themselves, find mates and so on; hence we can explain the success of animals that can see, in living longer and reproducing, by appeal, in part, to their having vision. To use an evolutionary explanation to show that innate beliefs are reliable, one needs to show at least the following:

(i) the beliefs help us to survive;
(ii) not only do the beliefs have to be conducive to survival, but their accuracy needs to be important to our survival;
(iii) there is some mechanism that explains how these beliefs could have been selected.

Point (iii) is slightly technical, but in some ways the easiest to understand. We can explain how natural selection can pick out traits of organisms that have a genetic basis. In such cases, organisms with the relevant genes are more successful in producing offspring who survive. Other traits can be communicated to offspring culturally: parents can teach behaviours or ideas to their children. Those behaviours or ideas that are successful in helping children survive and multiply will get passed on and on and on. These are mechanisms that explain how some traits are selected. If we are to use an evolutionary explanation to show how innate beliefs are justified, we need a mechanism whereby such beliefs are inherited and on which natural selection can be said to work.

The first two points are very interesting from the point of view of epistemology. It is not always clear how certain beliefs aid in our survival. Suppose for a minute that Leibniz is right and that we have the innate belief that the world is made up of substances in which properties inhere. It is implausible to say, without very good empirical evidence, that substance philosophers survive longer or produce more children than sceptics about substance. If we do want to use an evolutionary argument to support nativism, then we have to pick the beliefs that are involved rather carefully.

With regard to point (ii), not all beliefs that are conducive to survival need to be true to help us survive. Some philosophers and cognitive scientists have argued that our moral beliefs are the product of natural selection. But some of them, such as J. L. Mackie, Michael Ruse and Richard Joyce, think that despite the fact that these beliefs have helped humans to survive, they are false. In this case, it is the having and acting on the beliefs that is important, not their truth. In effect, they use an evolutionary argument to help undermine our confidence that our moral beliefs are true. The truth of a belief is often part of the explanation of why we hold it. Mackie, Ruse and Joyce try to show that evolution provides us with an alternative explanation of why we hold our moral beliefs. We have them because they have, in the past, helped humans to survive. There is no need, these philosophers claim, to add to this that our moral beliefs are true. We shall discuss this view again in Chapter 9.

The biologists Stephen Jay Gould and Richard Lewontin argue that even when an explanation based on natural selection seems plausible we should be wary of it. They say that many claims about traits being produced by natural selection are "just-so stories". The notion of a just-so story is taken from Rudyard Kipling, who wrote a series of stories such as "How the Camel got his Hump" and "How the Leopard got his Spots". The point is that Kipling made up explanations to amuse children. A just-so story for Gould and Lewontin is a plausible evolutionary explanation that is not backed up by any tested evidence. Gould and Lewontin point out that many apparently useful traits may have been produced not by being selected themselves but as by-products of other biological processes (Gould & Lewontin 1979).

If we have an argument that supports the truth of our innate beliefs, then these innate beliefs can be incorporated into our system of beliefs in the manner required by coherentists. Thus, it is no more difficult to think of ways in which innate beliefs can be incorporated into a coherentist epistemology than into a reliabilist epistemology.

The relationship between nativism and foundationalism is rather difficult to discern. Although some supposed foundationalists, such as Descartes, are nativists, there does not seem to be any direct connection between the two views.

Note that our innate beliefs can be defeasible. Some cognitive scientists claim that we have an innate physical theory, which is sometimes called "folk physics". This folk physics includes beliefs such as the belief that things do not disappear when they go behind other objects.[2] Our folk physics will also include the idea that ordinary objects are completely solid: that they contain little or no empty space. This latter belief is defeasible. It has been overthrown by modern science. Taking a belief to be basic just because it is innate does not seem reasonable. It must have some other quality to make it a candidate for a foundation for other beliefs. One such quality may be that we are not able to deny it, as in Descartes' clear and distinct beliefs.

4.4 The *Meno* argument

Our first argument for nativism comes from Plato's dialogue *Meno*. In the *Meno*, Plato's protagonist, Socrates, argues for the existence of innate beliefs. His argument consists of an illustration. Socrates questions an uneducated slave about some particular facts regarding geometry. Socrates is careful just to ask questions of the slave. Eventually the slave gives the answer to the question asked. The point is that we too can *see* what the answers are to the various questions that Socrates asks.

Here is a simplified version of one of Socrates' questions. Consider a square. Using only a straight edge and pencil (no measuring devices), how can we divide the area of the square in half? An answer to this is to draw a diagonal line from one corner of the square to its opposite corner, like this:

You may have known the answer before I gave it. But even if you did not think you knew it, you certainly can see that it is correct, even if you cannot remember the equation that determines the area of a triangle. Plato's problem concerns how we recognize the truth in cases like these.

Plato raises this problem as a paradox about the nature of "enquiry". When we enquire to find the answer to some question, we assume that we can recognize that answer when we are presented with it. But if we do not know what this answer is before we make the enquiry, Plato asks, how can we recognize it when we find it? Plato puts this in terms of a dilemma:

- If we do not know what the answer to our enquiry is, then we cannot know when we have found the correct answer to it.

• If we do know what the answer is, then enquiry is pointless.

In either case, it seems that we should not bother enquiring into anything, for all our attempts to find answers are impossible or pointless.

Plato's claim that we cannot recognize correct answers unless we already know them is central to his defence of nativism. It is also a claim that most of us find very strange. As Julius Moravcsik (1978: 54–5) points out, the *Meno* problem does not concern empirical queries. For example, Plato thinks we can recognize correct answers to empirical questions such as "Is it cold right now in Montreal?" without any difficulty. We know what cold is and we can know what it is like to be in Montreal, so if we are taken to Montreal we will be able to tell whether it is cold and satisfy our enquiry. But problems concerning mathematics and other supposedly a priori matters are different. Consider again the dividing of a square. You can recognize that the procedure of drawing the diagonal line works, and not only for that particular square, but for all possible squares. You can recognize this without difficulty. How do we do that?

Plato's answer is that we have mathematical knowledge innately within us. That would seem, however, by Plato's own reasoning, to entail that all enquiry into a priori matters such as mathematics is pointless; we already know the answers. Plato's reply is that although we do know the answers, they are buried deeply within our minds. In a successful enquiry into a priori matters such as mathematics, we *recall* something. But what? There is some ambiguity in Plato's view. Plato claims, as we have seen, that we have knowledge of the Forms before we are born and that we recall this knowledge while we are alive. The word "knowledge" here is ambiguous. We could know the Forms in the sense of being familiar with them, in the same way that we are familiar with people or our surroundings. We could also know them in terms of having specific beliefs about them. Does Plato think that we have specific beliefs about squares innate within us?

It is hard to believe, however, that we all know mathematics this well. Mathematicians know mathematics better than non-mathematicians. This does not seem to be a matter of their recalling beliefs that the rest of us have not bothered to remember. They have more mathematical ability. Seeing a mathematical genius explaining what she does can be quite fascinating. They usually have an extremely clear grasp on their very complicated subject matter. This is an extraordinary ability and only some people seem to have it. It would seem more reasonable to say that we all have certain mathematical concepts innately within us, but that some people are better at reflecting on the nature of these concepts than others.

The central problem that we are concerned with here is whether Plato's *argument* really supports nativism. We do have the ability to recognize general truths in certain circumstances. It seems plausible that something about this ability is innate, but do we really need very specific innate ideas, such as the idea of being a square, to explain how we do this? As we shall see, Aristotelians think we can abstract such ideas from experience or imagination. Plato would argue against Aristotelians that these ideas are *idealized*: we never come across perfect squares, circles or other geometrical shapes in experience. Aristotelians reply that we have a general ability to idealize, rather than specific innate ideas. We shall look at this debate in much more depth in Chapter 8. For now, we need to note that problem: how do we recognize general truths of certain sorts so easily?

4.5 The poverty of stimulus argument

One of the most important arguments for nativism is the poverty of stimulus argument. This argument has historical antecedents in Plato, Descartes, Leibniz and others. The modern version is due to Chomsky. According to Chomsky, we have innate knowledge of human languages. He claims that the evidence with which a child is presented is inadequate to allow him or her to abstract the rules of his or her language.

In the literature, there are many versions of the poverty of stimulus argument for an innate grammar. All of them contain premises about the success of children in learning language and the nature of the evidence available to them. The argument contrasts the speed with which children pick up language with the poor evidence available to them about what is grammatical. In particular, given a set of words, there are infinitely many different ways of combining them into sequences of words (called "strings"). Sometimes children produce an ungrammatical string and we correct them. This is called *negative linguistic evidence*. Children are presented with relatively little negative evidence, considering that there are infinitely many possible strings that they could produce. Most of what we present to children is *positive evidence*: grammatically correct speech. Positive evidence is inadequate to teach children language.

What children learn is the ability to produce *new* sentences by themselves. No finite set of grammatically correct sentences determines the rules of a grammar. This is a version of a problem due to Nelson Goodman (1983). He called his problem *the new problem of induction*, but these days it is commonly known as the *grue problem*. Goodman asks us to consider a date, let us say 31 December 2020. A thing is said to be grue if it is green before 31 December 2020 and blue afterwards. Now consider all the emeralds in the world. What colour are they? Normally we would say that they are green, but how do we know (now, in 2010) that they are not grue? For any set of objects of finite size or with any time limits, we can construct a problematic "gruish" property. The same is true for language. For any finite set of sentences, we can find a rule that fits all of them but may not be correct. Suppose that a child hears "Lola is happy" and then produces "Lola is dog". The second sentence is wrong because in English "is dog" is not a correct verb phrase. The word "dog" is not an adjective, like "happy", but a noun. Chomsky thinks that we need to have grammatical categories such as these innately and an innate (although rudimentary) idea about how they can go together. If we already have rudimentary categories and grammatical rules innately within us, explaining how we learn the rules of grammar becomes much easier.

Here is a schematic version of the poverty of stimulus argument.

1. Children learn to do x very quickly and efficiently.
   (empirical premise)
2. The evidence that children are presented with is inadequate to explain how premise 1 is possible.
3. The only plausible explanation of 1, given 2, is that an ability to do x is to some extent innate.
4. If there is one plausible explanation for a phenomenon, we should accept that explanation.
5. Therefore, we should accept that the ability to do x is to some extent innate.

Philosophers and cognitive scientists have raised important issues to do with premise 2 with regard to Chomsky's use of this argument. The adequacy or inadequacy of evidence can be determined only if we have some sort of theory of how we learn things. Fiona Cowie (1998: ch. 2) has argued against Chomsky that attempts to prove premise 2 have used theories of learning that are too weak to explain many cases of actual learning. For example, we learn very easily what a curry is despite perhaps only having tasted a few, but we certainly are not tempted to say that we have innate distinctions between a curry and a casserole. Perhaps, Cowie suggests, we need a more complicated view about our general learning processes rather than postulating domain-specific innate ideas. I shall leave it to the reader to decide whether he or she sides with Cowie or Chomsky, but I think we can all agree with Cowie that a good defence of premise 2 requires a substantial theory about how we learn.[3]

4.6 Summary

In this chapter we examined the doctrine of nativism: that we have innate ideas, beliefs or epistemic capacities. We looked at two arguments for nativism: Plato's *Meno* argument and the poverty of stimulus argument. Although both arguments make a plausible case for some degree of nativism, only serious empirical research can determine whether nativism is true and which, if any, concepts, beliefs or capacities are innate. Moreover, it is difficult to assess claims about innateness without first looking at alternatives. In Chapter 8, we shall look at a view that rivals Plato's innatism in particular. I suggest that the reader wait until having read Chapter 7 on Aristotelianism before making any final assessment concerning nativism.

Further reading

A good general resource on nativism is Peter Carruthers, Stephen Laurence and Stephen Stitch's edited collection *The Innate Mind* (2005).

On the *Meno* argument, good sources are chapters one and two of Michael Welbourne's *Knowledge* (2001) and Julius Moravcsik's article "Learning as Recollection" (1978).

On the poverty of stimulus argument: Massimo Piattelli-Palmarini's edited collection *Language and Learning* (1980) and Steven Pinker's *The Language Instinct* (1994) are excellent books on the case for our having innate knowledge of language.

There is an interesting debate between Fiona Cowie and Jerry Fodor on nativism. Cowie's view is in her *What's Within* (1998) and Fodor's is in his very long review of Cowie's book, "Doing Without What's Within" (2001). An excellent survey of technical issues to do with the poverty of stimulus argument is Geoffrey Pullum and Barbara Scholz's article "Empirical Assessment of Poverty of Stimulus Arguments" (2002).

5 Analyticity

5.1 Analytic–synthetic distinctions
Consider the following sentences:

(i) A vixen is a female fox.
(ii) The cat is on a mat.

The first of these is a paradigm *analytic* sentence and the second is a paradigm *synthetic* sentence. Sentence (i) seems to be made true by facts about language or about our concepts, but sentence (ii) is made true largely because of something about the world.

There are many ways to make these notions of analytic and synthetic precise. A full map of the different conceptions of analytic and synthetic, unfortunately, would be an unintelligible mess. Even giving a guide to the most influential concepts, as I try to do in this chapter, may overwhelm the reader with distinctions. I thus advise caution and care on the part of the reader when approaching it.

Having said that, there are three main versions of the analytic–synthetic distinction. The first of these employs *metaphysical conceptions* of analyticity. Metaphysical conceptions of analyticity hold that an analytic sentence is made true by the meaning of the words in it and the way in which they are arranged. A synthetic sentence on metaphysical theories, if true, is made true by virtue of something other than the meanings of the words involved in it or their arrangement. The second distinction employs *epistemological conceptions* of analyticity. According to epistemological notions, a sentence is analytic if and only if understanding it is sufficient to justify the claim that it is true. A true synthetic sentence according to epistemological theories requires more than just the understanding of it to determine that it is true. The third distinction uses *stipulational conceptions* of analyticity. On this conception, a sentence is analytic if and only if it is true because someone has stipulated that it is true.

As we can see, these are three very different ways of making the analytic–synthetic distinction. But they do have something in common. Either the way in which they are made true or the way in which analytic sentences are known to be true has to do with the meaning of the terms used in the sentences. On the face of it, the metaphysical and stipulational conceptions of analyticity are notions that belong to semantics. Semantics is the theory of truth, reference and meaning. All three of these conceptions on analyticity, however, do have interesting epistemological uses. All three of these conceptions give rise to means of justifying beliefs. Often I shall use the term "analytic justification" to refer to one or other of these methods of justification. These means of justification are often, but not always, a priori, and we need to be careful to distinguish those that are from those that are not.

In this chapter I talk about the primary object of a priori knowledge, not as a proposition as in the other chapters, but as a sentence. Sentences should be distinguished from statements and propositions. We met propositions in Chapter 2. A statement is a sentence when considered in a particular context of use. Consider, for example, the sentence "I am hungry". Without knowing who is saying it, you cannot determine what proposition it expresses. But when I say "I am hungry" it becomes a statement and expresses a particular proposition.

There are two reasons why I consider sentences when discussing the analytic–synthetic distinction. A sentence is supposed to be analytic (on the metaphysical conception) if it is true by virtue of the meanings of the words used in it. In a statement, words can take on added meaning because of the context in which they are said. When we consider the word "I" in abstract we know only that it refers to whichever person says it. If we consider it in a context in which, for example, Elvis Presley says "I" then we know it refers to the King of Rock and Roll. When considering the analyticity of a sentence, we need to abstract away from particular contexts of use.

I state again my warning before we begin the chapter. Discussions of the analytic–synthetic distinction are full of other distinctions. It is just that sort of topic. You may need a scorecard to keep track. I am sorry about this. I have tried to keep the distinctions to a minimum, but the best I can do is warn you.

5.2 The history of analyticity

Perhaps the earliest philosopher in whom we find a serious discussion of analytic sentences is Locke. Locke distinguishes "trifling propositions" from other sentences. (By "proposition" Locke means a sentence, not a proposition in the sense of Chapter 2.) These trifling propositions are what we would call analytic sentences. As we see in greater depth in Chapter 8, Locke holds that some of our ideas are simple and others are complex. Complex ideas are constructed from simple ideas. If we predicate an idea of a complex idea, we get a trifling proposition. In saying that "all gold is fusible", we are expressing a trifling proposition. The complex idea of gold includes the less complex idea of being fusible. Other trifling propositions are what Locke calls *identical propositions*, such as "whatever is, is" (*Essay* bk IV, ch. 8).

Kant is perhaps the first to use the terms "analytic" and "synthetic". Kant's distinction is not about sentences but about judgements. Judgements are sorts of thoughts: they are acts of believing propositions. A judgement is analytic for Kant if and only if the concept of the predicate is contained in the concept of the subject. Although this is a view about thoughts rather than about sentences, Kant is here appealing to a traditional view about grammar. A sentence is supposed to have a subject and a predicate. In "All bachelors are male", the subject is "bachelors" and the predicate is "male". The concept *bachelor* does contain the concept of *male*, so this judgement is analytic. Kant makes the analytic–synthetic distinction in part to show how little analytic knowledge we have. He tries to show that certain arguments used in metaphysics, such as the ontological argument for the existence of God, are attempts to give analytic justification for claims that go beyond the reach of our sense experience. Kant holds that all such justification is spurious and that all analytic knowledge is rather trivial.

Gottlob Frege (1848–1925), in opposition to Kant, wants to show that some mathematical knowledge is analytic. In particular, Frege thinks that arithmetic – the theory of the natural numbers, 0, 1, 2, 3, ..., together with addition, subtraction and multiplication – is analytic. Frege, however, has an understanding of analyticity different from Kant's. Frege rejects the view that all analytic judgements are of subject–predicate form. For Frege, all proper definitions are analytic, as are all the laws of logic. Showing that arithmetic is analytic, for Frege, amounts to showing that it is reducible to logic, that is, showing that all the principles of arithmetic are principles of logic. This view is known as logicism, and we shall discuss it in some detail in Chapter 11.

The logical positivists in the early part of the twentieth century use analyticity in order to have a "cheap" route to apriority. On their view, the only a priori knowledge that we can have is analytic. Unlike Kant, and even Frege, they think that all of mathematical knowledge and a good deal of scientific knowledge is analytic. For example, the positivist Hans Reichenbach (1891–1953) is famous for holding that our knowledge of the geometry of physical space is analytic. Like Kant, however, the positivists think that we cannot get any substantive knowledge about the world analytically. The positivists reconcile these two views by holding that analytic "truths" are not really substantive truths about the world; rather, they are conventions. We stipulate that they are true, but their truth consists in nothing but this stipulation. They are not supposed to represent accurately the way things really are. Conventions, for the positivists, allow us to frame our experiences in convenient forms. We shall look at conventionalism in detail later in this chapter.

Quine attacks the view of the logical positivists, and the notion of analyticity more generally. Like the positivists, he holds that the only plausible understanding of a priori knowledge is analytic knowledge, but comes to reject analyticity. Thus he rejects a priori knowledge entirely. In Chapter 6 we shall look at his "master argument" against a priori beliefs and his attempt to avoid apriority in his own epistemology. In Chapter 10 we shall look at his argument against the positivists' view that logical truths are true by convention. And in Chapter 12 we shall examine his argument that Rudolf Carnap's version of the analytic–synthetic distinction is hopelessly circular.[1]

Although Quine's attack on analyticity remains influential, many philosophers have tried to make the notion respectable again. In this chapter, we look at several such attempts.

5.3 Truth by virtue of meaning

Gillian Russell claims that all true sentences are made true in part by virtue of what they mean. Some true sentences – synthetic ones – are also made true by particular facts about this possible world.[2]

On metaphysical conceptions of analyticity, an analytic sentence is made true merely by virtue of the meanings of the words in it and the way in which they are arranged. This characterization of analyticity can be read in various different ways. Recall the concept of double indexing from Chapter 2. On that theory, there are in effect two very natural notions of necessity. We say that a sentence is necessarily true if it is true in all possible worlds. But this can mean two things. First, it can mean that the *proposition* that the sentence expresses in some particular context of utterance is true in all possible worlds. Second, it can mean that the sentence, in whatever context it is uttered, is true. Using this distinction, let us consider the sentences:

- If it exists, Venus is Hesperus.
- I exist.

The name "Hesperus" refers to the planet Venus. Following Kripke, many philosophers think that the sentence "If it exists, Venus is Hesperus" expresses a necessarily true proposition. A proposition, moreover, is the meaning of a sentence. Thus, there is a sense in which "If it exists, Venus is Hesperus" is made true by its meaning and not by some peculiarity of this possible world, because it is true in all possible worlds.

The second sentence never expresses a proposition that is necessarily true. If I say it, then it expresses the proposition <Exists, Ed>. Clearly, this proposition is true in some worlds and not in others. I do not exist in all possible worlds. But in any context in which someone utters "I exist", then they do exist; you have to exist in order to say anything.

These two notions of necessity suggest two different types of theories of analyticity. Let us call the first of these *propositional theories of analyticity*. According to the propositional theories, the meaning of a sentence somehow determines that the proposition it expresses in a given context is necessarily true. Let us call the second type of theory of analyticity *utterance theories of analyticity*. According to utterance theories of analyticity, the meaning of a sentence somehow determines that it will be true whenever it is uttered.

A worry is raised by Boghossian (1997) for metaphysical conceptions of necessity. On metaphysical conceptions, a sentence is analytic if it is true by virtue of its meaning alone. He points out that sentences have meanings and that these meanings are propositions. As we saw in Chapter 2, a sentence has a truth-value by virtue of its expressing a proposition that is true or false. Moreover, propositions do not themselves have meanings. He puts these points together in the following argument:

1. A sentence is true if and only if the proposition that it expresses is true.
2. Sentences have meaning, but propositions do not.
3. Thus, sentences cannot be true by virtue of meaning alone.

(from 1 and 2)

Propositions are the primary bearers of truth or falsity. The truth or falsity of a sentence depends on which proposition it expresses; to be true, sentences must express true propositions. But the sentence itself is not responsible for its own truth. Thus, we cannot really talk of truth by virtue of meaning.

Here is a counter-argument to Boghossian's argument.[3] Suppose that I tell you that the phrase "trifactored sable merle" is a meaningful categorization for collies. You have no idea that this is a colour, but you believe me (correctly) and you know that:

Zermela is either a trifactored sable merle or she is not.

You know this without knowing what (structured) proposition this sentence expresses, since you do not know what "trifactored sable merle" means. You can use the meanings of other parts of the sentence – in particular, "or" and "not" – to determine that the sentence is true.[4]

Let us say that you know that the truth condition for "not" is:

> The sentence "not-S" is true when uttered in context c if and only if S fails to be true in c.

And you know that the truth condition for "or" is:

> The sentence "S_1 or S_2" is true when uttered in context c if and only if at least one of S_1 and S_2 is true in c.

Then you can reason as follows:

1. For any context, "Zermela is a trifactored sable merle" is either true in that context or it fails to be true.
2. For any context either "Zermela is a trifactored sable merle" is true in that context or "Zermela is not a trifactored sable merle" is true in that context.

   (from 1, by the truth condition for "or")
3. For any context, "Zermela is either a trifactored sable merle or she is not" is true in that context.

   (from 2, by the truth condition for disjunction)

The point of this example is to show that we can determine whether a sentence is analytic in the utterance sense without knowing which proposition it expresses. It seems that we can. In some circumstances we only need to know the meanings of some of the parts of the sentence together with the fact that the sentence does express a proposition.

I think this shows that Boghossian's argument fails against utterance theories of analyticity. Boghossian, however, can point out that the example above does not show that sentences can be true by virtue of their meanings alone, but only that in some cases we do not need to understand a sentence in order to know its truth-value. His point that a sentence needs to express a proposition in order to have a truth-value still stands.

But the example does show that the propositional content can be almost irrelevant to the truth-value of a sentence. The short argument given above shows that any meaningful sentence of the form "*S* or not-*S*" is true in any context in which it is uttered. What *S* means is almost irrelevant. It is only relevant that *S* means some proposition.

5.4 Epistemological conceptions of analyticity

There are various epistemological conceptions of analyticity. The one we shall begin with is the following:

> Understanding an analytic sentence is sufficient to justify one's belief that it is true.

Moreover, all analytic sentences are true. This conception is very closely related to the notion of self-evidence that we examined in Chapter 3. According to that notion, understanding a self-evident proposition itself is sufficient justification to hold that it is true. As I argue in Chapter 3, we can claim that a proposition is self-evident only against the background of certain reasoning abilities. The same, as we shall see, is true of analyticity in the epistemological sense.

Let us look at a simple example to see how this conception works. Clearly the sentence "A vixen is a female fox" is analytic in this sense. To understand the word "vixen" is to know that it means "female fox". If one were to deny this sentence, then one could be accused of failing to understand the sentence.

Williamson, however, has put forward several arguments against all forms of the epistemological conception. He gives a series of rather similar arguments, all employing the idea that people with false theories accept sentences as analytic different from those accepted by people who hold correct views. Let us examine one of these arguments.

One sort of false theory that Williamson employs is a logic different from the standard one taught to undergraduates (see §5.6). The alternative logic that Williamson considers is a *three-valued* logic. On this logical theory, a sentence can take one of three values: true, false or indeterminate. Also on this view, the truth condition for negation changes:

> The sentence "not-*S*" is true if and only if *S* is false.

And we add a "falsity condition" as well that says

> The sentence "not-*S*" is false if and only if *S* is true.

If *S* has the indeterminate value, then "not-*S*" is neither true nor false, so "not-*S*" also has the indeterminate value.

What are we to say about sentences such as the following?

> Either it is raining now or it is not raining now.

The proponent of standard, or "classical", logic says that this is true and self-evidently so (and so counts it as analytic). The proponent of three-valued logic says that it is not self-evident (and so counts it as empirical).

We could say that the proponent of three-valued logic has concepts of "not" and "or" different from those of the proponent of classical logic. Thus, when they consider the proposition that the sentence expresses, in fact they are considering different propositions. The concepts of negation and disjunction in those propositions are different. But Williamson thinks there is something wrong with this analysis. Williamson assumes in his example that classical logic is correct in the sense that this is the logic that underlies the way we actually think and speak. To tell three-valued logicians that they do not understand negation and disjunction is "irrelevant and gratuitously patronizing" (2007: 91). He thinks they understand these concepts in the same way that others do. Their disagreement with classical logicians, claims Williamson, is about logic, not about the meanings of words. Although I disagree with Williamson that we can distinguish between logic and semantics in this way, let us grant him this point.

The reasoning that allows the classical logician to find the proposition expressed by this sentence is not open to the three-valued logician. What is different about the two logicians, on this story, is not that they have different concepts but that one has the background reasoning ability to find the proposition self-evident and the other does not. But if, say, classical logic is correct and three-valued logic is not, then the classical logician is right in saying that the proposition is self-evident, and the three-valued logician is wrong. And so the sentence is analytic. Similarly, if the three-valued logician is correct, then the sentence is not analytic.[5]

Williamson is wrong in claiming that the epistemological conception is untenable, but his argument does make us realize that we have to read the claim that understanding an analytic sentence is sufficient to justify one's belief in it against the background of what we consider to be *normal* reasoning abilities. By adopting three-valued logic, a person deprives themselves of certain types of reasoning that they could otherwise use. Hence this person does not find all the same sentences to be analytic.

Thus we should amend the definition of our epistemological conception of analyticity to read:

> Understanding an analytic sentence is sufficient to justify one's belief that it is true given that one has normal reasoning abilities.

There are, of course, worries about what should be considered normal with regard to reasoning abilities, but I shall leave those worries to the reader.

5.5 Truth by stipulation

The last conception of analyticity that we examine is the *stipulational conception*. According to this notion, a sentence is analytic if and only if it is true because it is stipulated to be true. We cannot merely stipulate any sentence to be true. I cannot just stipulate that the Taj Mahal is purple and thereby make it purple. Rather, certain conditions must hold before a stipulation can be successful.

A stipulation is a sort of *speech act*. A speech act is an action that we do by uttering (saying, writing, etc.) something. For example, making a promise is a speech act. If you promise someone else that you will do something, you do an action that affects others. Speech acts often have conditions that must be fulfilled in order for them to be successful. Naming something is a sort of speech act. For instance, suppose that you smash a bottle of champagne on the side of a ship and say, "I name this ship the *Rudolf Carnap*". If you are empowered by the owner of the ship to name it, then this speech act may be successful, but if you just walk up to a random ship and perform this speech act, then it will not be successful. You need to have the right to name it.

Likewise, stipulating can only be successful under certain circumstances. Suppose that you want to stipulate that the word "chewerrier" is to stand for the dog breed that comes from crossing chihuahuas with fox terriers. This stipulation can be successful (in the dog-breeding world) if you are empowered by some important society of dog breeders (such as the American Kennel Club) to name a breed and the word "chewerrier" is not already in use for a breed. (If it is in use, then we shall need some way of distinguishing different meanings of the same word, or we may just deem the stipulation to have failed and search for another name for chihuahua–terrier crosses.)[6]

More generally, a stipulation can be successful only if it is *conservative* over the existing uses of words. This means that it cannot conflict with the existing truths and falsehoods of a language. In the Taj Mahal example, the problem is that the words "Taj Mahal" and "purple" are already in use and have accepted meanings. People already accept the sentence "The Taj Mahal is not purple", and unless they agree to change the meanings of "Taj Mahal" or "purple" the sentence "The Taj Mahal is purple" cannot be deemed to be true in English. Moreover, we cannot now stipulate that "The Taj Mahal is white" is true, even though it is true. It was true independently of our stipulation. We cannot make stipulations about sentences that already are true or false.

In his famous article "Two Dogmas of Empiricism", Quine (1980b) asks what makes a stipulation into an analytic truth. This, I think, is an extremely good question. As we saw in Chapter 2, we can stipulate certain non-analytic truths (such as "the first child of 2020 will be named 'Tui'"). What makes some stipulations analytic truths and others not?

Some stipulations determine necessary truths. Consider again the truth conditions for "not" and "or" that we discussed earlier in this chapter. These are stipulations of a sense and they make all meaningful sentences of the form "S or not-S" true. When someone invents a new logical operator, they stipulate in effect that it will be used in a certain way when talking about any possible world. The difference between this sort of speech act and the one that named the first child born in 2020 is that the latter only *fixes the reference of a name* in this possible world. It is not meant to be a necessary truth. Only those stipulations that create necessary truths in the right way are analytic.

The stipulational conception is epistemologically important for several reasons. First, all language is to some extent conventional. What words and phrases mean is to some extent stipulated by us. This does not imply that we always know all the consequences of our stipulations. In the case of the meaning of the word "water", someone chose to use it to mean the stuff that we drink, bathe in and so on, but he or she did not know that it is H_2O. But there is always a choice – a stipulation – that determines what words and phrases mean. Thus, any view of analyticity has to account for truth by stipulation to some extent. Second, we often, although not always, know what we have stipulated. If we set up a convention, we often have epistemic access to the contents of that convention. Sometimes this access is rather difficult, as in the case of complex conventions such as laws and regulations.

5.6 Implicit definitions

An important class of stipulations is those that give *implicit definitions* of terms. There are different ways to define a phrase. For example, there are *explicit* and *implicit* definitions. An explicit definition is the sort that we find in a dictionary. It states the meaning of a term in a sentence or two. The examples that we have been using up to now of analytic sentences have all been based on explicit definitions.

A term is implicitly defined if there is some theory in which the term occurs and the role of the term in the theory defines it. The notion of an implicit definition first comes to prominence in the field of geometry in the late nineteenth century. In this period the great mathematician David Hilbert (1862–1943) produces the first logically complete axiomatization of Euclidean and various non-Euclidean geometries (see Chapter 2). In Euclid's own axiomatization of his geometry, there are logical gaps. In order to prove the facts about geometry that Euclid wants to prove, he needs occasionally to use principles and techniques that are not explicitly in his list of axioms or definitions. Hilbert's system is complete in the sense that it does not require the use of anything that is not explicitly stated in his axioms or rules.[7] Unlike Euclid, Hilbert does not begin by stating a series of explicit definitions of geometrical notions such as point and line. Instead, these notions are taken as undefined and their meaning is taken to be determined by the role that they have in the geometrical theories. Thus, for example, a point can be said to be between two other points, or on a line, and so on. The notion of a point is not given any meaning apart from the sentences that can be proved about it in the theory. The same is true for the concept of line, the concept of being between and all the other geometrical notions.

Frege criticizes Hilbert's view that geometrical terms are defined in his geometrical theories. According to Frege, a proper definition gives the meaning of a term. Moreover, the meaning of a term determines the referent of that term. For example, the meaning of "vixen" is "female fox" and this definition determines exactly which things in the world can correctly be called vixens. (Of course this assumes that the meanings of "female" and "fox" are already determined.) But Hilbert's theories do not determine which objects in the world can correctly be called points and lines.

Consider an easier example: the theory of the integers (the positive and negative numbers). We can take the true sentences of this theory and reinterpret all of them. We can take each number and reinterpret it as referring to its negative. Thus "2" will refer to "–2" and "–2" will refer to "2", and so on. Then all the true sentences about the integers will still come out as true. "$2 \times 2 = 4$" in this inverted theory means that $-2 \otimes -2 = -4$. The operation $\otimes$ is not normal multiplication, but is changed so as to make all the sentences about multiplication seem to come out the right way. The point is that sentences that make up the theory of the integers ("$2 \times 2 = 4$", and the like) do not fully determine which entities they are about. These sentences can all be taken to be true, but about things that are completely different from the things to which we intended them to refer. Therefore the theory of the integers (i.e. the true sentences about the integers) does not by itself determine the things to which its terms refer. For Frege, this means that these terms are not defined by that theory.

The notion of an implicit definition, however, is still alive in philosophy. Frank Jackson uses the notion as a basis of his metaphysical and ethical theories. Jackson begins with an almost universally held theory, which he calls a "folk theory". There are (supposedly) folk theories of morality, of psychology and so on. The meanings of terms that are particular to the topic covered by the theory – for example, "good" and "bad" in morality – are determined by the roles these terms play in the relevant theory.

There is an important difference between Jackson's approach and Hilbert's. Jackson does not claim that all the terminology in a folk theory is implicitly defined by that theory. In folk moral theory, for example, there are moral terms such as "good" and "bad", and non-moral terms such as "kill" and "preference". Only the moral terms are defined by folk morality. Other terms may have their meanings determined in other ways. The meanings of the non-moral terms help to determine meanings of the moral terms.

5.7 Conventions in science

The logical positivists, in particular Carnap and Reichenbach, use the stipulational conception of analyticity very heavily in their philosophies of science. According to Carnap, we choose a way of speaking about our experiences. This is called a "linguistic framework". This linguistic framework will determine that certain sentences are true. For example, if we choose Carnap's physical language, then we in effect stipulate that the sentence "everything that exists is material" is true (i.e. that there are no immaterial minds, ghosts, deities, etc.). According to Reichenbach, in choosing a geometry scientists stipulate that the geometry that they choose is right.

The frameworks or theories that are adopted as conventions, according to Reichenbach and Carnap, implicitly define certain theoretical terms, such as "point" and "line", but also "electron", and even "physical object". These terms mean nothing when taken out of the context of the framework or theory.

Carnap and Reichenbach also claim that their conventions are analytic. There is, however, a tension here. It would seem that even in stipulating that we will talk as though everything is physical, for example, we do not commit ourselves to the claim that it is impossible for there to be anything except physical objects. Similarly, even if we stipulate that actual space is Euclidean, say, we do not thereby claim that all possible spaces are Euclidean.

But what we have said, on Carnap's view at least, is to ignore an important distinction. For Carnap, picking a linguistic framework does set the limits to what can be considered possible within that framework. We can think of possible worlds as containing ghosts and other spirits, but we can do so only outside this framework.

In order to adopt Carnap and Reichenbach's view of conventions in science, we need to think that stipulations of this sort are appropriate. As we said in the previous section, a stipulation is appropriate only when it does not conflict with an existing fact. We cannot stipulate that there are no ghosts if there are in fact ghosts, and we cannot stipulate that physical space is Euclidean if in fact it is not Euclidean. Carnap and Reichenbach deny that there are any facts about these matters. On this view, physical space does not in and of itself have a geometry. We decide which geometry it has.

We can adopt conventions only where we think that there are no matters of fact. Recall that we cannot stipulate the colour of the Taj Mahal. It already has a colour. To adopt conventionalism in science requires that we hold anti-realist views about what we are stipulating. We cannot claim that space already has a specific geometry and then say that we are stipulating what that geometry has. If it has a geometry, then it has it regardless of what we say. Thus, in order to be a conventionalist about geometry, we have to be an anti-realist about geometry. This is not to condemn conventionalism, but it is always good to remember the commitments of a theory when considering it.

5.8 Analytic justification

All three types of analyticity – metaphysical, epistemological and stipulational – support forms of justification. The resulting types of justification are similar to one another in that they all involve appeals to the meaning of the words involved. When people appeal, for example, to the definition of a word or phrase (the extremely overused "by definition") in a reasoning process, they are using some form of analytic justification. Similarly, when I "calculated" that "Either Zermela is a trifactored sable merle or she is not" is necessarily true, I used a form of analytic justification.

My justification of that sentence about Zermela is a priori. Knowing the meanings of some of the words involved, together with a little bit of logical reasoning, is sufficient to discover the necessary truth of the sentence.

Understood in a certain way, analytic justification is not defeasible. If we have correctly understood a sentence and correctly analysed the concepts expressed in it, then we have proved that the sentence is true. But of course we can be in error about the concepts and we can be mistaken in our analyses of them. Thus our judgements about whether we are analytically justified are clearly fallible. If we want to retain the label "analytic justification" for cases in which one's understanding and analysis are both correct, then we have a form of a priori justification that is indefeasible. If we want to say instead that we are analytically justified when it merely seems to us that a sentence is true on the basis of our (perhaps faulty) understanding of the words that make up the sentence, then we can hold that analytic justification is both empirically and a priori defeasible.

It is an interesting question as to the limits of analytic justification. Consider, for example, the sentence "Anything that is coloured is extended". This sentence is not usually considered to be analytic. But it is analytic in either of the metaphysical conceptions that we have discussed. It seems hard to justify this sentence by appeal just to the meanings of the words involved. It seems that we need something else, such as the claim that we cannot imagine anything that is coloured and fails to be extended. Here we reach a grey area. Can our imagination be involved in this way in understanding the meanings of words? It seems that there may not be a fact about this. It may be that epistemologists need to make a stipulation about this.[8]

5.9 Summary
In this chapter we have discussed three notions of analyticity: the metaphysical conception, the epistemological conception and the stipulational conception. Although we did not explore the stipulational conception fully – this will be done in Chapters 7 and 10 – we found them all to be viable conceptions. And all are, in some cases, good bases for analytic justification.

Further reading
Carnap's theories of analyticity (and there are at least two of them) are in his *Meaning and Necessity* (1947). Quine's most famous attack on Carnap's views of analyticity is in his article "Two Dogmas of Empiricism" ([1951] 1980b). For

interesting background to the debate between Carnap and Quine take a look at their correspondence in *Dear Carnap, Dear Van* (1990).

Gillian Russell has an extensive defence of her metaphysical conception of analyticity in her *Truth by Virtue of Meaning* (2008).

Paul Boghossian and Gilbert Harman have an interesting debate about the viability of the epistemic conception in their articles "Analyticity Regained" and "Analyticity Regained?" in *Noûs* **30** (1996).

Tim Williamson's attack on the epistemological conception and his own defence of a metaphysical conception is in his *The Philosophy of Philosophy* (2007). A forthcoming issue of the journal *Philosophy and Phenomenological Research* is devoted to articles about this book. Some of these articles, such as Boghossian's, analyse Williamson's criticism of the epistemological conception.

6 Radical empiricism

6.1 The burden of proof

William James coined the term "radical empiricism" to mean a philosophy that includes as objects of experience particular things, relations and values. But I use the label to designate something quite different; it is the view that there are no a priori beliefs.

In order to evaluate the theories of apriority that we are examining, I need to put them into context. We need, in particular, to see whether philosophy without the a priori is viable and what, if anything, one needs to relinquish in order to get rid of the a priori. In this chapter, we shall look briefly at the history of radical empiricism and then in some depth at four radical empiricists – Mill, C. S. Peirce, Quine and Gilbert Harman.

The main question we need to ask in this chapter is: why do we need to think that there are a priori beliefs? In Chapter 1, we said that the a priori is useful in helping us understand how we can have knowledge about necessity and about certain types of normativity, especially moral obligations. Mill, Quine and Harman think we cannot know about what is necessarily true. Quine goes so far as to attack the notion of necessity itself. Harman thinks there are no moral facts in any strong sense, and he thinks moral knowledge is easily obtained, but is not the sort of knowledge many philosophers have taken it to be.[1] Quine says very similar things about the nature of epistemology itself: it is a normative theory in a very weak sense, according to him. Life without the a priori also seems to require that we do philosophy without much in the way of necessity or normativity.

The notion of necessity is a central notion in philosophy. It is central in the way in which philosophers think about subjects such as logic and metaphysics. The study of these fields should tell us not only about what is the case, but also about what has to be the case. Similarly, the notion of normativity is strongly associated with other branches of philosophy such as epistemology and ethics. To weaken the sort of normativity that is involved in philosophy is to do serious damage to views that are near and dear to many philosophers. Thus, the burden of proof is on the radical empiricist to show us why we should reject the idea that we can know about what is necessarily true and what is morally obligatory.

This analysis of the burden of proof reverses the usual understanding of the debate. Radical empiricists adopt more parsimonious ontologies. They claim that we cannot know about other possible worlds, moral facts and so on, so they do not include them in their lists of what exists. Because they have less in their theories, they claim that the onus is on the opposition to prove that these entities are really required. But if we think about the matter in terms of epistemology rather than ontology, the onus reverses. Philosophers and non-philosophers alike think they know something about what is necessarily true and what is morally required of us. The burden of proof is on those who deny such knowledge to show that we do not have it.

This chapter looks at radical-empiricist reasons for abandoning the a priori. We begin by looking at three radical-empiricist methodologies: Mill's inductivism, Harman's inference to the best explanation and Quine's theory of belief revision. I put Quine's view last (and out of chronological order) because it connects closely with the next topic: Quine's master argument against the a priori. This argument appears many times in Quine's writings. It tries to show that certain theses that come out of his view of belief revision justify a rejection of the idea that there are any a priori beliefs. The chapter ends with an analysis and rejection of the master argument.

6.2 Mill's inductivism

One form of radical empiricism claims that all justification is some form of empirical induction. This position is held by Mill, who claims that even most of our logical and mathematical beliefs are justified by induction.

For Mill, induction is a form of "colligation": the bringing together of various particular facts to give them a single explanation ([1843] 1974: bk III, ch. 2, §4). Thus, in doing induction one provides facts with an explanation as well as predicting future or general facts.

Let us look at Mill's view of the laws of logic. As I shall discuss in depth in Chapter 10, a logical theory is somewhat like a geometry. There are various logical systems, just as there are rival geometrical systems. Like geometries, logical systems have a set of axioms, which we shall call the "laws" of the logical system. They also have rules that allow us to make deductions from these axioms. The laws of a logic are usually claimed to be necessarily true. Mill, however, denies that we can know whether the laws of a logic are necessarily true. He considers the law of non-contradiction, which for many philosophers is obviously necessarily true. This law says that for any sentence S, it is not the case that both S and not-S.

Mill claims that we may not be able to imagine a case in which a contradiction is true, but just because we cannot conceive of something does not mean that it is impossible. And so it might be possible that there are true contradictions (*ibid*.: bk II, ch. 7, §5). We are justified in believing the law of non-contradiction, but not that it is necessarily true, by induction. We have never perceived a contradiction and so we hold that no contradictions are true, nor will there ever be a true contradiction.

One problem with the inductive view of the epistemology of logic is that our inductive methods seem to have deductive logic built into them. For example, according to most canons of scientific method, if we test a hypothesis inductively, what we test are the *consequences* of the hypothesis. To derive the consequences of a hypothesis we need logic.[2]

Mill recognizes the need for "demonstration" to be included in our inductive methods (*ibid*.: bk II, ch. 4, §6), but he denies that this is what we normally call deductive logic. He claims to have reduced what we normally think of as logical inference to reasoning about the similarity of things. The inference from "All people are mortal" and "The Duke of Wellington is a person" to the conclusion "The Duke of Wellington is mortal" should not be seen as an instance of the form: "Certain individuals have a given attribute; an individual or individuals resemble the former in certain other attributes; therefore they resemble them in the given attribute" (*ibid*.: bk II, ch. 3, §7).

Thus we read the purported deductive argument as in fact saying that other certain individuals who are people are mortal, and the Duke of Wellington resembles these individuals in being a person, so he resembles them in being mortal. This reconstructed inference has a character very different from the original one. The original one purports to be deductively valid: the conclusion seems to follow necessarily from the premises. The reconstructed argument seems only to give us a probable conclusion even if the premises are correct. So according to Mill, even what we normally think of as deduction is in fact a form of induction. *His inductive methods are inductive all the way down!*

Mill thinks there is something incoherent about the way in which logicians usually think about logic. He says they consider deductive logical inferences to be "proofs", but they also hold that in a valid argument there is "nothing in the conclusion which was not already asserted in the premises" (*ibid*.: bk II, ch. 3, §2). He thinks that a proof, to be a real proof, has to show us something new. Thus, the claim that proofs are deductive inferences is inconsistent with the claim that in a valid deductive inference the conclusion introduces nothing new.

Mill has hit on something interesting. The claim that the conclusion of a deductively valid argument does not introduce anything new has to be interpreted carefully. In terms of possible worlds we do this as follows. Let us consider the premises and conclusion of an inference to be unstructured propositions in the sense of being sets of possible worlds (see Chapter 2). Take the set of worlds that belong to all the premises and call this set X. If the inference is valid, then the conclusion will be true in all the worlds in X. Thus, the premises taken together in a sense necessarily make true the conclusion of the inference. In this way we can understand the claim that the conclusion of a valid argument is implicit in its premises.

We can also understand the sense in which the conclusion introduces something new. The set of worlds in which the conclusion is true need not exactly match X. It needs to include X, but it might contain other worlds too. It may, then, select only certain aspects of what is in all the premises. Moreover, often in deductive arguments what is in the conclusion is not in a single premise. The conclusion shows us what happens from the combination of the premises.

Mill's approach to the problem of deductive logic is really to reject the question. One problem is to determine how we know that the laws of logic are necessarily true. His reply to this is that we have no such knowledge. The other problem is to determine how we know that the logical rules necessarily preserve truth. Once again Mill denies that we know this at all. Furthermore, our reasoning, in so far as it is good reasoning, is not really deductive. It is all inductive.

Mill justifies induction by claiming that we must use it. We are psychologically constructed so as to use it. The question is how this fact is epistemologically relevant. What Mill needs to argue is that we should use induction. It is often claimed by philosophers that if we ought to do something, then we can do it. Using a little logic, we can infer from this principle that if we must do something, then we are permitted to do it. But Mill seems to rely on a stronger principle, that is, *if we must do something then we ought to do it.*[3]

It is not clear that we ought to do something just because we cannot help doing it. If a psychopath kills someone because he is deranged and cannot help himself, then it may be that we cannot blame him for his action (hence it is permissible in some very weak sense), but it would seem strange to say that he ought to have killed that person. Thus, it seems that the "must implies ought" principle is not obviously true. But, as we have said, we may weaken Mill's conclusion to say that the use of induction is permissible.[4]

Induction, however, has its limitations. Charles Sanders Peirce (1839–1914) suggests that induction needs to be supplemented by other reasoning processes. In particular, we need a process whereby to generate hypotheses that can be confirmed or rejected by induction. Peirce claims that this reasoning process is captured by his conception of abduction, which is the topic of the next section.

6.3 Peirce and Harman on abduction

Strictly speaking, Peirce is not a radical empiricist. He believes that mathematical reasoning is a priori. In contrast, he believes that our knowledge of logic is a posteriori. I include him in this chapter because he has a strong influence on radical empiricists – especially Quine and Harman – and because he is the discoverer of abduction.

Abduction is the process of reasoning from data to an explanation. In its more contemporary form, due to Harman, given a set of data we choose between the best of the available explanations of the data. The best explanation is the one that has the most favourable combination of being the simplest, most intuitive and so on. In short, we choose between the available explanations for a given set of data on the basis of their theoretical virtues, in the sense of Chapter 2. Harman calls this process *inference to the best explanation*, and it is known as that in the literature, or by its initials (IBE).

Peirce claims that scientific method is made up of induction, deduction and abduction. Induction gives scientists a data set to explain; in abduction they devise hypotheses to explain the data; and deduction allows them to analyse concepts and "refine hypotheses".

These three reasoning methods are, for Peirce, normative theories. He calls logic (in the wide sense, which includes all three of these methods of reasoning) the "ethics of the intellect" (Letter to Lady Welby, 14 March 1909, in Peirce 1958: 415). Ethics, for Peirce, does not concern moral principles in the usual sense (see Chapter 9) but rather methods for obtaining one's goals. Reasoning is a method for obtaining our intellectual goals. Peirce sees our chief intellectual goal as the removal of doubt. Thus, the methods of reasoning are successful or unsuccessful depending on how well they help us answer our questions about the world. The justification of reasoning methods is, for Peirce, an empirical matter; the success or failure of a method of reasoning in this regard can only be judged empirically.[5]

Harman's view of reasoning is, in many ways, like Peirce's theory, but Harman takes inference to the best explanation to be the central reasoning method. Deduction is not really a reasoning method, according to Harman. Deductive logic gives us a set of general truths and it tells us about what sentences follow from what other sentences. For example, it tells us that the rule of *modus ponens* is valid:

If S_1, then S_2
S_1
_____

Therefore, S_2

This rule is not a rule of inference, according to Harman. It does not tell us that if we believe its premises we should believe its conclusion. It leaves open the possibility that we may reject one or both of the premises if we do not wish to accept the conclusion.

Harman also thinks that the traditional way of understanding induction is incorrect. Typically we characterize induction as a process of enumerating a series of similar events and then concluding that either a simple generalization is true or that the next event that we come across will be similar to the ones we have already found. Induction, then, is usually taken to be a simple projection on the basis of a sample. Harman thinks this is wrong. We may do various things with a sample in an induction. We may use it to show that a belief we currently have is incorrect, we may use it to provide data to test a theory, and so on.

According to Harman, the best way to think about induction is as an element of abduction. What we want is to have the "best total explanatory account" of our experiences. Induction helps by providing us with data that our beliefs are to explain. The best system of beliefs that we can have is one that provides the best available explanation for our experiences. For Harman, all our epistemic practices are elements of the process of inference to the best explanation. This means that all our beliefs are to be judged in terms of how they relate to experience. This is clearly a form of radical empiricism.

We can see in Harman's epistemology a development of Peirce's view. According to Peirce our overall goal is to settle doubts. On Harman's view, inference to the best explanation allows us to do this in a systematic and unified manner.

Although Peirce and Harman think of abduction and inference to the best explanation as empirical methods, there are ways of using them in a priori reasoning. Suppose that one has several a priori beliefs that she wishes to explain together. She may choose a single "explanation" of those beliefs on the basis of the theoretical virtues that this explanation has compared with the alternative explanations. For instance, mathematicians have used such explanations to explain their beliefs about mathematics. They believe that $2 + 2 = 4$, the square root of two is irrational, and so on. As we shall see in Chapter 11, mathematicians have postulated a unified ontology of objects (called "sets") that, together with some definitions, allows the deduction of all of these particular beliefs. This postulation can be viewed as a form of abduction. It gives us a single theory from which a huge number of particular beliefs may be deduced. The choice between rival theories has been made by some mathematicians on the basis of the simplicity, elegance, strength and ease of use of the alternative theories. Thus, we have non-empirical uses of abduction as well.

6.4 Quine's web of belief

In "Two Dogmas of Empiricism" ([1951] 1980b), Quine uses the metaphor of a web to describe how we organize our system of beliefs. The beliefs at the centre of the web have very widespread consequences and we are less likely to abandon these beliefs than those at the edge of the web. At the edges are our perceptual beliefs.

Let us call the relationship between beliefs in the web "epistemic entrenchment".[6] When we change beliefs, we do so in accordance with two principles:

- *Conservativeness*: all other things being equal, abandon a less entrenched belief rather than a more entrenched belief.
- *Consistency*: when integrating new beliefs into our web, maintain consistency. If the new beliefs are not consistent with all the old beliefs, then we have to abandon some beliefs until we construct a consistent system.

Quine does not argue for the correctness of these rules. As we shall see later when we discuss his naturalized epistemology, Quine does not think it is possible to give such a justification.[7]

If we relinquish beliefs in the centre of the web – those beliefs that are the most entrenched – we have to modify the relationships between other beliefs. Suppose that we believe that the following logical rule is valid:

$$S_1 \text{ and } S_2$$

$$\text{Therefore, } S_2$$

This rule affects all our beliefs about sentences of the form "S_1 and S_2", and, typically, we have many of these. It tells us that any sentence of the form S_2 is more entrenched than any sentence of the form "S_1 and S_2". This might seem strange, but it is correct. If we maintain our belief in this logical rule and reject the belief in S_2, we also have to reject our belief in "S_1 and S_2". But the reverse does not hold. This view of how we revise our beliefs is *holistic*. In the web, there are very widespread interconnections between beliefs. Beliefs tie other beliefs together.

Entrenchment is not only a logical matter. In some cases we may have other reasons to hold on to certain beliefs in the face of apparent counter-evidence. In the discussion of the inverted master argument later in this chapter, we shall see how one can use this feature of the web in order to attack the notion of apriority.

In the next four sections, we look at Quine's "master argument" against the a priori.

6.5 The Duhem–Quine problem

Central to Quine's thinking about how we revise beliefs is a view known as *confirmational holism*. According to confirmational holism, our experience does not confirm or refute beliefs individually; rather, it refutes them in groups. Quine is famous for holding a radical form of holism. He claims often that single experiences can refute our system of beliefs as a whole. As we shall see, this radical form of confirmational holism is not essential to his argument.

Consider an example. As we saw in Chapter 2, Einstein's theory of relativity was confirmed by what happened during an eclipse. A star appeared to shift position. This apparent shift was explained by the mass of the sun bending the light from the star. But the experience of what happened during the eclipse did not by itself confirm the theory of relativity. Instruments, such as telescopes and cameras, were used. Telescopes and cameras have optics, mirrors and other parts. The behaviour of these instruments must be taken into account when assessing the experiment. For example, we have to assume that the telescopes and cameras were accurately recording the light from the star and from the other stars used to locate the particular star. Only if we make this assumption can we assess relativity theory and its rival (Newton's theory of gravity) against one another using data from the eclipse.

Sentences about the instruments used in experiments and other background that is needed to assess experiments are called "auxiliary hypotheses". Pierre Duhem (1861–1916) claims that the use of auxiliary hypotheses is unavoidable. He also claims that when an experiment does not give a predicted outcome, it may not falsify that theory. It may, in fact, be one or more auxiliary hypotheses that need changing rather that the theory that is being tested. The logical situation is quite straightforward. We can think of the relationship of a theory and a collection of auxiliary hypotheses to a prediction in terms of a deductive argument:

Theory
Auxiliary hypotheses
_____

Therefore, Prediction

If the prediction turns out to be false, given only this deductive argument, we cannot tell whether the theory is wrong or one or more of the auxiliary hypotheses are false. This is the Duhem–Quine problem.

6.6 Quine's master argument

In this section, we discuss an argument due to Quine that pervades his writing and provides a basis for his rejection of apriority. This argument has a place in Quine's thought that is similar to what André Gombay calls "Berkeley's master argument".

Before we give a schematic version of the argument, let us look at a simple example. Suppose that you have the following beliefs:

(i)   John is a bachelor.
(ii) All bachelors are unmarried men.
(iii) Everyone who wears a wedding ring is married.

Suppose also that you find out that John wears a wedding ring. You have a choice about which beliefs to revise. You could reject belief (i) and believe that John is married. You could reject belief (iii) and hold that at least one person who wears a wedding ring is unmarried. According to Quine, you could also reject belief (ii) and come to believe that at least one bachelor is married. On Quine's view, the only difference between belief (ii) and the other two beliefs is that it is more entrenched in your web of belief. You probably will not revise that belief, but only because, all things being equal, one chooses to revise less entrenched beliefs over more entrenched beliefs.

We can see in this example how Quine uses the Duhem–Quine problem to motivate what I call his "free-choice principle". The free-choice principle says that, given a situation in which a set of beliefs entails a false empirical prediction, we are free to choose to revise any of these beliefs. The Duhem–Quine problem says that it is not clear which of a theory or our auxiliary hypotheses are responsible for a false prediction. Quine thinks that this lack of clarity allows us to choose to reject any of the principles used to derive a false prediction. Our choice of which premise to reject may be determined by the entrenchment relations between those beliefs, but in principle there is no norm that tells us that any of these beliefs is immune from revision.

Here is the free-choice principle stated in typical Quinean prose:

> What then of the holistic doctrine that *every* sentence is vulnerable? This claim is tenable in legalistic principle. Even a truth of logic of mathematics could be abandoned to hold fast some casual sentence of ephemeral fact: "could" in the sense that the thus altered system of the world could still save the appearances. Could be abandoned – very well; but *would* be? Yes, in an extremity; there are the two oft-cited examples, intuitionist logic and the deviant logics that have been proposed for quantum mechanics. In principle, thus, vulnerability is universal.
> ("Reply to Jules Vuillemin", in Hahn & Schilpp 1986: 619–20)

The passage "this claim is tenable in legalistic principle" means that in principle we can choose to revise any of our beliefs, even if we rarely revise those that are traditionally called "a priori". This is an expression of the free-choice principle.

Another idea that is incorporated into the master argument is Quine's view that all our beliefs entail empirical predictions. This means that we use each of our beliefs, together with other beliefs, to derive particular predictions. Some of our beliefs seem "remote" from experience, such as our beliefs about logic and mathematics. Quine claims that even these have an impact on what experiences we think we will have. I think we can see here the influence on Quine of the American pragmatist school of thought. According to pragmatism, the value of a belief is in its application in experience. It is pointless to have a belief, on this view, if it has no observable consequences. Let us call the view that all our beliefs are used to derive empirical predictions the "derivation principle".

Putting together the free-choice principle and the derivation principle, we can construct the master argument:

1. The belief in *S* is a priori.   (hypothesis)
2. We cannot falsify *S* by experience.

       (from 1 and the empirical immunity notion of apriority)
3. The belief in *S* is used together with other beliefs to make
    empirical hypotheses.   (derivation principle)
4. These empirical hypotheses can turn out to be false.   (fact)
5. We are free to choose to reject *S* rather than the other beliefs
    to accommodate false predictions.   (free-choice principle)
6. 5 contradicts 2.
7. Hypothesis 1 must be false.   (from 6 by a *reductio ad absurdum*)

I use *S* for the belief in question because Quine thinks that to believe something is to accept a sentence. Thus, to believe that dogs are mammals is to accept the sentence "Dogs are mammals", or some sentence like this. Quine rejects the view that there are propositions in addition to sentences. This is important for us, and I shall examine it in detail in my analysis of the master argument in the next section.

6.7 Analysis of the master argument

Let us return to the short example in the previous section. If we reject our belief that bachelors are unmarried men, then what are we to make of the belief that John is a bachelor? If beliefs are just sentences, as Quine holds, then the rejection of the belief that all bachelors are unmarried is independent of the belief that John is a bachelor. One can believe just one of these sentences, or both of them, or reject both. But if we think that beliefs are about propositions, then there is a real difficulty with the example.

To understand what this difficulty is, consider another example, due to my late colleague George Hughes. If I decide that I shall use the word "pig" to refer to birds, then my belief in the sentence "Pigs fly" will be easy to justify:

1. I use "pig" to refer to birds.
2. I believe that birds fly.
3. I should believe that "pigs fly" is true.   (from 1 and 2)

This argument gives me a good reason to believe that the sentence "Pigs fly" is true. But instead of showing that I should believe that pigs fly, it shows that there is something odd about taking beliefs to be about sentences. Suppose that prior to deciding to use "pig" to refer to birds I believed that pigs do not fly. Does this mean that I should reject this prior belief? If we accept the view that beliefs are about propositions, then we can think of the content of this prior belief as:

$$\langle Not, \langle Some\ x, \langle And, \langle\langle Pig, x\rangle, \langle Flies, x\rangle\rangle\rangle\rangle\rangle$$

In this representation of the proposition, "Pig" stands for the *property of being a pig*, not for the word "pig". Coming to believe that "pig" refers to birds need not change my relationship to this proposition. Whatever we call it, a pig is a pig. It is not a bird.

Returning to the master argument, suppose that you accept the sentence "Some bachelors are married". We can say one of two things about you. Either you are saying something that is false or you are using the word "bachelor" to express a property different from the one it usually denotes. A defender of the a priori against the master argument should say that in contradicting the definition of "bachelor" – that is, "a bachelor is an unmarried man" – one is not using the word "bachelor" to refer to the property of being a bachelor.

The propositional view of beliefs together with the idea that there are necessary conditions for one's being able to refer to specific properties undermines the free-choice principle. It is not the case that one can merely abandon beliefs such as "all bachelors are unmarried men". Denying that sentence, on the view that we are contemplating at present, indicates that one is using "bachelor" in a non-standard way. Thus, if one denies that sentence, one cannot be denying the proposition that all bachelors are unmarried men. Rejecting that proposition from one's belief system is impossible.[8]

In the passage given in the previous section, Quine claims that even logical and mathematical theories can be considered empirical because people have given "empirical reasons" for revising them. Quine's examples are rather dated, so let us look at a different one due to Penelope Maddy.

In quantum physics, there is a problem concerning the view that space is made up of non-dimensional points. The physicist Richard Feynman claims that we should regard space as made up of many tiny pieces, which have positive length, width and depth. The problem concerns the treatment of very small phenomena in physics, the radius of which is less than 10^{-14} cm. The equations that treat larger-scale phenomena give absurd answers for phenomena smaller than that (for example, in classical particle physics, the energy mass of an electron goes to infinity). Feynman and others solved the problem by developing a procedure called "renormalization". Feynman, however, does not think renormalization is legitimate. At best it is *ad hoc* and at worst it is inconsistent. He says:

> The shell game that we play … is technically called "renormalization". But no matter how clever the word, it is still what I would call a dippy process! Having to resort to such hocus-pocus has prevented us from proving that the theory of quantum electrodynamics is mathematically self-consistent. It's surprising that the theory still hasn't been proved self-consistent one way or the other by now; I suspect that renormalization is not mathematically legitimate.   (1990: 128)

Feynman claims that the belief that space is made up of infinitely many dimensionless points is at fault: "I rather suspect that the simple ideas of geometry, extended down to infinitely small space, are wrong" (1967: 166). Feynman thinks we need to think of space as made up of tiny pieces. Maddy (1997: 149) takes this to be a potential empirical refutation of the belief that space is made up of dimensionless points.

The belief that space is made up of dimensionless points is supposed by many to be a priori. This argument is supposed to show that it is empirically defeasible. But it is not clear to me that it does this. In this situation, scientists have a choice between at least three different theories: (i) the original theory with renormalization; (ii) Feynman's proposal of a theory with space made up of tiny bits; (iii) a theory in which space is made up of dimensionless points, but in which physical processes cannot take place in regions of less than a certain size.

If the renormalization theory is consistent, then these three views are empirically equivalent. That means that they make the same empirical predictions.[9] Thus, one *might* say that the choice between them is not empirical. Each theory may have different theoretical virtues. One may be more elegant, simpler or more intuitive than the others. Thus, at this stage the choice of theories is made on a priori grounds. According to two of the theories, space is made up of dimensionless points. Looked at in this way, the choice between whether to retain the belief that space is made of dimensionless points or to reject it is made for a priori, not empirical, reasons.[10]

This example should teach us to be cautious about judging too quickly about whether the refutation of a belief is empirical or a priori. There are many cases, such as the one above, in which an apparently empirical refutation of a belief can, in fact, be seen on closer inspection to be an a priori refutation.

6.8 Inverting the master argument

Quine suggests that the Duhem–Quine problem can also be used to show that any belief can be insulated against empirical falsification. As we shall see, it may be true that a wide range of beliefs can be protected in this way, but it is not straightforward that this has as much to do with apriority as Quine suggests. A belief is a priori in the empirical-immunity sense if it cannot be empirically refuted. The Duhem–Quine problem does not indicate that there are any beliefs that cannot be falsified by empirical evidence, but rather that for any empirical evidence we can choose not to falsify a given belief.

In order to make sense of Quine's claim, let us introduce a distinction. The master argument is supposed to show that an *absolute* notion of the a priori is untenable. On this conception of the a priori, a belief is a priori if there is no possible empirical refutation of it. There are also *relative* notions of apriority. Kantians, for example, utilize various relative concepts of the a priori. We shall examine some of them in Chapter 7. Here we shall look at a different notion that can be distilled from the work of the philosopher of science Imre Lakatos (1922–74).

According to Lakatos (1978), science is organized into various research programmes. In a research programme, a distinction is made between its core theories and a "protective belt" of auxiliary theories. If the programme makes empirical predictions that turn out to be false, then the scientists within the programme alter its auxiliary theories. In Lakatos's view, the core theories of a research programme are a priori relative to that programme.

From Lakatos's view we can extract an inverted form of the master argument. According to Lakatos, there are many theories T that are such that the following argument holds:

1. For all possible empirical evidence E, there are auxiliary hypotheses that allow T to predict that E will happen.

   (hypothesis)
2. There are research programmes that scientists could create in which T is a core theory. (from 1)
3. In these research programmes T is a priori – it is immune to empirical falsification.

   (from 2 and the definition of a "core theory")

This inverted master argument seems to show that many theories can be considered to be a priori in the sense that they are empirically indefeasible. This argument seems to show that the empirical indefeasibility conception of apriority is useless. For a great many theories are empirically indefeasible. But note that the notion of indefeasibility used here is rather weak. It is not only a relative notion. What this argument says, in effect, is that there are many theories that we can choose to defend regardless of the empirical evidence.

We also run into this problem outside science. For example, people who believe in conspiracy theories often invent new auxiliary hypotheses to counter any evidence that you present them with in order to maintain their core beliefs. If you argue with someone who does not believe that humans landed on the moon in 1969, they will tell you that the television coverage was faked. You could counter by pointing out that this would have involved many people, and the likelihood is that at least one of them would have confessed the truth. But they may counter by claiming that some of these people have come forward, or that they were all murdered, or whatever. We need a way of determining when altering auxiliary hypotheses is permissible and when it is not.

On Lakatos's theory, a research programme is considered *degenerate* if it keeps on changing auxiliary theories to protect the core beliefs. The goal of research programmes is to make successful bold predictions. If it constantly has to play "catch up" with the empirical evidence rather than predict it, a research programme is not doing its job. Clearly, there are degrees of degeneracy in this sense, and it is sometimes impossible to tell whether a programme is in serious difficulty unless we compare it with another research programme that is trying to explain the same empirical data.

Suppose that we have two competing research programmes and one is chosen over the other on Lakatos's grounds. This would seem to be an empirical argument for one programme over the other. For if the empirical evidence had been different, perhaps, the other programme would have been the one that was seen as degenerate. But should we think that the core theories of these programmes are empirical just because the choice between the programmes is empirical? The answer to this is not clear. It may be that the problem with a research programme is that the original auxiliary theories were wrong and that they really need radical change, and that this is the reason for the apparent degeneracy of the programme. Surely this should not affect the status of the core theories.

The conclusion that we should come to from all this is the one I stated earlier. We need a fairly subtle view about when it is permissible to alter auxiliary hypotheses. Only against the background of such a theory can we really judge when a theory or belief is empirically defeasible.

6.9 Norms and necessities

In Chapter 1, we said that much of our knowledge about norms and necessity seems to involve a priori belief. The obvious question to ask of radical empiricists is how they deal with norms and necessity.

Necessity is easier than norms, so let us start with that. Radical empiricists generally deny that we have any knowledge about what is necessarily true. Quine goes so far as to deny that the concept of metaphysical necessity is coherent. He thinks there is a reasonable notion of relative necessity, but this is an extremely weak notion. According to Quine, we can say that a sentence is necessarily true relative to a theory if we can derive that sentence from the principles of the theory. Thus, for example, $2 + 2 = 4$ is necessarily true relative to the principles of arithmetic. But there is no sense to be made of the claim that $2 + 2 = 4$ is metaphysically necessary.

We shall not look here at Quine's arguments against metaphysical necessity. I do so briefly in Chapter 12. But let us consider why philosophers want to have a notion of metaphysical necessity.

Having metaphysical necessity and possible worlds in our theory is extremely useful. Consider the usual definition of a logically valid argument as one in which the premises *cannot* be true and the conclusion false. It is not just that we do not have an argument with true premises and a false conclusion, but the premises and conclusion are such that there is no possible way in which the former are all true and the latter is false. This notion of validity is modal. The notion of a valid inference is also usually thought to be a central concept of philosophy. As we have seen, many philosophers use possible worlds in their theories of meaning.

Moreover, there are other notions, such as that of a hypothetical conditional, that seem to require possible worlds for their analysis. A hypothetic (or "counterfactual") conditional is an "if ... then" sentence that has an antecedent that we know to be false, but want to entertain anyway. For example,

> If dogs did not bark, Ed would be able to hear what is said on the phone.

We all know that dogs do bark, so the antecedent of this conditional is known to be false. According to the most widely accepted views of conditionals, what we do to evaluate this conditional is consider possible worlds that are very similar to our own but in which dogs do not bark. If in those worlds Ed is able to hear what is said on the phone, the conditional is true (and otherwise it is false). If we were to reject possible worlds, then we would have to reject this way of evaluating hypothetical conditionals. Such conditionals play an important role in our thinking and in philosophy. Thus, we need some way of thinking about them. Unfortunately for the radical empiricists, there seems to be no reasonable alternative theory currently available.

Let us now turn to the other topic of consideration: normativity. The problem with normativity for radical empiricists is similar to the one they have with necessity. In order to determine what should occur, one needs to find out not what happens to be the case but what should be. This does not seem to be a matter for empirical investigation.

Radical empiricists have typically adopted one of two solutions to this problem. First, radical empiricists may deny that we can know about norms. This solution takes the form of denying that there are any facts about the norms in question. For example, a radical empiricist may claim that moral claims are really expressions of our own values or emotional responses to events.

Second, radical empiricists may maintain that we can have empirical knowledge of norms, but that norms are the rules of some institution. For example, we can have empirical knowledge of various sorts of norms. We can know empirically the rules of games such as chess or Monopoly. We find them out from reading rule books. Applying this idea to moral norms, we obtain a version of moral relativism. Different moral institutions (such as different societies) have different moral rules. According to the radical empiricist, we cannot know which institution is correct in any absolute sense, and most radical empiricists deny that there is any correct moral institution.

6.10 Naturalized epistemology

In this book we have been treating epistemology as a normative field. It tells us what we should believe, how we should treat evidence and so on. But some radical empiricists treat it as largely descriptive. The most influential descriptive epistemology is Quine's *naturalized epistemology*.

Quine abandons the task of dealing with traditional epistemological problems such as the problem of the existence of the external world. He thinks that if we play the game of attempting to prove there is a world outside our minds, we will lose. The sceptic will always win. Quine sums this up in one of his famous slogans: "the Humean predicament is the human predicament" (1969: 72). Quine thinks we should abandon the grand task of trying to justify all our beliefs. Instead, we should appeal to our best scientific theories in order to say which beliefs we should adopt or which methods we should use to justify our beliefs. This is a much more modest programme.

The psychology of perception, for example, can tell us under which conditions our senses are reliable and in which circumstances they are unreliable. Thus, we can use psychology to help us evaluate our experiences. Naturalized epistemology allows us to find justification for individual beliefs. It does not give us global justification for our belief system as a whole.

Nor does naturalized epistemology justify the appeal to scientific method, except perhaps in a circular manner. We could appeal to scientific methods, such as induction or abduction, to justify our use of science, but Quine does not do this. What Quine does do is appeal to science as an institution.[11] There is no independent justification of that institution. Scientific method is our only systematic way of treating evidence and modifying our beliefs, so we have no independent way of justifying it.[12]

Quine is fond of repeating the positivist Otto Neurath's (1882–1945) ship analogy. Neurath says that gathering knowledge is like rebuilding a ship while at sea. We have no place to put the ship that is secure and dry. We have to stand on one section while fixing others. When we collect or alter our beliefs, we have no firm dry foundation on which to stand. We have to use scientific methods to help us to improve other scientific methods.

6.11 BonJour's argument against Quine's naturalized epistemology

As we have seen, Quine thinks the norms of consistency and conservativeness drive belief revision. But what is the status of these norms? BonJour (1998: §3.7) argues that Quine cannot give an adequate answer to this question.

Consider the norm of consistency: one should not accept a contradiction. This norm is driven by the belief that no contradiction can be true. This is the *principle of non-contradiction*. So a question arises: is the principle of non-contradiction itself empirically defeasible? Quine holds that all beliefs are empirically defeasible so this one must be too. To reject the principle of non-contradiction on Quinean grounds, we must have a new belief that contradicts it. This new belief is (or logically implies) that there is at least one true contradiction.

Now, suppose that we believe that there is at least one true contradiction. Why should we reject the belief that there are no true contradictions? Not just because these beliefs contradict one another. For we now believe that contradictions can be true. BonJour suggests that we might have a third belief, one that says that it is not true both that no contradictions are true and that there are some true contradictions. (He calls this the "meta-principle of non-contradiction".) But BonJour asks why we should not accept all three of these beliefs: (i) the principle of non-contradiction; (ii) the belief that there is at least one true contradiction; (iii) the meta-principle of non-contradiction. If the answer is that we have a further belief (iv) that we cannot accept (i), (ii) and (iii) at the same time, then we can just ask why we cannot accept (i), (ii), (iii) and (iv) at the same time. And so on.

This infinite-regress argument shows that it cannot be that our acceptance of the principle of non-contradiction alone motivates the norm of consistency. For consider what happens when we come into contact with any information that contradicts our existing beliefs. We do revise our old beliefs so that they are consistent with the new ones. But why not just accept the new belief and all of the old beliefs? This would be inconsistent. In such a system the belief that there are no true contradictions is just another belief that causes a contradiction, perhaps among many.

Our obeying the norm of consistency, in Quine's theory, distinguishes belief revision from mere belief accumulation. The norm itself does not seem revisable. If it is not revisable, then the principle of non-contradiction is not defeasible, for any belief that contradicts the principle is itself a contradiction, and so is barred by the norm. Thus, if we already believe the principle of non-contradiction, we can never adopt any belief that contradicts it, so we have no reason to abandon it.

We can adopt norms that are weaker than the norm of consistency. For example, Graham Priest (2006) has put forward views of belief revision that, in effect, have us revise our beliefs to be consistent *all things being equal*. There might be some cases in which there are overriding reasons to accept contradictions. But the fact that there are weaker norms available does not alter BonJour's point. These weaker norms also support logical principles,[13] in the way that the norm of consistency supports the law of non-contradiction. In order to show that every belief is revisable, however, we need a theory of belief revision that does not presuppose any particular logic. I do not know of any such theory, and so I say very tentatively that BonJour's argument seems strong.

6.12 Assessing radical empiricism

At the beginning of this chapter I claimed that the burden of proof is on the radical empiricist to show that we do not have a priori knowledge. I have attempted to show that the most influential argument against a priori knowledge – Quine's master argument – does not prove this. Thus, it seems that those of us who claim that we do have a priori knowledge can continue to reject radical empiricism.

But radical empiricism is an interesting view in its own right. At the beginning of this chapter we looked at the views of Mill, Peirce, Quine and Harman. These all have in common the attempt to formulate a general theory of inference that explains how we can know about mathematics and logic as well as about empirical matters of fact traditionally understood. Formulating such a theory is a very interesting and difficult project.

Another feature that is common to radical empiricisms is the rejection of normative epistemology in the traditional sense. Mill and Peirce, as well as Quine, all reject the claim that we can give any strong justification for their general methods of belief acquisition or belief revision. Mill claims that we have no choice but to use induction and Peirce and Quine treat epistemology as a descriptive empirical science that tells us how we actually reason. To those of us who think of epistemology as a more robustly normative discipline, this is rather disappointing. But if, like Quine, you see traditional epistemology as a game that one cannot win, then perhaps radical empiricism is the philosophy for you.

Further reading

A very good overview of empiricism is Robert Meyer's *Understanding Empiricism* (2006).

Mill's central work on induction is *A System of Logic* ([1843] 1974). Although this book looks formidable, it is not too difficult to understand.

Harman's *Thought* (1973) sets out his ideas on abduction very clearly. For the more technically minded reader, his *Change in View* (1986) is a very interesting book about belief revision that refines some of the ideas in *Thought*.

Quine's more radical views about belief revision are in "Two Dogmas of Empiricism" ([1951] 1980b). A more moderate position can be found in his and Joseph Ullian's book, *The Web of Belief* (1978). The standard source on Quine's naturalized epistemology, naturally, is his paper "Epistemology Naturalized" (1969). The first chapter of his *Pursuit of Truth* (1990) is perhaps a clearer presentation, and more appropriate for students not yet initiated into reading Quine. Peter Hylton's book, *Quine* (2007), is perhaps the best secondary source on any of Quine's views. It is especially good on naturalized epistemology.

For an overview of attempts to create formal theories of belief revision along Quinean lines, see Peter Gärdenfors's book, *Knowledge in Flux* (1988).

7 Kantianism

7.1 Introduction

In this chapter I discuss the epistemology of Immanuel Kant (1724–1804) and of a Kantian, Michael Friedman. Kant is a nativist. He holds that there are certain innate concepts, intuitions and beliefs that we use to organize our understanding of the world. According to Kant, these concepts, intuitions and beliefs are a priori in two senses. First, they are not learned. Second, the possibility of our having experience depends on our having these concepts, beliefs and intuitions. As we shall see, within Kant's system his innate beliefs are not empirically defeasible. Moreover, they provide many of our other beliefs with a priori justification.

Nativism, however, is only one of Kant's doctrines. As we shall see, some modern Kantians abandon nativism. For them, the important aspect of Kant's epistemology is the idea that we construct the world according to principles that we do not extract empirically from the world. They think that we impose these principles on the world. For Kantians, as for Kant, these principles are a priori.

In this chapter I discuss "theoretical philosophy" only in the Kantian sense of this term. Theoretical philosophy includes only metaphysics and epistemology. Kantian ethics, on the other hand, is what he calls "practical philosophy". I examine Kantian ethics – or, rather, metaethics – in Chapter 9.

7.2 Kant on phenomena and noumena

Kant's theoretical philosophy has two central aims. First, he wants to defeat scepticism about the external world. He does so by making the external world not very external. He thinks that the world of objects in space is, to a large extent, a human construct. The existence of the external world is something we can be sure of because we build it in our minds. Second, he wants to limit the scope of metaphysics. In the introduction to his great work, the *Critique of Pure Reason*,[1] he states that we cannot prove the existence of God, we cannot prove that we have free will, and nor can we demonstrate that there is life after death. Throughout the book Kant argues that attempts to prove these things on the part of philosophers have been misguided. They consist of the misapplication of certain a priori beliefs and concepts.

The key to both of his aims in the *Critique of Pure Reason* is Kant's distinction between the *phenomenal* world and the *noumenal* world. The phenomenal world is the world we experience. It does not just contain the aspects of the world that we actually perceive, but everything that we can experience and that we know exists on the basis of what we do experience. So, for example, atoms and subatomic particles are in the phenomenal world, since we know that they exist on the basis of what we perceive.

The phenomenal world is a mental construct.[2] Kant argues that space and time cannot exist outside minds. They have a paradoxical nature. For example, space and time are constructed from points. A point has no length. But when very many points are collected together we get something that has length. According to Kant, this does not make sense: adding together many things with length zero should give us no length. Thus, Kant concludes, space and time cannot exist except as what he calls "intuitions" in our minds. But this means that when we perceive things and events as being in space and time we are adding the spatiotemporal element to them.

What things are in themselves when extracted from how we perceive them is what Kant calls the noumenal world. In one sense, our minds are part of the empirical world. In introspection we "perceive" our own thoughts occurring in time. But there is an aspect of our minds that is noumenal as well. As we have seen, Kant says that our minds construct the phenomenal world. It cannot be a purely phenomenal object that is doing this construction. Whatever is constructing the phenomenal world is noumenal.

Note that this does not mean that we can know a noumenal object by looking into our own minds. We have no idea what the thing that underlies the construction of the world is like in itself.

Kant agrees with the sceptic about the external world if "the external world" is interpreted as the noumenal world. As we shall see, however, he thinks that we can defeat scepticism about the world that is studied by the empirical sciences.

Kant claims that we cannot know whether we have free will or immortality, nor whether God exists, because these topics are about the nature of noumena (the things in the noumenal world). Thus, he rejects traditional metaphysics.

7.3 Intuitions, concepts and beliefs

Kant draws a sharp distinction between concepts and intuitions. The exact nature of this distinction is the subject of some controversy between commentators. This is not a book of Kant scholarship, so I am not going to get embroiled in that debate. But we do need to understand this distinction in order to comprehend Kant's view of a priori knowledge.

There are various species of intuition, according to Kant. First, there are empirical intuitions. These are just our sense experiences. Second, there are our intuitions of space and time: our so-called a priori intuitions. What do these two sorts of intuition have in common? One way to think of intuitions is that they show us what individual things (either physical objects or space and time) are like. Intuitions are particular. Concepts, on the other hand, are general. They can each apply to many things. You might have a concept of a cat. This concept can apply to any cat. But your intuition of a cat is of a particular cat. It is not just any cat. It is *that* cat. Even if you have a concept of a particular cat, it is made up of general concepts (according to Kant), such as the concept of a particular type of cat, the name of the cat, and so on.

Our intuitions of space and time are like mental containers into which we fit our experiences. We place all our experiences in time, and we use our experiences of the outside world to fit them together in this intuition of space to construct a four-dimensional mental map or picture of the world. This map or picture is always partial; we never experience the whole world.

We can also use this intuition to get information about the properties of the whole of space. According to Kant, we can justify our belief that the angles of a triangle add up to 180 degrees by appealing to our intuition of space. By mentally drawing a triangle in our intuitions, we can determine that its angles add up to 180 degrees. This is called a "mental construction" of a triangle. The idea is that from our intuition we know that space is uniform. It might contain different things in different places, but if one considers the intuition of space itself, on Kant's view, one can come to realize that one bit of space is just like any other bit of space.

One of Kant's aims is to show that we can know the real nature of space. By considering our intuition of space, on his view, we can know about the geometry of space. There is not the problem that we saw with the strong rationalist. Kant does not have to justify that our intuition of space is just like real space. Our intuition of space *is* space.

Like his rationalist predecessors, Kant thinks we have certain concepts that we cannot learn from experience. As we saw in Chapter 3, Leibniz thinks the concept of substance is one of these. And so does Kant. For Kant these innate concepts – his famous *categories* – are not to be applied beyond experience. We impose concepts such as that of substance on the things we experience, but whether these represent how things really are as noumena we have no idea.

These innate concepts are closely related to certain beliefs. Kant supposedly derives his categories from a list of basic forms of judgement. The nature of this derivation and whether it really works is not our concern here. What is of more interest to us is the way in which Kant thinks these concepts are related to experience.

In order to apply a category to an empirical thing or event, we need a rule of sorts. Let us take Kant's category of cause and effect. The rule that Kant proposes is that we can say that one event causes another if the second follows the first in accordance with some universal principle. This principle is a law of nature. Thus, what Kant is saying is that we can judge one event to cause another if we can relate the two events to one another by some law of nature. For example, we can say that one billiard ball's hitting another causes the second to move because we know there is a law of nature about the transfer of energy from one ball to the other, and that energy will be expressed in these circumstances as motion.

The judgement that a particular event is the cause of another particular event is not a priori, according to Kant, but the belief that all events have causes and effects is. Kant attempts to establish the apriority of the principle of causation and many other such principles using "transcendental arguments". It is to these that we turn next.

7.4 Transcendental arguments

A transcendental argument starts with a proposition that is assumed, that is, it is not being questioned. Then the argument attempts to show that the truth of this proposition assumes certain other propositions. In the *Critique of Pure Reason*, the proposition that is assumed is that we have experience. Then a series of transcendental arguments are used to show that our experience requires certain concepts and beliefs. These concepts and beliefs, since they are assumed by experience and not learned from it, are said to be a priori. We shall return later to discuss their a priori status in terms of our understanding of that notion given in Chapter 1.

Kant sometimes talks about experience as our experience of things and events in space and time – that is, external things and events – and sometimes he talks about experience in terms of the train of one's own sensations. There is no inconsistency here. These two notions are intimately interconnected, according to Kant.

Of course, we need to have sensations in order to construct the world around us in space and time. Thus, there is a sense in which the subjective train of sensations is prior to our experience of external things and events. But, according to Kant, we could not have knowledge of this inner train of sensations if it were not for the external things and events. If we were merely to relate our sensations to one another, any order that we came up with would be arbitrary. It could not count as *knowledge*.[3] On Kant's view, the only way we can justify the relationships that we claim these sensations have to one another is by appeal to the events that they represent and the way that they are obtained. So, for example, in the past few minutes I saw one of my dogs lying on the floor and then I saw the other asleep on my sofa. The two events of one dog's lying and the other's sleeping are simultaneous, but I can explain why I saw one before the other by appeal to the motion of my head (which is another event that occurs in the external world; see *Critique* Bxl–xli, B226, B274–5).

Kant's presupposition that experience in this sense is possible might seem to beg the question against the sceptic. In Kant's writings, however, the line is often blurred between the claim that we do have experience that allows for knowledge in this sense and the claim that we must interpret our experience in a way that allows us to have knowledge. If we interpret Kant as making this second claim, he can be seen to avoid the criticism of assuming something the sceptic questions.

Let us turn now to the examination of one of Kant's transcendental arguments: his argument for the principle of causation. For Kant, as we have seen, the notion of a cause is closely connected with the notion of a law of nature. To say that one event causes another is to say that the second follows the first according to a law of nature. The principle of causation thus says that events in nature came into being from other events and give rise to other events in accordance with the laws of nature.

The historical background for Kant's discussion of laws is the discussion of causation and induction in the work of Hume (1711–76). Hume thinks that there is no good reason to believe that the future will be like the past, but that we believe this anyway. Hume says we are what we would now call association machines: we see one sort of event always follow another sort of event, and we come, because of habit, to form the idea that events of the first sort will always follow those of the second sort in the future.

Kant thinks things are more complicated than that. If we consider exactly what we perceive, then the world seems rather chaotic. Our visual fields change quite radically, often with a mere movement of our heads or if we close our eyes for a minute. This chaotic stream of sensations is what Kant calls the "subjective succession of apprehension" (*Critique* A190/B234ff.). As I have said, we make sense of this swirling world of sensation by thinking of the sensations as being caused by objects and events external to ourselves.

I see my visual field change colour throughout the day because of the path of the sun and its angle to my windows. Late in the evening I turn on the lights, and the strong shadows and sharp contrast that I saw before are replaced by a warm even light. I can justify my judgements about these changes by judgements about my relationship to the sun, the window in this room, the positions of the various pieces of furniture and so on.

In order to understand my perceptions as perceptions of objects, I (tacitly) use laws of nature. I use laws that govern the way in which light moves (i.e. in straight lines) and how it reflects off surfaces. The change in the colour of the light in my room is determined by the fact that the tungsten in the light bulbs gives off a particular wavelength of light that is closer to the red end of the spectrum than the cooler blue light that is caused by the filtering of sunlight through the atmosphere.

This transcendental argument, then, begins with the assumption that we experience a world of things in space and events in time, in a way that can ground judgements that can be justified by means of other judgements about things in the external world. The argument ends with the conclusion that we need to have the (perhaps tacit) belief that events occur in a law-like way. This belief, moreover, is a priori. It is not learned from experience, and our ability to have experience depends on it.

What exactly is going on in this argument? It seems that the form of a transcendental argument is the following:

1. P
2. P presupposes Q
3. Therefore, Q

In the transcendental argument that we just examined, P is the sentence "We have experience of objects in space and time" and Q is the sentence "We have the a priori belief that events follow one another in time according to laws of nature". On the face of it, this looks like a version of the argument form *modus ponens*. If so, it is a valid argument form, but not that original.

There is, however, something rather different about transcendental arguments. It has to do with the second premise and the interpretation of the concept of presupposition that is used here. To interpret transcendental arguments as mere instances of *modus ponens*, we must read "P presupposes Q" as meaning "if P

then Q". But this reading does not do justice to Kant's notion of presupposition.

Friedman treats the relation of presupposition in terms of the meanings of the propositions involved. That is, he claims that P presupposes Q if and only if the truth of Q is necessary so that we can even make sense of P. This may make sense of some of Kant's use of "presupposition" but does not seem to work well for the argument that purports to establish the apriority of the principle of causation.

Kant, surely, is not claiming that it is *meaningless* to talk about perceiving a spatiotemporal world without assuming that there are laws of nature. Rather, it would seem that, from Kant's point of view, the only way we can *explain* how we perceive objects and events in space and time is by our assuming that there are laws of nature.

There may in fact be other notions of presupposition in Kant as well. Another sense of "presupposition" that one finds in Kant (and in other Kantians) is that of the presuppositions of an epistemic practice. Consider scientific method. According to Kant, a science can only be a science if it has precise mathematical laws. Thus, it could be said to be a presupposition of *doing* science of this sort that there are such laws.

That there are various meanings of "presupposition" in Kant should not bother us. If each of these meanings is legitimate and, in particular, allows us to infer from a statement to what it presupposes, then it does not matter that not all of these uses of "presupposition" represent exactly the same concept.

Before we leave the topic of transcendental arguments, we should consider whether they are themselves a priori. This is an interesting question. The first premise is that we have experience of things and events in space and time. This cannot be a priori in the strict sense. It is not *very* empirical, though! It is something we can assent to without much thought and certainly without any serious empirical investigation. But this is enough to show that transcendental arguments are not, strictly speaking, a priori.

7.5 Different notions of apriority in Kant

In order to relate Kant's notions of the a priori to the concepts we are employing in this book, we have to ask whether these a priori beliefs are justified independently of experience and whether they are empirically defeasible. Both of these questions are interesting and difficult.

For Kant, some a priori beliefs are justified independently of experience. For example, according to Kant, our mathematical beliefs appeal only to our innate intuitions of time and space. We know that $3 + 15 = 18$ because we can think of units lined up and counted successively in time: first three and then fifteen to get a total of eighteen. Our belief that the angles of a triangle add up to $180°$ comes about from our consideration of our intuition of space. These are clear cases of a priori justification.

But what of our belief that events follow one after another according to laws? The belief seems without justification and without need of justification. It is something we use to construct the world that we perceive. We may be justified in holding that we do have this belief, and such a justification (for Kant) is a transcendental argument. But this is not the same thing as justifying the belief itself.

Thus, we cannot say that Kant's a priori beliefs are all a priori in the standard justificational meaning of the term. But they do have a very important role in providing a priori justification for other beliefs. For example, our belief that we can find laws of nature by doing science is justified by the belief that there are such laws. Thus, we have an a priori foundation for the doing of science and the belief that natural science can be successful.

On the other hand, are Kant's a priori beliefs empirically defeasible? Mathematical beliefs are not, according to Kant. Any experience that we have will conform to mathematical beliefs (if they are correct) because these beliefs describe the nature of space and time themselves. As we have seen, some philosophers and most scientists think that Euclidean geometry is a false theory of physical space. This disagreement, as we shall see below, this has caused a problem for Kant's theory.

Is the belief that events follow one another according to laws or the belief that there is some permanent matter out of which all bodies are made empirically defeasible? It depends on exactly what we mean by "empirically defeasible". In a sense Kant thinks that we cannot have experience that contradicts the principle of causation, because our ability to have experience depends on that principle.

Kant's view, however, has struck some philosophers as implausible. C. I. Lewis (1883–1964) apparently once asked whether Kant ever had any dreams. In dreams things happen in a haphazard way, and do not seem to obey any rules. It would seem that our waking experience could be like that as well, and so falsify this a priori belief. But if we interpret "experience" in Kant as referring to the sorts of experiences we can use as the basis of judgements that can be justified or used for justifications, then dream-like perceptions will not do. In dreams we do not have this sort of experience, and so dreams cannot contain experiences that falsify Kant's view.

7.6 Absolute and relative a priori

Lewis might reply to Kant that we may not always have experience in Kant's sense. Kant could then say that his argument shows only that *if* there is experience, then we have laws of nature. Here we have a distinction between Kant's a priori beliefs taken as being *absolute* or as *relative to a particular way of understanding the world*.

If we take Kant to be arguing for beliefs that are a priori relative to our experiencing a coherent spatiotemporal world in the sense that we have been discussing, then we should understand the logical form of transcendental arguments in a slightly different way.

Those readers who have learned a natural deduction style of proof in a formal logic course will find this very familiar. In deductive arguments there are two sorts of hypotheses. There are premises, which are assumed to be true, and there are hypotheses that are "discharged" in the course of the argument. Premises are familiar to all philosophy students (and everyone else, I hope), but hypotheses that are to be discharged may not be as well known.

Suppose we want to argue that if the sky is blue and not blue at the same time, then the moon is made of green cheese. We can do so in the following way:[4]

1. The sky is blue and the sky is not blue.   (hypothesis)
2. The sky is blue.   (from 1)
3. The sky is not blue.   (from 1)
4. The sky is blue or the moon is made of green cheese. (from 2)
5. The moon is made of green cheese.   (from 3 and 4)

6. If the sky is blue and not blue, then the moon is made of green
   cheese.   (discharging the hypothesis)

The hypothesis in this argument is not a premise. It is not something anyone would ever believe. Rather, it is assumed only for the sake of the argument, and it is discharged and made part of the "if … then" statement in the final step. So we can amend our representation of transcendental arguments to being of the following form:

1. P (hypothesis)
2. P presupposes Q
3. Q (by 1 and 2)
4. If P, then Q (discharging the hypothesis)

Thus, we can think of Kant's transcendental arguments in this way as having a conditional ("if … then") as their conclusion. Whereas transcendental arguments traditionally construed are not a priori, it seems that they can be turned into a priori arguments by treating the first premise (which is empirical) as a hypothesis. The second premise seems to be a priori, and so are all the logical moves in the argument. We shall return to this view of Kant's project when we look at Friedman's Kantian view of science later in this chapter.

7.7 Kantian crises

There have been various crises regarding Kantian philosophy. The first of these crises occurred in the late eighteenth and early nineteenth centuries. In fact there were two such crises that occurred at almost the same time. One of these crises concerned the starting-point of Kant's *Critique of Pure Reason* and the second concerned the existence of noumena.

The crisis over a starting-point for the *Critique* was initiated by Karl Reinhold (1757–1823). According to Reinhold and, following him, many German philosophers of the late eighteenth century, Kant's philosophy should be deduced from a single indubitable principle. Reinhold's own proposal for such a principle does not concern us here, but the reasons why he made this criticism do interest us. The demand for a single principle from which we derive all our other philosophical views about a given topic is ubiquitous in that period. This perhaps dates back to Descartes' claim that he could derive the whole of philosophy from the single principle that he knows that he is a thinking thing. But Descartes used other ideas, rules of reason and so on. And this is true of Reinhold as well.

From a modern point of view, the concern with the certainty of the premise that we have experience is rather odd. Kant's a priori arguments are far more dubious than this premise, but his contemporaries seem more worried about this premise.

The second Kantian crisis concerns the heart of Kant's philosophy – his distinction between phenomena and noumena. The criticism that sparked the crisis is due to Friedrich Jacobi (1743–1819). According to Jacobi, noumena play an active role in Kant's system, so Kant contradicts himself when he claims to have no knowledge about them. Jacobi has a good point. Kant claims that *we* construct the empirical universe. Who is this *we*? As we have seen, it is not our phenomenal selves that do this construction. What we are in our own experience is bodies and streams of consciousness. Neither of these sorts of things construct the universe. They are empirical objects in time and space, so are themselves constructed by our noumenal selves. Thus we do know something about noumena: we know what they do.

This is a deep problem. Kant says:

> What, then, is to be understood when we spoke of an object corresponding to, and consequently also distinct from our knowledge? It is easily seen that this object must be thought only as something in general $= x$, since outside our knowledge we have nothing which we could set over against this knowledge as corresponding to it. (*Critique* A104)

Our comprehension of noumena is supposedly quite empty. We have no real concepts that we know we can apply to them. They are just things about which we know nothing. We cannot even apply the categories to them. One of the categories is that of unity. We cannot say that noumena are the sorts of things that can be counted. The notion of a single object is understood by us in terms of a rule that allows us to consider it placed in a time series with other things (in a process of counting these things). The notion of a unity is forced by us on the things that we experience. We cannot

say objects satisfy it in themselves. Thus, it seems that even referring to noumena as "something in general $= x$" is misleading. This
characterization seems to presuppose that noumena are individual things (and can be represented, say, by variables). Kant has an
utterly unintelligible reality constructing the world of experience.
To sum up, what seems paradoxical to Jacobi (I suggest) is Kant's
claim that something is constructing reality, but this something may
not be a thing in any sense of the word that we understand. Surely
there is something pathological about this assertion, but exactly
what is not that easy to discern. It does not seem to be an outright
contradiction.[5]

Some of Kant's followers, in particular Johann Fichte (1762–
1814) and Friedrich Schelling (1775–1854), assert that in fact we
do have knowledge about our noumenal selves. They claim that
we have "intellectual intuition". Intellectual intuition is a form of
direct perception of noumena. When we have any experiences,
according to Fichte, we are also aware of our noumenal selves.
For Schelling, when we perform any actions we intuit ourselves as
noumena. Postulating a new form of awareness in order to avoid
Jacobi's criticism, however, seems rather desperate.

The third crisis is of most interest to us. It came much later and
is concerned with the a priori status of mathematics. According to
Kant, geometry and the theory of numbers are a priori disciplines.
Many present-day philosophers of mathematics hold this too, but
they mean something very different from this than Kant does.
According to contemporary philosophers of mathematics, there is
a difference between pure mathematics and applied mathematics.
Pure mathematics is about structures that may or may not exist in
the physical world. Applied mathematics is only about structures
that do actually have some physical reality. For example, in pure
mathematics one might study geometrical spaces with more dimensions than space and time have put together. In applied mathematics, one studies mathematical structures that are used in scientific
theories about the real world. For Kant, mathematics is only a
means for studying the physical world. Thus his claim that mathematical truths can be known a priori is startling.

Kant thinks that the principles of Euclidean geometry are all
true of actual physical space and known a priori. As we saw in
Chapter 2, modern physics treats space in terms of a non-Euclidean

geometry. The fact that Kant turned out to be wrong about the geometry of space is not the only lesson that Kantians should learn from this crisis. Another is that scientists should be free to choose the mathematical framework for their theories. This is essential to the progress of modern science. Our philosophy of mathematics should allow them this freedom. Kant's use of innate intuitions as a foundation for his philosophy of mathematics, together with his view that we impose space and time on to our experience, restricts science in ways that cannot be allowed.

7.8 Michael Friedman's Kantianism

For Kantians, one response to the crisis about geometry is to abandon the notion that there is one way only of constructing the natural world. Kantians who take this approach think there are various different sorts of schemes that we can use to understand the world. As in Kant, these schemes are imposed by us on the world. So there still is a strict distinction among Kantians between phenomena and noumena, between how we construct the world and what the world is like in itself. But these Kantians are not nativists. They believe that we choose the way in which we interpret the world. Thomas Kuhn, Putnam and Friedman are Kantians of this sort. I have written about Kuhn and Putnam elsewhere (see Brock & Mares 2007). Here I discuss Michel Friedman's view from his book, *Dynamics of Reason* (2001).

Friedman rejects Kant's nativism and Kant's claim to have discovered the general principles that underlie all reasoning. Rather, Friedman takes particular scientific theories and finds within them principles that he claims to be a priori with respect to the rest of the theory.

For Friedman, a principle is a priori relative to a theory if it is not possible to empirically confirm or refute that principle, but it allows other parts of that theory to be empirically tested. One of Friedman's examples of an a priori scientific principle is the principle in Einstein's theory of relativity that light always travels at the same speed in a vacuum regardless of its source or direction. Having light travel at a constant speed gives us a method by which to measure other things (consider the notion of a light-year as a measure of distance). Without these a priori laws, other laws are empty of empirical content; they are just mathematical equations.

Let us consider a similar example in more depth. One of Newton's laws is the law of universal gravitation. This law say that every mass attracts every other mass in the universe according to the equation:

$$\text{force of gravity} = (\text{gravitational constant} \times \text{mass of body} \\ 1 \times \text{mass of body 2}) \div \text{distance between} \\ \text{body 1 and body 2}$$

How can one test this law? Unless there is a way of measuring the force of gravity between two bodies, we cannot tell whether the equation is true. This is where another of Newton's laws comes in: force on a body = mass of the body × its acceleration. Now we can tell what the force of gravity is on a particular body. The force on body 1 from body 2 can be measured by measuring the mass of body 1 and its acceleration towards body 2 (that is, if there are no other forces on body 1).

The point of this is that Newton's second law of motion – force = mass × acceleration – helps to make Newton's theory of gravity empirically testable. But how can we test the second law of motion? According to Friedman (2001: 36), we cannot. It has the status of a stipulation. It gives us, in effect, an empirical meaning for the word "force" as it is used by Newton. In other words, Newton's second law of motion is a priori relative to his theory of gravity.

One challenge to Friedman's view comes from Quine's master argument (see Chapter 6). According to Quine, we always have a choice about which postulates to reject when we come upon data that does not fit with our theory. On Friedman's view, some parts of theories (or paradigms or research programmes) are immune to empirical refutation. On Friedman's view, these are the postulates that make the theory empirical. These allow for empirical refutations of other parts of the theory but are themselves not capable of being falsified by empirical data.

We might be tempted to think of a framework as itself being refuted empirically. The data from the 1919 eclipse, for example, might be taken to have refuted Newtonian physics as a whole. But Friedman would contest this suggestion. The only way the eclipse can be taken to be evidence against Newton's theory of gravity is by assuming that light travels in straight lines. Of course, even Friedman would agree that a sentence made up of a conjunction of all the sentences that make up Newton's theory of gravity and the sentence "light travels in a straight line" and all the sentences that make up all the other background theories used to determine the apparent position of the star should have remained in the same place before and during the eclipse is empirically testable. But this is a very artificial way of interpreting science and has little to do with how scientists understand their theories.

This is one way to understand the disagreement between Quine and Friedman. Quine treats our beliefs *holistically*. He thinks of our beliefs as making up one big theory. This big theory survives or is refuted by the empirical evidence. Friedman, in opposition, is willing to separate out different elements in the way in which scientists confirm or refute theories.

As we saw with regard to Feynman's suggestion that we reject the idea that space is made up of dimensionless points, it may be that the empirical data have restricted our choices between theories, but that this choice can be made only a priori grounds. Friedman's description of the progress of science through changes in frameworks reinforces this distinction. Scientists do abandon frameworks and give empirical reasons for doing so. But looking closely at their arguments often shows that they could have maintained the old frameworks, but at a cost of elegance, simplicity, intuitiveness and so on. That is, the cost is to be measured in terms of the theoretical virtues.

7.9 What should we say about Kant and Kantianism?

This chapter outlines Kant's views on a priori knowledge. We saw that Kant holds that we have innate concepts, such as those of substance and causation and innate intuitions of space and time. We also have innate beliefs, such as belief in the principle of causation: events follow one another according to laws of nature.

Kant's nativism, as we saw, restricts scientific practice. Scientists, according to Kant, must use Euclidean geometry to describe space. Kant's views about innate beliefs may also cause similar problems. The way in which Kant interprets the principle of causation is as demanding that there be *deterministic* laws that describe nature. But our best contemporary theories – especially quantum mechanics – describe nature in terms of probabilistic laws. It may be that determinism is not an essential part of Kant's views, but it may be that it is. If it is, then that is another problem for Kant's view.

Friedman rejects the absolutist interpretation of the a priori and Kant's nativism. He replaces it with a theory of the relative a priori. This view seems more defensible. It allows for scientific freedom.

But both Kant's and Friedman's views come with a price. The price is the adoption of a form of anti-realism. Friedman thinks we can stipulate, for example, that the speed of light is constant in a vacuum. As we saw in Chapter 5, stipulations are allowed only where they do not contradict pre-existing facts. Thus, if we are allowed to stipulate that the speed of light is constant, there cannot be a pre-existing fact about the speed of light. The absence of facts like this characterizes one form of scientific anti-realism. For those of us who want to think of science as telling us about the nature of things (rather than stipulating what it is), this is disappointing. Now, this does not mean that Friedman or Kant thinks scientists make up everything about reality. Both think there are serious empirical constraints on the truth of theories. But this may not be enough for those of us with strongly realist leanings.

Further reading

Henry Allison's *Kant's Transcendental Idealism* (1983) is one of the best systematic interpretations of the *Critique of Pure Reason*. This book is slightly dated now, but it is perhaps the best overall study of Kant's theoretical philosophy.

Friedman's *Kant and the Exact Sciences* (1995) is not an easy read, but an excellent book on Kant's philosophies of science and mathematics.

An influential attack on transcendental arguments is Barry Stroud's "Transcendental Arguments" (1968). His arguments are repeated in his *The Significance of Philosophical Scepticism* (1984). James Chase and Jack Reynolds present a survey and analysis of the literature on transcendental arguments in their "The Fate of Transcendental Reasoning in Contemporary Philosophy" (2010).

Ernst Cassirer's *Einstein's Theory of Relativity* (1923) explores the problem of the use of non-Euclidean geometry from a Kantian perspective.

Friedman's views discussed here are in his *Dynamics of Reason* (2001). This outlines Friedman's philosophy of science. It is difficult, and presupposes a lot of background in the history of philosophy and some understanding of physics.

8 Aristotelianism

8.1 Introduction

Aristotelianism holds that we gain some of our knowledge from the abstraction of concepts from our experience and reflection on these concepts. This may sound more like empirical knowledge than a priori knowledge, but the justification involved is remarkably similar to analytic justification. In analytic justification, we learn the meanings of words empirically. Then using these meanings together with only our reasoning abilities we determine if a particular sentence is true. According to Aristotelianism, we first abstract concepts from experience and then reason by reflecting on these concepts. We can characterize Aristotelian justification as the process of reasoning using concepts that are abstracted from experience (rather than, say, concepts that are innate or those that we associate with the meanings of words).

Aristotelian justification is very much like the rationalists' rational insight. Aristotelian justification, unlike rationalists' justification, is restricted to those cases in which the concepts involved are abstracted from experience.

Aristotelianism is an attractive theory of the a priori. It does not involve innate concepts. It allows a priori justification about objects that are independent of our minds. It also fits well with empiricism.

I begin the chapter, as usual, with a history of the theory. Then I defend Aristotelianism against the charges that it is not a form of a priori reasoning and that it is not reliable. The chapter ends with a brief discussion of the relationships between Aristotelianism and coherentism, reliabilism and foundationalism.

8.2 History of Aristotelianism

Aristotle famously holds that in perception our minds take on the form of what is being perceived. This is his theory of abstraction. Aristotle's scientific method is to explore the essences of things. In effect, scientific method is to reflect on the forms of things. His logic – in particular his modal logic, which deals with the notion of essences – is a part of his theory of reflection.

It is natural to complain about Aristotle's view that it is implausible to think that our minds literally take on the forms of the objects they perceive. The implausibility of this view is only one problem with it. It is difficult to explain how mistakes are possible regarding the forms of things if we have the forms in our minds.

On Locke's view, we extract ideas from experience. These ideas are often complex, that is, they can be constructed from other ideas. As I write this sentence, I am sitting in a library that has brightly coloured bookshelves. I am looking right now at a red bookshelf. According to Locke, I have a sensation of a red bookshelf and at least two ideas: the simple idea of red and the complex idea of a bookshelf.

Locke's notion of reflection largely consists in the extraction of simpler ideas from more complex ones. But in reflection we get not only simpler ideas, but more abstract ideas. Berkeley criticizes Locke for his view of abstract ideas by claiming that an idea must be of a particular thing. Berkeley's critique, however, assumes a certain view about ideas that Locke did not share. For Berkeley, unlike Locke, is an imagist. An imagist holds that an idea is a mental image (a mental "picture"). Consider an example of an image of a triangle. We cannot have an image of a *triangle in general*. Rather, we have an image of a particular triangle: a right-angled isosceles triangle, say. But, since Locke does not think of ideas as images, he does not have this problem.[1]

Another philosopher who does think that ideas are images, but also accepts that we form mental abstractions, is Hume. His *Treatise of Human Nature* begins with a statement of agreement with Berkeley that there are no abstract ideas. Almost immediately after this passage, however, Hume presents a theory of abstract ideas. He is, however, being consistent in all of this. Hume uses the word "idea" to mean a copy of a sense-impression. These copies cannot be abstract. They are about the original sense-impression, either because they are causally linked to them (a tricky notion in Hume) or because they resemble them. But he also has a second notion. We can have an abstract conception. This abstract conception is a cluster of similar ideas. He puts this view rather succinctly in his *Enquiry into Human Understanding*: "All general ideas are nothing but particular ones, annexed to a certain term, which gives them a more extensive signification, and makes them recall upon occasion other individuals, which are similar to them" (*Enquiry* bk I, §vii, 17). The view is that an abstract idea is a cluster of similar ideas that we tag with a term. For example, my concept of *dog* is, according to Hume, all my specific ideas of dogs collected together under the label "dog".

Locke thinks that a priori reasoning can be used to derive truths about a wide range of topics, such as mathematics, ethics and even politics. Hume, however, thinks that mathematics is the only a priori science: "It seems to me that the only objects of the abstract sciences or of demonstration are quantity and number, and that all attempts to extend this more perfect species of knowledge beyond these bounds are mere sophistry and illusion" (*Enquiry* bk I, §xii, iii, 163). As Barry Stroud (1977: 47–50) points out, there is a problem understanding how Hume can account for "reasoning from mere ideas" at all. How we derive anything from a cluster of images, on Hume's view, is unclear. Although his is the earlier view, in some ways Locke's theory of reflection is superior to Hume's. The analysis of complex ideas into simpler ones is a relatively easy process to understand.

Edmund Husserl (1859–1938) holds that in our experience we are aware of both the particular objects of perception and the universals that are instantiated in them. In Husserl's philosophy after 1903, however, he is unwilling to commit himself to any specific metaphysical views. He wants to bracket the problems of metaphysics and merely describe our experience. It is part of our experience, according to Husserl, that we intuit universals.

In Husserl, there is no metaphysical description of how we abstract universals from experience. Moreover, he thinks we can isolate a universal in consciousness and reflect on it directly. This reflection on a universal is called "eidetic intuition". In it the universal itself comes before the mind and we can (or feel we can) discern its properties. Through this process we attain our understanding of logic and mathematics. This is clearly an Aristotelian theory.

Bertrand Russell (1872–1970) famously changed his mind often. In 1910–1915, Russell adopted a form of Aristotelianism that was quite similar to Husserl's. According to Russell, the immediate object of perception is a sense-datum. A sense-datum is a mind-independent object. In perception, we not only perceive sense-data themselves, but also the universals that are instantiated in the sense-data. In Russell's terminology, we are "acquainted with universals" in perception. Russell also thinks we can be acquainted with universals in imagination. All a priori knowledge, for Russell ([1912] 1959), results from our reflecting on universals and on the relations between universals. Once again, this theory clearly fits our characterization of an Aristotelian epistemology.

8.3 Is Aristotelian justification really a priori?

In this section we shall look at two parallels, with Aristotelian justification. The first of these is a parallel with analytic justification. This is supposed to support the thesis that Aristotelian justification is a priori. The second is a parallel with the use of memory in justification. This is supposed to create a worry about the apriority of Aristotelian justification. I argue, however, that the parallel with analytic justification is accurate and the parallel with memory is misleading, at best.

Let us begin with the parallel between Aristotelian justification and analytic justification. Aristotelian justifications can be represented as having the following form:

The analysis of the concepts used to think about p implies p

Therefore, p

We could run a parallel with either metaphysical or epistemological conceptions of analyticity, but we shall look at only one of these here. Analytic justification has the form:

The analysis of the meaning of the words in sentence S implies S

Therefore, S

These justificatory arguments look very similar. Both have one premise that asserts that a form of analysis implies a sentence or proposition. We could make the parallel even closer if we wish by adding a premise to the argument concerning analytic justification that states that S represents p and alter its conclusion to say that p.

Aristotelian justification is sometimes thought to be empirical because it deals with empirical concepts. But similar worries could be raised about analytic justification. For we learn the meanings of words empirically. As we said in Chapter 5, this problem disappears if we distinguish between experience's justifying a belief and its enabling a belief. It enables a belief if it makes it possible, or even possible for the belief to have justification. I can be justified about the truth of a sentence only if I understand that sentence (or at least think that I understand it). And to do so, I need to learn the meanings of the words involved. Similarly, I can have beliefs about propositions on the basis of the concepts used to represent them only if I have those concepts and I get them empirically. But in neither case does the justification itself refer to the experience I need to learn meanings of the words or obtain concepts.

It is useful, as Carrie Jenkins has done, to understand a priori justification in the framework of a general theory of how we have "knowledge of the mind-independent world". She characterizes such knowledge as having three steps:

- "An input step in which the world somehow gets into our minds";
- "A processing step" in which what is in our minds is somehow made so that we can understand it;
- "A belief formation step" (forthcoming: 3).

Although she does not label herself an Aristotelian,[2] the process of forming an a priori belief fits my characterization of this position. She claims that the "world gets into our mind" by our having experience. She says that this process "grounds" these concepts in external reality (2008: ch. 4). In the processing step, concepts are abstracted from this experience. In the belief formation step, the reasoning about the relationship between the concepts takes place.

On the face of it, however, a similar parallel can be drawn between Aristotelian justification and the use of memory in justification.

Consider a common case. I want to find my keys. I remember that I put them on my table. I am therefore justified in believing that I put them on my table. This justification can be represented, somewhat artificially, as having the form of an argument:

I remember that *p*

Therefore, *p*

There is no mention here of experience. Of course, experience enables us to have memories, but the experience is not involved in the justification of the belief (at least at this time).

The parallel with memory justification, however, is misleading. We can see how misleading it is if we consider the input and processing steps of knowing about the world through memory beliefs. In the input stage, we have experience. The experience is processed through either being remembered as it seemed at the time (perhaps somewhat faded) or in terms of remembering propositions that were experienced. Thus, what gets in and stays in the mind are not concepts but propositions. We remember the propositions that were originally learned through experience. This is an important difference between memory justification and Aristotelian justification. In Aristotelian justification, connections are understood between concepts. In memory justification, what was learned through experience is recovered. The nature and content of memories make them more of an extension of experience than is the faculty of conceptualization that is being used in Aristotelian justification. The point here is that in Aristotelian justification, the having of certain concepts, and certain reasoning abilities, is sufficient for justifying certain beliefs. This sounds very much like other forms of a priori justification we have examined in this book.

8.4 Aristotelian concepts

One way in which Aristotelian justification differs from analytic justification is in the sorts of concepts it uses. In analytic justification, the concepts that are used are ones that represent the meanings of words or phrases. In Aristotelian justification, the concepts are ones that are abstracted from objects of experience, and which refer to those objects. In some versions of Aristotelianism, such as Russell's and Husserl's, the concepts involved refer to universals, but for both of these philosophers universals are (at least in some sense) objects of experience.

The fact that Aristotelian concepts refer (largely) to entities that are external to our minds makes them particularly interesting. In Aristotelianism, we have a way to make sense of a priori justification about objects that are independent of us. It is this feature of Aristotelian justification more than any other that distinguishes it from, say, analytic justification. Of course rationalists claim that rational insight can give us a priori knowledge of mind-independent objects. This may be true, but rationalists have to rely on some other link between concepts and their objects than experience. The use of experience in the Aristotelian concept-forming process makes it particularly attractive as an epistemological theory. Experience is something we all think we have, and the vast majority of us think that experience is generally reliable. The use of experience in the Aristotelian explanation of a priori reasoning makes a priori reasoning easier to understand and accept.

Consider the following example. We learn the concepts *round* and *square* through experience. Using our imaginations and intellects, we can be justified in claiming that nothing can be both round and square at the same time in the same sense. This justification is a priori because it does not require that we check instances of round or square things. It only requires that we have the concepts and the relevant reasoning abilities. This belief is about things that are independent of our minds. It is a belief about all things that can have a shape.

8.5 Empirical defeasibility

Although there are close similarities between Aristotelian justification and analytic justification, there is also one rather important difference. Suppose that one comes to believe that nothing can be both round and square at the same time in the same sense, but then perceives something that is both round and square at the same time in the same sense. What should one believe? Under these circumstances it would be rational to be suspicious of one's senses and examine the object more closely, of course. But it would also be rational to reject one's previous reasoning that came to the belief that no object could have both these properties in the same sense at the same time. Aristotelian justification is empirically defeasible. It can be undercut by observation.

Aristotelian justifications can turn out to be wrong because the person's reasoning is faulty, but they may also turn out to be false because the concepts themselves are inaccurate. It may be that the person making the false judgement had in fact abstracted a concept from an experience of the right sort of object, but that the concept abstracted was incorrect.

For example, from experience we abstract the concept of a solid object as being completely solid, as containing little or no bits of empty space. Modern science, however, tells us that this conception is inaccurate. Physical objects are largely made up of empty space.

Our sense organs are set up so as to present to us a picture of physical objects such as tables and chairs that we naturally interpret as being without gaps (except those filled with air). That there are bits of completely empty space in them is surprising to most of us when we learn that there is.

Although our concept-forming mechanisms are fallible, they must be generally reliable if they are to enable justification to take place.[3] That is, if the concepts we formed were not generally reliable, our Aristotelian justifications would be suspect. The likelihood that they would be wrong would be too high to trust that form of justification. It is an empirical matter whether our concept formation process is reliable, but it is clear that the case for Aristotelian justification depends on it.

8.6 Idealization

Among those concepts that it would be *nice* to count as Aristotelian are mathematical concepts, such as "line" and "point". But we never perceive perfectly straight lines. And we cannot perceive dimensionless points: they are not big enough to see or feel.

We can think of this issue in terms of a debate between an Aristotelian and a nativist. The nativist claims that we must have these concepts innately within us, because we have them and we never perceive objects that match them. The Aristotelian, on the other hand, will claim that we perceive objects that approximate straight lines or points (such as lines and dots on paper) and we have a general cognitive mechanism that allows us to idealize from them. As I said at the end of the chapter on nativism, only empirical research can tell us which of these hypotheses is right. But we can understand a bit more about the case for Aristotelianism without getting out of our armchairs.[4]

We have a large number of ideal concepts: concepts that are idealized versions of properties that we perceive. It would be simpler to postulate that we have the ability to idealize from things that we do perceive than to claim that we have each of these ideal concepts innately within us.

Moreover, our stock of concepts seems to grow. When I was a child I was taught the concept of a set by my teacher as part of the "new maths" education of the 1960s. We collected together objects into clusters of pencils, erasers, children with brown eyes, children with blue eyes, boys, girls and so on. From these examples, we abstracted the concept *set*. Something interesting happened after that. My teacher had us think of a set with nothing in it, although we did not (and could not) experience that. We did so and came to have the concept *empty set*. This is an idealized notion in the sense that it idealizes (and generalizes) a concept that we abstracted more directly from experience.

This process of coming to learn the concept *set* and then the concept *empty set* is a multi-level process of idealization. The concept *set* idealizes from the actual collections that we perceive. We perceive a collection in terms of a group of pencils or children gathering in one part of a classroom. The concept *set*, as we learned it even in primary school, is more abstract than that. It does not require that the members of a set be spatially contiguous to one another. But we got the idea rather quickly. Moreover, we did not have any trouble generalizing from this concept – making a further idealization – to the concept of an empty set.

A nativist could complain that this story could equally be explained by our having the concepts of *set* and *empty set* innate within our minds. The teacher's actions, on this view, just made us recall or triggered the use of these concepts. Of course, we can only really decide the debate between the Aristotelian and the nativist by serious empirical research, but we can indulge ourselves by doing a little armchair philosophy while we are waiting for some neurologist or cognitive psychologist to do the right experiments. Surely the Aristotelian view that we actually learn these concepts is more intuitive than the nativist view that they are innate. Moreover, the view that we have a general mechanism that idealizes from experience is a simpler explanation that that we have a huge number of innate concepts. Thus, the Aristotelian hypothesis is better than its alternative, and abduction (as characterized in Chapter 6) directs us to accept it.

8.7 Connections between concepts

In a famous passage in his *Treatise of Human Nature*, Hume admits that we can have ideas that are not copies of sense-impressions. The particular idea he discusses is that of a "missing shade of blue". According to Hume, if we are shown samples of two different shades of blue, say, we can conjure up in our minds a third colour that fits between those two: the missing shade of blue (*Treatise* bk I, pt I, §1, ¶10).

The point that is of interest to us is not that we can invent ideas, but rather that we can invent ideas to connect other ideas. It can help us in certain cases to have concepts that contrast with, or are similar to, the ones we are currently analysing. Similar to Hume's missing shade of blue are many concepts of qualities close to those we have actually experienced. Suppose that you are cooking and you taste the food and decide it would be nicer if you added a bit more oregano or other herb. You have an idea what it would taste like, even if you have never tasted anything with exactly that mixture of herbs. This invention of an idea might be explained in a Lockean theory by the assembly of simple ideas in a new way into a complex idea.

We also have concepts that compare concepts. These can be of two forms. First, we can have relations between the things that concepts represent. For example, from reflecting on two colours one can extract relations between them, such as the realization that one colour is brighter than another. But we can also decide that one concept is more difficult than another to use, one is more general than another and so on.

8.8 Infinite sequences and mathematical knowledge

One of the most influential contemporary philosophies of mathematics is *structuralism*. According to structuralism, mathematics studies patterns of objects. These objects might be abstract objects – things that are not in space or time – or they might be concrete objects – things that are in space and time. There are several motivations for structuralism, but the one that is of interest is that, on the structuralist view, we can attain at least some mathematical knowledge by abstraction from our experiences of patterns of concrete things. This can provide the basis for an Aristotelian epistemology of mathematics.

Consider the following simple picture:

This pattern of objects can be seen to be two objects, but it can also represent two points on a vector. We perceive different mathematical patterns in the objects around us. On the Aristotelian view, we abstract at least some of our mathematical concepts from these patterns.

One type of pattern is especially interesting. Consider the following sequence:

You probably think you know what the next line in this sequence is: ★★★★★. And you probably think you know what the one after that is and the one after that. You know, at least potentially, an infinite pattern of lines of stars. This seems to be a very simple pattern that goes on for infinity. The Aristotelian, it would seem, can point to sequences like this one to show how we abstract our idea of an infinite progression. We do seem to learn infinite sequences like this. We teach children how to count by counting with them to higher and higher numbers. Eventually, they see how to go on and to keep counting, potentially forever.

There is a problem, however, with the characterization of mathematical learning given above. When we have a finite segment of an infinite list of things, as we have above in the first bit of a sequence of infinitely many lines of stars, then it is not fully determined what rule properly describes the entire sequence.

Consider the sequence of lines of stars given above. As we said, people usually continue the sequence with a line of five stars. But we could come up with a rule that dictates the next choice to be a line of fifteen stars:

> If n is less than 5, write n stars. If n is 5 or more, write $n \times 3$ stars, where n is the number of the line of the sequence in the vertical list (the top line is the first in the list, and n gets higher as we move down the list).

In fact, for any choice of a number of stars for the fifth line in the sequence, we could come up with some rule that fits that choice.[5]

Interestingly, some rules "feel natural" and others do not. This could be an effect of our generalization mechanism. For example, some rules may be more easily represented in our brains than others. But it also could be that we have innate structures in our brains that allow us immediately to choose some rules and not others. There is also a third possibility: which rules seem natural to us may be an effect of learning of other sorts. On this view, the naturalness of rules is a "social construction", that is, an effect of certain beliefs or institutions that are common in our society. If judgements about which rules are natural vary from society to society, then it seems likely that naturalness in this sense is a social construct.

8.9 Aristotelianism and rationalism

Both Aristotelians and rationalists think that we can reflect on properties, and determine their properties and relationships between them. We can, for example, reflect on red and green, and realize that nothing can be both red and green all over at the same time. So is Aristotelian reflection just a form of rational insight?

How an Aristotelian or a rationalist answers this question will clearly depend on what she means by "rational insight" and "reflection". Most philosophers who label themselves as rationalists do not allow imagination to count as an element of rational insight. Most of the philosophers whom I have labelled as Aristotelians, on the other hand, claim that imagination is an integral part of means we use to reflect on properties. Aristotelians tend to eschew talk about a special faculty of pure reason that is responsible for all of our a priori judgements. Rationalists, on the other hand, tend to rely on there being such a faculty.

8.10 Is abstraction reliable?

One reason for Descartes' assertion that the intellect is more reliable than the senses is that the science of his time claims that the external world is quite unlike the way that we perceive it.

Our science still tells us this. Apparently solid objects largely contain empty space. Perhaps the colours we see are really just our way of interpreting different wavelengths of light. Our apparently stationary earth is in fact hurtling through space and spinning all the while. And, of course, our natural concept of space is Euclidean.

So the question naturally arises: is our empirical concept formation really reliable?

Clearly, the concepts that we abstract from experience are defeasible, in a sense. Of course this is a misuse of the term; only beliefs and perhaps processes of justification can be defeasible. Concepts are not defeasible. But the idea is that a concept can be undercut in the sense that it can be shown to be accurate using further experience or a priori reasoning (or both). A very long and difficult process of reasoning, together with experimentation, has gone into the development of our current theories of physics. These theories, in turn, imply that ordinary solid objects are in fact largely made of empty space. And this has undercut our previous concept of a solid object as something that is truly solid.

The problem here, however, is not whether concepts are defeasible in this sense. It is perfectly compatible with the theory of Aristotelian justification that they are defeasible. Rather, the problem is whether empirical concept formation is so rife with error that we should not trust Aristotelian justification, or take abstracted concepts actually to refer to external objects.

Although some of the concepts we abstract in a naive way *may* not be reliable, we do seem to have the ability to correct them. Our concepts can be modified. For example, we use our scientific theories to modify our concept *solid object* even though this concept is first abstracted from experience. In order to show that Aristotelian justification is unreliable because the concepts it uses are not reliably accurate, one must show that our process of updating our concepts is unreliable, not just that the concepts that we first abstract from experience are not reliable.

8.11 Aristotelianism and other epistemologies

If our discussion in the previous section is right, then abstraction is a reliable concept-forming process. Then, if the ways in which we unpack concepts and relate them to one another using logic and other tools of reasoning are also reliable, Aristotelian justification is a reliable belief-forming process. Given these assumptions, then, Aristotelian justification fits in well with a reliabilist epistemology. Reliabilists, recall, hold that a belief is justified if and only if it is formed by a reliable process.

As we have seen in previous chapters in this book, if we have good reason to think that a justification process is reliable, then we can also recommend it to coherentists. In this case, a coherentist need only accept the beliefs formed by the process of Aristotelian justification and add to her belief system the beliefs that seem to show that the Aristotelian process is reliable. The coherentist can have an explanation of the beliefs formed in this way.

Foundationalists often take perceptual beliefs – often of the form "it seems to be ..." – as basic. There is perhaps a relationship between these beliefs and empirical concept formation that can in some sense justify our empirical concepts. Of course, in epistemology we usually talk of beliefs, not concepts, being justified. But here I mean that we are justified in assuming that our empirical concepts are accurate. Our empirical concepts would be treated as capturing how things appear to us. Our a priori knowledge, then, would be about how things appear and not about how they are in themselves. Thus, integrating Aristotelian justification into a foundationalist epistemology may change the nature of Aristotelian justification. In particular, it may not give us a priori knowledge about mind-independent things.

8.12 Summary

In this chapter we have discussed Aristotelianism. The process of Aristotelian justification is just a priori conceptual analysis of the same sort that we saw in Chapter 3. The only thing new about Aristotelian justification is that it uses empirical concepts. Aristotelianism is often overlooked as a form of a priori justification because people think of it as a form of a posteriori reasoning. So, one of the main problems concerning Aristotelianism is to defend its credentials as a priori reasoning, and I have done this in this chapter. I have also tried to set the scene for a defence of Aristotelianism as part of an epistemology of mathematics. This defence will be continued in Chapter 11.

Further reading

Carrie Jenkins's *Grounding Concepts* (2008) is a good contemporary defence of Aristotelianism.

There are various good introductions to Aristotle. One is John Evans's *Aristotle* (1987).

A good although slightly dated general book on Locke is Richard Aaron's *John Locke* (1971). Also good is Peter Alexander's *Ideas, Qualities, and Corpuscles: Locke and Boyle on the External World* (1985).

Good books on Hume and his theory of ideas are Barry Stroud's *Hume* (1977) and David Norton and Jacqueline Taylor's edited collection *The Cambridge Companion to Hume* (1993).

Russell's own presentation of his views in *The Problems of Philosophy* ([1912] 1959) is easy to read. Husserl's work, on the other hand, is full of jargon and bad writing. His views on eidetic intuition are in his *Ideas Pertaining to a Pure Phenomenology* ([1913] 1982). A very clear account of Husserl's theory is in Mattheson Russell's *Husserl* (2006).

9 Moral knowledge

9.1 Moral epistemology

This is the first of four chapters on applications of theories of a priori knowledge. Moral knowledge is particularly interesting. There is no consensus among philosophers about whether moral knowledge is possible and what an object of moral knowledge is. There is, however, widespread use of the method of *reflective equilibrium*.[1] The process of finding a reflective equilibrium consists of taking some putative moral principles and testing them against our moral judgements about particular situations. Those readers who have studied ethics will recognize this method. When a lecturer discusses some moral principle she will often bring up a counter-example and then discuss ways in which the principle can be modified to treat the counter-example. For example, when students are taught in their first ethics course the utilitarian principle that we should strive for the most overall happiness among people, they are almost invariably also taught a counter-example that concerns the hanging of an innocent person to calm a large crowd of people who are upset about a grisly murder. We can modify the utilitarian principle to make allowances for rights or make other changes to it. We can also defend the principle and claim that there is something wrong with the counter-example. In any case, all these moves are part of the attempt to find a point at which we have a cognitively stable moral view, and this stable view is called "reflective equilibrium".

The process of finding reflective equilibrium is an a priori method in the same sense that logical deduction is an a priori method. Once we have the inputs – the putative principles and the particular situations – we can do the rest without empirical input. We should ask, however, where the putative principles and particular situations come from. The origin of the putative principles is the main topic of this chapter. The particular situations can be ones that someone has experienced, or they can be hypothetical situations that we create in imagination.

The use of reflective equilibrium is another case in which principles that we have (perhaps) discovered a priori are treated as fallible (see Chapter 2). The need to test our moral principles against individual cases shows that we do not treat the reasoning that invents these principles as perfect.

In what follows, we shall look at attempts to develop moral epistemologies for each of the attitudes to a priori belief that we have discussed in the first eight chapters of this book.

9.2 Radical empiricism

As we saw in Chapter 6, radical empiricists typically make norms dependent on norms, or they treat one's normative claims as expressions of one's emotions or values. This is particularly true in metaethics.

Two philosophers who take typically radical-empiricist views of moral knowledge are A. J. Ayer[2] and Gilbert Harman. Ayer is an emotivist. He claims that our moral claims are in fact expressions of our emotional reactions to events. So when we condemn a person's action we are just expressing our disdain for that action. We are not expressing a belief, and we are certainly not stating any fact of the matter. This is a non-cognitivist position. It claims that our moral attitudes towards things are not beliefs about facts. Thus, we cannot really have moral knowledge; there are no facts to make what we claim true or false. The non-cognitivist, therefore, has no problem about moral knowledge, since she denies that there is anything to know.

Harman takes the other radical-empiricist route. He claims that morality is a social institution that varies from society to society. He is a *social relativist*. This position makes the problem of moral knowledge easy, not by denying that it exists, but by making an empirical problem about societies. We can use empirical means to investigate what norms are enforced in different societies, or which norms are adopted in the population.

Of course it is open to the empiricist to claim that there are no real moral truths. This position is called "error theory". J. L. Mackie (1917–81) is an error theorist. We shall look at two of his arguments for error theory in the section on rationalism and Aristotelianism later in this chapter.

Mill, on the other hand, gives a very strange but interesting argument for his version of the principle that we should seek to maximize the overall happiness in the human population. He gives an empirical argument for the claim that we should seek happiness. He says:

> The only proof capable of being given that an object is visible, is that people actually see it. The only proof that a sound is audible, is that people hear it; and so on of the other sources of experience. In like manner, I apprehend, the sole evidence it is possible to produce that anything is desirable, is that people actually desire it.   ([1861] 1969: 234)

Here what is desirable is placed on the same footing as what is visible and what is audible. But the "-able/-ible" suffix on these three words does not mean the same thing in each case. For a thing is visible if one can see it. Similarly, it is audible if one can hear it. But a thing is desirable, in the sense important for moral theory, if it *should* be desired, or rather if it should be sought.

Mill may rather be arguing here that the only thing that people *can* desire is happiness. If he is making this point, then he may be invoking again the principle that "must implies ought" (see Chapter 6). In this case we can rewrite the argument as follows:

1. The only thing that people actually do desire is happiness.

    (empirical fact)
2. The only thing that people can desire is happiness.   (from 1?)
3. If one cannot help but do something, then he or she ought to do it.   (must implies ought)
4. Therefore, people ought to desire happiness.   (2, 3)

The inference from steps 2 and 3 to the conclusion is valid, but the inference from 1 to 2 is invalid. We need some way of inferring from what we always do to there being a law of nature (or something of that sort) that we do it. Thus there is a missing step in Mill's argument.

As I said in Chapter 6, however, the "must implies ought" principle is itself dubious. It is especially doubtful when we are discussing moral obligation. We sometimes exempt people who are compelled to do bad actions from punishment, because we think that they *have* to do these bad actions, but we never say that they *ought* to do these actions. The "must implies ought" principle just seems too strong.

There may, however, be another way of interpreting Mill. Mill says that "questions of ultimate ends do not admit of proof, in the ordinary acceptation of the term" (*ibid.*). Given this, he may not be trying to prove that we must seek happiness. Recall the discussion of naturalized epistemology in Chapter 6. Naturalized epistemology is a "natural" position for radical empiricists to have. Since they cannot argue for general norms in epistemology (or anything else), they instead describe how we form beliefs and extract more localized claims about what we should or should not do from these descriptions. We should trust certain sorts of experience, for example, if they are reliable (according to the natural sciences), and we should not trust, say, wishful thinking because it has been shown empirically not to be reliable.

Similarly, Mill may only be making the claim that we do actually seek happiness. Mill may be describing an actual (empirical) feature of people and then telling us how they should regiment their behaviour to get what they want. Unfortunately, this does not seem to be adequate grounds to justify Mill's principle of utility, which claims that we should seek the most net happiness for the entire human population of the world. Mill argues that individuals want happiness *for themselves*, not for everyone else.

Regardless of the success or lack of success of Mill's argument, we can see that radical empiricists do not have a moral epistemology that delivers moral knowledge in the strong sense of knowledge about opinion-independent moral principles. Radical empiricists generally abandon the search for such principles and claim that moral knowledge, if it exists at all, is about actual human institutions or what people actually want.

9.3 Are moral principles innate?

In arguing against the existence of innate moral principles, Locke says:

> Whether there be any such moral principles wherein all men do agree, I appeal to any who have been but moderately conversant in the history of mankind, and looked abroad beyond the smoke of their own chimneys. Where is that practical truth that is universally received, without doubt or question, as it must be if innate? (*Essay* bk I, ch 2, §2)

The variation between societies in the moral principles they accept convinced Locke that we do not have an innate morality. But those who argue for nativism think there is some empirical evidence that we do all share certain norms. For example, there are in all cultures and societies rules against harming others. We can explain why this is so by postulating innate moral principles.

Shaun Nichols points out, however, that there may be some good evidence for nativism about moral principles. He points out that people are usually emotionally predisposed to finding harm to people upsetting. Moreover, we are more likely to make rules against actions that we find upsetting. But Nichols thinks this evidence is not enough to support nativism. He says that perhaps instead of postulating innate moral principles, we should merely think that we are born with tendencies to have certain emotional reactions. These tendencies, moreover, provide a more plausible explanation for the universality of rules against harming people (Nichols 2005: 362–4). A tendency to have a particular reaction may give rise to the sort of intuition we often use as a justification for accepting or rejecting moral principles.

If nativism is true, is there any good evidence that it provides us with knowledge or even justified beliefs about moral truths? As we saw in Chapter 4, one way of showing that innate beliefs provide us with justification about external facts is to use an argument based on evolution. Evolutionary arguments of this sort attempt to show that we have innate beliefs as the result of natural selection. Having knowledge of the relevant facts helps us to survive, and nature put certain beliefs in our minds to aid us in this regard. But, as we saw in Chapter 4, we need to establish at least three facts about the beliefs in order to make an evolutionary argument plausible:

- the beliefs help us to survive;
- not only do the beliefs have to be conducive to survival, but their accuracy needs to be important to our survival;
- there is some mechanism that explains how these beliefs could have been selected.

There is no doubt that moral beliefs help us to survive.[3] Without moral beliefs such as *it is bad to harm others*, human societies could not thrive. Societies require cooperation, and it is difficult to cooperate with others if you think they are going to harm you if they see some advantage in doing so. Moreover, the existence of societies is crucial for our survival as a species.

The question, however, is whether moral beliefs need to be accurate in order to help us survive. Do there need to be true moral principles that are represented by our innate beliefs in order for these beliefs to help humanity survive? Mackie, Ruse and Joyce claim that the truth of moral principles is irrelevant to the survival of our species. To understand why, compare innate beliefs about which animals can harm us. We probably do not have such beliefs, but if we did they would help us to survive only if they are at least somewhat accurate. If we believed that squirrels could harm us but that bears could not, then we would be in serious trouble. Accuracy in our beliefs about what animals can harm us is crucial to our survival. Our moral beliefs, on the other hand, help us to cooperate with one another. It does not seem, however, that the truth of these beliefs matters at all to our survival.

In fact, nativism may help to undermine the claim that there are independent moral facts. Nativism explains why we have moral beliefs: we are born with them. We can construct arguments based on natural selection to explain why we have innate moral beliefs *despite the fact that there are no true moral principles.*[4]

9.4 Are moral principles analytic?

It is plausible that at least some moral principles are analytic. One such is John Rawls's famous slogan "justice is fairness".[5] This slogan refers to the principle that any just society is a fair society. Rawls uses this principle to justify the adoption of certain elements of the welfare state.

The real question, however, is whether we have analytic sentences about moral terms that define them in terms of what are usually thought to be non-moral terms. The claim that justice is fairness connects two moral terms, but what we really need in order to provide a moral epistemology are propositions that link moral terms with empirical or scientific terms so that we may really know what morality is all about. Defining one moral term in terms of others does not help very much with this task.

Many philosophers, however, hold that no sentences defining moral terms using non-moral terms are analytic. One famous argument against the analyticity of moral principles is G. E. Moore's *open question argument*. According to Moore, the word "good" cannot be given any definition except using other moral terms. Suppose, for example, that we say with Mill that a good action is one that produces the most overall happiness for all of humanity. Moore (1903) points out that we can ask why a good action is one that produces the most overall happiness. According to Moore, if it makes sense to ask this question, then the principle cannot be just a matter of the meaning of the terms involved. For one can understand the principle yet still think that the question is appropriate.

Clearly Moore's argument is using "analytic" in the epistemological sense. One way of avoiding the problem, then, is to claim that moral principles are analytic in the metaphysical sense. If we do so, it might be that the meanings of moral principles might alone make them true, even if we cannot always tell that they are true.

We might read Richard Boyd (1988) as doing this. According to Boyd, the way in which we use the word "good" and other moral terms makes them refer to clusters of properties. Moreover, "good" refers to the same cluster of properties in all possible worlds, in just the way that "water" refers to H_2O in all possible worlds. Boyd thinks we can discover empirically what these property clusters are, but we may not at this time know what they are. On one view of meaning, the meaning of a term is what it refers to in all possible worlds. On this theory, the meaning of the term "good", then, is the cluster of properties that it refers to in all possible worlds. Let us call the cluster of properties that "good" refers to G. Then the sentence "*G* is good" is true by virtue of its meaning alone, and so is analytic in the metaphysical sense.

Boyd thinks we can discover the meaning of "good" empirically. But recall our discussion of "water is H_2O" in Chapter 2. Although we can discover empirically that the word "water" refers to H_2O, we need a priori premises to show that "water" picks out H_2O in every possible world. I think something similar is true here. It may be that we can discover what "good" refers to empirically. But to establish that "good" refers to this same cluster of properties in all possible worlds it would seem that we need an a priori premise. This premise may, as in the case of "water" and H_2O, concern how we use the words involved (i.e. it might concern our stipulations about what the words mean). In any case, it is difficult to see what sort of empirical premise will allow us to establish a necessary connection between "good" and a particular cluster of properties.[6]

J. O. Urmson (1950) claims that views like the one that I am basing on Boyd's position commit a fallacy. Suppose that "good" is defined in terms of natural properties *A*, *B* and *C*. The term "good" is an evaluative term: it is used to praise people or actions. The terms *A*, *B* and *C* are, by hypothesis, descriptive terms. They are used only to describe people or actions (or other things). Thus, Urmson claims, it would seem that any definition of "good" just in terms of *A*, *B* and *C* is missing something. We cannot apply "*A*, *B* and *C*" in the same way that we apply "good" to things, because "*A*, *B* and *C*" does not provide us with an evaluation of an action or person. So it is not a proper definition.

John Searle claims that Urmson himself is guilty of a fallacy. He is confusing the content of a statement with the way in which it is used. We use the statement "This action is good", say, in a different way from "This action has properties *A*, *B* and *C*". We may use the statement "This action is good" to evaluate or praise an action, and the statement "This action has properties *A*, *B*, and *C*" merely to describe the same action, but this does not mean the two statements express different propositions. The definition "an action is good if and only if it has properties *A*, *B*, and *C*" may be a proper definition, for it need only tell us the necessary and sufficient conditions under which an action is good (Searle 1969: 135–6).

Jackson (1998) also claims that moral principles are analytic. He says that moral terms are implicitly defined by the moral theory that ordinary people hold, which he calls "folk morality".[7] (In fact he claims that an idealized form of folk morality is what actually defines our moral terms.) Moral principles are then derived logically from folk morality. This strategy avoids the open-question argument, since implicit definitions are often extremely complicated, so unobvious.

What if there is not one theory of folk morality but many? It could be that people in different cultures or societies have different folk moral views. If this is so, and we accept Jackson's view that folk moral theory implicitly defines moral terms, then it would seem that people in different societies use the same moral terminology ("good", "bad", etc.) in different ways and the moral principles that contain them are analytic, in the stipulational sense.

Jackson's view, however, is that it is not any actual version of folk morality that determines what is right and wrong, but what he calls "mature folk morality". This is a theory that is based on actual folk moral views, but is tidied up in a certain way. First, moral theories often include non-moral claims. For example, advocates of slavery or genocide have often held that the people they were enslaving or killing were inferior intellectually, or have a natural tendency to steal, or similar sorts of claims. These views were invariably false, but were important in allowing justifications of barbarous treatment of these other people. Thus, the first thing we need to do to tidy up folk morality is to remove all false statements from it and replace them with the relevant true statements (such as "no race of people is inferior to any other", or even "race is not a biologically significant category"). Next, we need to remove all contradictions from folk morality. And we need to make the view coherent in the sense that there are explanatory connections between the statements of the theory. There may be many other things we can do to make the view truly mature, but I think the reader gets the picture.

Whether this process will lead to a single theory is an open question. But it does seem at least reasonable to hold that even if there are several mature folk moralities that could be developed from the actual folk moralities people currently hold, there will be very widespread agreement between them. Consider, for example, the current tension between the moral views of divine-command theorists – who claim that we should do whatever God tells us to do – and those of atheists. Suppose that God does not exist. Then we will need to change the theist's folk morality to omit the statement "God exists" and we replace it with the statement "God does not exist". We then need to make the theory coherent. We cannot have statements such as "Act in accordance with whatever you are told to do in the Bible" floating around in the theory, since these will lack any explanation in the theory for their force (they will not express the will of God). So they too will have to be removed. And so on. Similarly, if God does exist, we might have to change the atheist's folk morality in similar ways.

9.5 Rationalism, Aristotelianism and moral intuition

Moral intuitionism is the view that people have an "immediate awareness" of right and wrong (Hudson 1967: 1). There are two sorts of intuitionism: rationalist intuitionism and moral-sense theory. Rationalist intuitionism is a form of rationalism and moral-sense theory can be interpreted as a form of Aristotelianism.

Rationalists, as we saw in Chapter 3, hold that we can grasp certain truths through some form of rational insight. Moral rationalism holds that we can grasp moral truths in this way. Kant is a moral rationalist, as are Aristotelians. But we are interested here in foundationalist moral rationalists, who, unlike Kantians and Aristotelians, think that we have an insight into moral truths that are independent of our opinions, and that insight need not be explained in terms of the physical workings of our minds and sensory systems.

One such foundationalist rationalist is Michael Huemer, a contemporary philosopher who holds an extreme version of this view. He believes that moral intuition is a direct awareness of moral truths; it is not something we infer from any other beliefs. Moreover, moral intuition is distinct from perception, memory and introspection (Huemer 2006: 102). Moral intuition is like perception, memory and introspection, however, in the sense that it yields "appearances" of some sort (*ibid*.: 99). Huemer is a moral realist. He thinks that moral facts are independent of what we believe them to be. Thus, Huemer is a strong rationalist in the sense of Chapter 3.

Huemer has to convince us (i) that we actually do have this rational insight into moral principles and (ii) that this insight has the content that he thinks it has. These problems are more difficult for the foundationalist rationalist like Huemer than the analogous problems for certain other philosophers. If moral principles are self-evident, then how can there be significant difference of opinion about what they are?

If we turn from foundationlist rationalism to its coherentist and reliabilist forms, we see other problems appear. Moral rationalism leaves itself open to an argument due to Mackie: the so-called "argument from queerness". There are two versions of the argument from queerness in Mackie. One is epistemological and the other is metaphysical. The epistemological argument is most relevant to these views. According to the epistemological version of the argument from queerness, moral realism is problematic because it requires some sort of relationship between our minds and moral truths that cannot be explained in terms of the theories of contemporary natural sciences.[8]

Another sort of moral intuitionism is moral-sense theory. According to moral-sense theory, in ordinary experience we can perceive moral qualities in actions and (perhaps) people. One proponent of this view is Francis Hutcheson (1694–1746). Moral-sense theory can be interpreted as a form of Aristotelianism. We abstract our basic concepts from experience and then develop moral principles by reflecting on these concepts.

Moral properties may be, as Boyd claims, natural properties.[9] If this is so, moral-sense theory is a form of naturalism. This view of moral properties would in some ways be welcome to the Aristotelian. This is nice, but there is still a problem.

As we have seen, some philosophers reject the attempt to reduce evaluative properties to non-evaluative ones. If they are reductionists, moral-sense theorists do have to explain why a particular set of natural properties can be used in the evaluation, rather than just in the description, of an action or a person. This is a problem for all reductionists, not just Aristotelians. Jackson is a reductionist, and he claims the evaluative nature of certain properties emerges for their roles in folk moral theories. For example, it might be part of our moral theory that it is bad if people are caused to suffer. Then actions that cause suffering will have natural properties that make them bad. This seems like a reasonable way of dealing with this problem, but it is not open to the moral-sense theorist. What is distinct about moral-sense theory is that we can come to know the goodness or badness of an action through experience; it cannot be part of a background theory that we use to interpret the experience. We come to know general features of goodness, badness and other moral properties through abstraction and reflection. The evaluative nature of moral properties has to be somehow evident to us, either in our perception of them or in our reflection on them after we have abstracted them. It is difficult to understand how this can be so.

For this reason, most moral-sense theorists reject naturalism. They say that moral properties cannot be reduced to natural properties. Thus they are "non-naturalists". Advocating non-naturalism, however, exposes the moral-sense theory to the metaphysical version of the argument from queerness. Non-natural properties cannot fit into the causal order as is understood by science. It becomes mysterious, then, how actions or people get these properties and how we perceive them (Mackie 1977: 38). This is a very serious problem.

9.6 Kantian moral epistemology

In his *Groundwork of the Metaphysic of Morals*, Kant gives a transcendental argument for his famous categorical imperative. We shall give a formulation of the categorical imperative later. Right now, recall the form of transcendental arguments:

1. *P*
2. *P* presupposes *Q*
3. Therefore, *Q*

The first premise tells us what fact needs to be explained. At the start of the *Groundwork*, Kant tells us that "It is impossible to conceive anything at all in the world, or even out of it, which can be taken as good without qualification, except a *good will*" ([1785] 1964: 61). Here Kant is telling us that actions and things cannot be good, except in a derivative sense. Rather, the only sources of good in the world are good people. As we shall see, it may be that there are no sources of good in the world, but we shall set that aside for now. What Kant wants to find in his transcendental argument are conditions under which a person can be good. He argues that one's acting in accordance with the categorical imperative is such a condition. Acting in accordance with the categorical imperative is a presupposition of good actions.

Kant claims also that in order for someone to do a good action, that action must be his or her own action. The person cannot be caused to do good by some external event. We cannot consider a person good if all they are is a link in a causal chain. Rather, they must be doing the action of their own free will.

Kant rejects the idea that a person is good or bad because of the effects of his or her actions. Once we perform an action, it takes on a life of its own. We do not possess or control it. Rather, our goodness has to come from ourselves. On Kant's view, we only control our own intentions, so it is only these that matter. Note that Kant here is assuming that we control our own thoughts. As we said in Chapter 6, Kant does not think we can prove that we have free will. This includes freedom to think what we will. Instead, Kant thinks that in order to be able to think of ourselves as morally responsible we need to assume that we have free will, but we do not know that we have it.

It looks like Kant has painted himself into a corner here. In the *Critique of Pure Reason* he claims that we must think of all events that take place in time and space as determined by laws of nature. But in the *Groundwork* and, especially, the *Critique of Practical Reason*, he says that only free actions can be considered morally good and that we have to assume we have free will. Kant's way around this tension is to accept a form of compatibilism between free will and determinism. He holds that we can describe our actions in two ways. On one hand, if we describe them in terms of ourselves as empirical things in space and time, then we need to think of ourselves and our thoughts as subject to laws of nature. If we think of our actions as the products of our noumenal selves, on the other hand, we can think of them as free. Recall that we do not know that our "noumenal wills" are free, but we also do not know that they are not free. What Kant is claiming is that we must assume that they are free. Thus, Kant claims that we cannot know whether we can actually do good things or be good people ([1781/1788] 1929: 45–59).

In order for an action to be considered good, the reasons behind it must appeal to our intellect alone. They cannot appeal, for example, to our desires, since desires belong to the empirical world and are subject to the laws of nature. Thus, in order to discover the laws of morality, we need to investigate what sorts of laws will appeal to reason. Kant claims that the only principles that reason could use to justify actions are the various formulations of his famous *categorical imperative*. It is easiest, given what I have said so far, to understand the end-in-itself formulation. On this formulation, we must act towards other people as if they are moral ends in themselves; we must not use them as means. The reason why we should do this is because, like ourselves, others are potential sources of good action. We should allow them the opportunity to do good actions – by using their reason to direct their decisions and to act on their decisions – and not force them (or manipulate them) into doing what we want them to do if they do not want that also.

I shall leave it to the reader to decide whether the deduction of the categorical imperative is successful. What is interesting for us is that the first premise of the argument – that only people can be good in an unconditional sense – is a priori, and that so is the argument. It is also important to note that the argument, as Kant gives it, depends on his distinction between the experienced world, which is controlled by laws of nature, and the noumena world, which we postulate to have free will.

Some contemporary Kantians give transcendental arguments for Kantian moral principles without appealing to any of Kant's theoretical philosophy for support. One such philosopher is Christine Korsgaard.

Korsgaard gives us a different transcendental argument for a version of Kant's end-in-itself formulation of the categorical imperative. Instead of beginning with the claim that only good souls can be good, she begins by claiming that the only sources of value are human beings. We create value by valuing things, actions, feelings and so on.

Korsgaard claims that in order to act, one must "endorse one's own humanity". In an action, one is carrying out an intention. In acting, one makes choices about what is better or worse (not necessarily in a moral sense); one must have a reason for acting. To act and be rational, one has to think that it is a good thing to act on reasons. Only humans can act on reasons. Thus, in acting one is endorsing one's own humanity: the ability to appeal to reasons.

It is not just one's own humanity, according to Korsgaard (1998: 139), that one should value, but everyone's humanity. Moral reasons – reasons we can give to justify our actions – are "public reasons". They are reasons that I can give to others.[10] Korsgaard argues for this by an appeal to a particular view about thought in general. She thinks that it must be capable of being made public. This is a very controversial view, but I do not think she needs to adopt it. There is an easier way to make her point. When one acts in public, one's actions should be justified not just for oneself but for others, because they too have to live with them.

In using one's humanity as a reason for acting, it is not the fact that *you* are human that matters, but rather the fact that one is *human*. Suppose that someone steals some food to feed himself because he is starving. In his own defence he says, "I am a human being and I have a right to survive". This is a convincing reason for stealing food. If he were to say "I am Joe Bloggs and *I* must survive" we would not find that compelling, unless we had reasons to value Joe Bloggs in particular. The public nature of reasons shows that humanity is in itself valuable. It is not just a particular person's humanity that we value.

In both Kant and Korsgaard we see attempts to derive a substantive moral principle from the assumption that it is only reflective human beings who can be, or create, things of moral value. These assumptions and derivations are a priori.

What is attractive about the Kantian approach to ethics is that it does not assume that there are any mind-independent moral facts, but still claims that there are objective moral truths. This means that there are moral principles that everyone should obey, even if these moral principles are not independent of us. Kantians seem to avoid the epistemological problems of moral rationalism and the metaphysical problems of non-naturalist moral-sense theory. The success of the Kantian project, however, rests on the derivation of the general moral principle from the supposed facts about good souls or humans as the source of values. I have not attempted any real analysis of this derivation – I shall leave that to the reader – but we can still see why Kantianism is supposed to have these virtues.

9.7 Summary

I shall not claim that any one of these moral epistemologies is correct. I certainly have not surveyed every theory of moral knowledge; perhaps I have not even given a representative sample. But what I have given is at least one illustration of each approach to a priori reasoning applied to the problem of moral knowledge.

We can see some interesting, but expected, results from this glimpse of moral epistemologies. Strong rationalists postulate a mind-independent moral reality of which we are supposed to have rational insight. This position has the usual difficulty of explaining how such insight can be reliable. Nativism may be plausible as a view about why there are certain commonalities between moral codes in different cultures, but it is difficult to show that nativism is a theory of moral *knowledge*. Aristotelianism, in the form of moral-sense theory, claims that we can perceive moral properties in ordinary sense experience. We abstract these moral properties from experience and realize moral principles by reflecting on the resulting concepts. We saw that both the naturalist and non-naturalist versions of this theory have serious epistemological and metaphysical difficulties.

Kantians reject the moral realism of the rationalists. They think that what is morally good is very closely tied to the way in which we understand good and bad. This is especially true of Korsgaard, who claims that human minds are the sources of all normativity and all value. As in the case of Kant's theoretical philosophy, we can criticize the transcendental arguments themselves, but the attempt to find objective moral principles without postulating a mind-independent moral reality is admirable. As we shall see in the next chapter, the attempt to do this in moral philosophy is much more plausible than Kant's very similar attempt to give a foundation for logic.

Analytic approaches to morality also seem reasonable. They have had a tough time recovering after the assault on them in the first two-thirds of the twentieth century. But perhaps some version of the view will deliver a defensible form of moral epistemology that allows us to use analytic justification as a way of supporting moral beliefs.

On the other side, radical empiricists have rejected moral facts in any strong form. Harman thinks that moral facts are social facts and that different societies are subject to different moralities. Ayer and Mackie deny that there are any moral facts at all. Ayer claims that our moral statements do not attempt to state facts about things or people, but rather express our feelings towards those things or people. Mackie rejects both non-cognitivism (Ayer's position) and moral facts. He thinks that moral statements do attempt to state facts, but he claims that there are no facts of the sort that moral statements attempt to state.

What we have here are the rudiments of a map of moral epistemologies and their commitments. I hope that such a map will be useful for the reader both to see theories of the a priori in action and to help him or her to navigate the difficult terrain of metaethics.

Further reading

Walter Sinnott-Armstrong and Mark Timmons's edited collection *Moral Knowledge?* (1996) is perhaps the best general book on the problem of moral knowledge. David Brink's *Moral Realism and the Foundations of Ethics* (1989) is also a good book, applying a coherence theory of justification to defend moral realism from an epistemological point of view.

A detailed presentation and defence of reflective equilibrium is Norman Daniels's *Justice and Justification* (1996).

Mill's moral views are in his *Utilitarianism* ([1861] 1969). Harman's theory is in his *The Nature of Morality* (1977). Mackie's error theory is spelled out in his *Ethics* (1977). A contemporary version of error theory can be found in Richard Joyce's *The Myth of Morality* (2001). Joyce's analysis of the evolution of our moral beliefs is in his *On the Evolution of Morality* (2006).

W. D. Ross is perhaps the best-known recent moral rationalist; see his *The Right and the Good* (1930). Robert Audi is also a moral rationalist; see his article "Intuitionism, Pluralism, and the Foundation of Ethics" (1996). Plato is a moral rationalist and a moral nativist. His *Republic* is largely a presentation of his moral rationalism.

Kant's ethics are to be found in his *Groundwork of the Metaphysics of Morals* ([1785] 1964) and *Critique of Practical Reason* ([1781/1788] 1929). Christine Korsgaard's position is in her *The Sources of Normativity* (1998). Good books on Kant's ethics are Onora O'Neill's *Acting on Principle* (1975) and *Constructions of Reason* (1989). Christian Illies's edited volume *The Grounds of Ethical Judgment* (2003) is a good collection on Kantian ethics. More dated but still good (and easier to read) is H. J. Patton's *The Categorical Imperative* (1948).

10 Logical knowledge

10.1 Introduction

In this chapter we explore how we know the principles of deductive logic. We could also discuss the principles of induction and abduction, but these topics are extremely complicated and I do not want to dedicate the rest of this book to discussion of the principles of reasoning.

Systems of deductive logic – such as the ones most undergraduate philosophy students learn in their first or second year – typically have two sorts of principles. First, there are the *laws of the logical system*. These laws are sometimes called "theorems" or, in the case of standard propositional logic, "tautologies". Laws are statements. In formal logical systems, these statements are formulas of various sorts. But we shall not be using the language of formal logic here. Instead, we shall write our laws in English or in a schematic form of English, writing, for example, "either S_1 or S_2" to stand for disjunctive statements such as "either it is going to rain soon or it will remain humid all afternoon" or "either dogs hate cats or dogs are afraid of cats".

A law of logic is a necessarily true statement. It is true in all possible worlds (see Chapter 2). Some philosophers think that laws of logic must have other characteristics as well. For example, some think that a law of logic must be necessarily true by virtue of its form. For example, the statement "red is a colour" is necessarily true. Red cannot be anything other than a colour. But its form "x is F" has *instances* that are not necessarily true. For example, the statement "red is my favourite colour" is not necessarily true. But the scheme "if S_1 and S_2, then S_2" has only necessarily true instances: "if my dog barks and whines, then she whines" is necessarily true. Thus, "if S_1 and S_2, then S_2" is considered to be a law of logic.

Some other philosophers, however, doubt the importance or even the coherence of the concept of logical form. They think that the words or phrases we choose as our logical words or phrases (such as "and", "or", "not", "if ... then", "all" and "some") are somewhat arbitrary. These are the words or phrases that remain fixed when we talk about the logical form of a statement. If there is nothing special about those words or phrases, then the concept of logical form has no real importance either (see Etchemendy 1999).

The second sort of logical principle is a *logical rule*. A well-known example of a logical rule is *modus ponens*:

If A, then B

A

―――――――

∴ B

The schematic statements above the line are premises and the one below the line is, of course, the conclusion of the rule. A logical rule, if it is a real logical rule, must be *valid*. This means that in all possible worlds, if any instances of the premises are true, then the relevant instances of the conclusion are also true. For instance, if in some possible world it is true that "if Lola barks, then Zermela will whine" and "Lola barks", then it will also be true in that world that Zermela will whine.

The problem of logical knowledge is the problem of how we know of particular statements that they are laws and of particular rules that they are valid. We could avoid this problem by denying that we do know either of these things. One way of doing so is to deny that logical principles are real objects of knowledge, either by adopting an *error theory* that says that there are no logical principles, or by holding a *non-cognitivist* theory that says that our logical assertions are expressions of our own attitudes or psychological tendencies and have no truth-value. If our statements about logic have no truth-value then they cannot be known to be true, and so the problem about how we know them disappears. I am not aware of any error theorists about logic and only a few non-cognitivists.

Thus, we shall assume that there are logical laws and that there is a substantive problem about our knowledge of them.

The topic of logical knowledge is particularly interesting for us. Recall that I claimed in Chapter 1 that the topic of apriority comes into its own when we are talking about normativity or necessity. Logical principles are supposed to be both normative and necessary. Laws of logic are supposed by most philosophers to be necessarily true, and valid rules of inference are supposed to preserve truth in all possible worlds. Moreover, the principles of logic, in some sense, give us standards of good arguments. They tell us what form our inferences should take.

We begin our discussion of the problem of logical knowledge with radical empiricism.

10.2 Are the laws of logic known empirically?

As we saw in Chapter 6, radical empiricists tend to reject or reinterpret our claims to know about necessity or norms. They claim that we cannot know what is necessarily true or, in the case of Quine, claim that there is no such thing as metaphysical necessity. Logic as it is usually understood is supposed to be normative – it tells us how we *should* reason – and its laws are supposed to be necessarily true.

Mill, Peirce, Quine and Harman all reject the view that logical laws are necessarily true. In Chapter 6 we looked in detail at Mill's views about logical knowledge. He thinks that it is a form of inductive logic. Moreover, on Mill's view, we cannot come to know necessary truths from induction. And so he denies that any of the laws of logic are necessarily true. Peirce thinks that our logical theories are just theories about how people actually reason. And Harman and Quine think that laws of logic are just general truths about the world. So much for necessity!

Interestingly, Quine gives logic a special normative status. He thinks that in order to assess scientific theories, we should translate them into the language of formal logic. Formal logic is precise. In particular, it makes the *ontological commitments* of theories clear. For example, in chemistry lessons all of us learned that each hydrogen atom has one proton and one electron. Thus, if there are any hydrogen atoms, the theory of chemistry commits us to saying that there are protons and electrons. Thus, given this fact about the world (that there is some hydrogen in it), we have a commitment to the formula $\exists xEx$ (there are electrons). The symbol $\exists$ means "there is" or "there are" and is called the *existential quantifier*. According to Quine, after formalizing our theory and seeing what formulas are entailed by it (and by the facts of the world) we should pick out those formulas with existential quantifiers at the start of them. They will tell us what our ontological commitments are. The theory of chemistry tells us that we are committed to the existence of electrons because it and the facts about the world entail the formula $\exists xEx$.

Quine thinks that one of the most important virtues a theory can have is to be *parsimonious*. This means that a theory is better if it is committed to fewer sorts of entities. What we want, according to Quine, are as few ontological commitments as possible.

Quine's view is interesting. It gives logic a special normative role, but this role is not based on a priori reasoning; nor does it assume that the laws of logic are necessarily true. It takes a particular fact about the structure of logic – its ability to represent in a very precise way – as the basis for a normative theory.

The main task of logic, however, is as a theory of reasoning. As we saw in Chapter 6, Quine says that our logical beliefs are close to the centre of our webs of belief. Changes in our logical beliefs can force very widespread changes in our system of belief. It is for this reason that we are unlikely to change our logical beliefs. The special status of logic as a theory of reasoning is due to the fact that our logical beliefs have this widespread influence on what else we believe.

This rather strict empiricist line on logic is very hard to maintain. Even Quine retreats from it on occasion. In his book *Philosophy of Logic*, Quine discusses philosophers who put forward non-standard logical systems. We have discussed alternative logical theories in Chapter 5 and we shall discuss them again later in this chapter. Quine considers someone who denies the law of non-contradiction: that no statement and its negation can both be true. He says that such a person must mean something else by "not" than he does. Now, this looks very much like an analytic justification. Quine is appealing to the meaning of "not" to justify his acceptance of a law of logic. One might object that Quine is appealing not to *the* meaning of "not", but to what *he* means by "not", but we can rephrase that as saying that he is appealing to the meaning of "not" in his own *idiolect* (his own language).

Quine is not alone in using a priori justifications for principles of logics. In debates about which logical system to adopt, few, if any, empirical arguments are used. Interesting exceptions are arguments for something called "quantum logic". Unfortunately, it takes almost a whole book to explain what quantum logic is, but roughly it is supposed to mirror the way in which quantum mechanics treats properties of atoms and subatomic particles. One feature of quantum logic is that it rejects the principle of distribution. In standard logic, we can infer from a statement of the form "S_1 and (S_2 or S_3)" to a statement of the form "(S_1 and S_2) or (S_1 and S_3)". According to quantum mechanics, the probabilities of the behaviour of particles do not obey the principle of distribution. We think that quantum physics is true, and we know this empirically, so do we have an empirical refutation of standard logic? Some philosophers, such as Putnam, have thought so.

The situation with regard to quantum logic, however, is quite similar to the situation regarding Euclidean geometry. There are other, more modern, interpretations of quantum physics and its logic that retain the principle of distribution. They do so by chaning the way in which we interpret properties and propositions to be related to the mathematics of quantum mechanics. We could retain the parallel postulate of Euclidean geometry by reinterpreting the way in which geometry is related to space (e.g. by rejecting the claim that light travels in straight lines). Similarly, we can retain the principle of distribution by reinterpreting the relationship between the mathematics of quantum mechanics and properties and propositions.

Because there is a real choice between which logics to use, while maintaining the central ideas of the physics, it would seem that the choice between quantum logic and standard logic is not really empirical. It has been made using theoretical virtues. In this case the main virtue that philosophers appeal to is ease of use. Classical logic is much easier to formulate and use to prove propositions. It is even easier to use in proving propositions about quantum physics.

10.3 Logic and analyticity I: logic and meaning

Given the way in which we have delimited the subject of logic, it is plausible to say that all the laws of logic and all the valid rules of logic are analytic. They follow from the meanings of the logical terms involved.

Consider, for example, the law of non-contradiction: "Not-(S and not-S)". This law tells us that us that every contradiction is false. We can prove this by means of a calculation using the truth conditions of the operators "not" and "and". First we note that either a statement is true or it is false. Then we can calculate as follows:

1. Either S is false or not-S is false.

   (from the truth condition for "not")
2. If S is false, then "S and not-S" is false.

   (from the truth condition for "and")
3. If not-S is false, then "S and not-S" is false.

   (from the truth condition for "and")
4. Therefore, "S and not-S" is false.   (from 1, 2 and 3)
5. Therefore, "not-(S and not-S)" is true.

   (from 4 and the truth condition for "not")

As we just seen, we use the principle of bivalence to support the law of non-contradiction. How can we justify our belief in the principle of bivalence? Here is a justifying argument for it:

1. "Not-(S and not-S)" is true for any statement S.

   (law of non-contradiction)
2. For any statements A and B, if "not-(A and B)" is true, then so is "not-A or not-B".   (*)
3. "Not-S or Not-not-S" is true.   (from 1 and 2)
4. "Not-not-S" is logically equivalent to S.   (**)
5. "Not-S or S" is true.   (from 3 and 4)
6. Either S or "not-S" is true.

   (from 5 and the truth condition for "or")

The principle used in line 2 is called "De Morgan's law", after Augustus De Morgan (1806–71). The principle used in line 4 is called the "law of double negation" and it allows us to remove a "not-not". The exact details of the proof are not that important.

What is important is that the law of non-contradiction together with these other principles and laws can be used to justify the principle of bivalence, which is stated in line 6.

We have, however, justified the law of non-contradiction using the principle of bivalence together with several other logical principles, and justified the principle of bivalence using the law of non-contradiction together with other logical principles. This sounds rather circular, and it is. The question is whether this circularity is problematic.

From the standpoint of a coherentist epistemology, this sort of circularity does not pose a difficulty. For the coherentist, all justifications are circular in the sense that one's beliefs are supposed to explain and support one another.

Perhaps more surprisingly, reliabilists are not always bothered by this sort of circularity either. For example, David Papineau (1993) and Peter Lipton (2004) justify the use of empirical induction using inductive arguments. Similarly, reliabilists have used abduction to justify the use of scientific method. Induction is itself an important element in scientific method. If induction and abduction are, in fact, reliable, then this sort of justification is all that is needed, according to reliabilism.[1]

The problem with circular arguments is that they are not at all convincing in debate. If someone does not accept, say, the principle of bivalence, then an appeal to the law of non-contradiction will not convince her. For example, proponents of three-valued logic (see Chapter 5 and later in this chapter) reject both bivalence and the law of non-contradiction. Any appeal to one to justify the other will not convince a proponent of that logical system. We shall return to this topic soon.[2]

10.4 Logic and analyticity II: logic and convention

There has to be something conventional about which laws and rules are valid. We stipulate the truth conditions for the logical operators. There are, however, limits to what we can stipulate. As we saw in Chapter 5, we can stipulate a sentence to be true only if it is not determined to be true or false before our stipulation. There are also other limits to how much of logic can be considered to be conventional.

First, there is what has popularly become known as the "tonk-problem", due to Arthur Prior (1960). In order to understand this problem we need a little background. As we have seen, modern symbolic logic studies (among other things) logical *operators*. Prior asks about the conditions under which we are permitted to add new operators to our logic with new rules. He considers adding an operator called "tonk" with the following rules:

$$\frac{S_1}{\text{Therefore, } S_1 \text{ tonk } S_2}$$

and

$$\frac{S_1 \text{ tonk } S_2}{\text{Therefore, } S_2}$$

The first rule is called "tonk introduction" because it introduces a tonk operator in the conclusion, and the second is called "tonk elimination" because the tonk in the premise disappears in the conclusion.

Given these two rules, we can perform the following derivation:

1. The sky is blue.   (empirical truth)
2. The sky is blue tonk the moon is made of green cheese.

(from 1 and tonk introduction)
3. The moon is made of green cheese.

(from 2 and tonk elimination)

We can see that the tonk rules, when added to logic, do not preserve truth in all possible worlds. They allow us to infer from a truth ("the sky is blue") to a falsity ("the moon is made of green cheese"). Prior is pointing out that logic cannot be purely conventional. We cannot choose any rules we wish. There are constraints that must be put on these choices, such as truth preservation.[3]

The second problem is what we will call the *Carroll–Quine problem*. It is originally due to Lewis Carroll (1895), of *Alice in Wonderland* fame, but is adapted to be an attack on conventionalism by Quine ([1936] 1976b).

The problem is that of seeing how a logical system can be stipulated as a convention. Usually when we formulate a logical system we state some laws (known as axioms) and some rules. This list of axioms and rules is finite, so that a human being can stipulate or understand it.[4] Logical systems, however, are understood as containing infinitely many statements called "theorems". A theorem is a statement that can be inferred from the axioms and rules. The Carroll–Quine problem concerns how we can stipulate a logical system so that theorems are, in fact, deducible from the axioms and rules.

Let us consider again the familiar rule of *modus ponens*. We might state this rule schematically by writing:

If *A* then *B*
A
_____

∴ *B*

The problem arises when we consider how we understand what this rule says. Clearly it tells that *if the premises are true, then the conclusion is true also*. But now suppose that we know that the premises are true. How can we know that we can derive the conclusion? Well, you now know that *the premises are true* and *if the premises are true, then the conclusion is true*. What you need to derive the conclusion is to know how to use *modus ponens*. But another "if … then" statement is not going to help. In order to use that, you need to know how to use *modus ponens*.

The point is that in order to understand rules of inference, you need to have already understood a particular rule of inference. In particular, you need *modus ponens*.[5] Thus, it seems that we cannot *stipulate* all the rules and laws of logic. Any such stipulation presupposes that we already know certain logical rules. We will not be able to understand the stipulation without this prior knowledge.

10.5 The innateness of logical principles

Robert Hanna (2006) motivates nativism about logic as a way out of the Carroll–Quine problem. If we have an innate understanding of logic, we will have no trouble using rules such as *modus ponens* in understanding the statement of logical systems.

As I said at the end of Chapter 4, serious empirical work needs to be done in order fully to justify claims about innate principles. According to Maddy (2007: III.5) – another nativist about logic – modern developmental psychology gives us good reason to think that our brains are hard-wired to pick up certain features of this world, including its logical features. Thus, it seems that there is good empirical evidence that some logical principles are innate.

An evolutionary argument in favour of innate logical principles also seems fairly natural. Consider again the list of features a set of beliefs or abilities should satisfy in order to be supported by an evolutionary argument:

- the beliefs or abilities help us to survive;
- not only do the beliefs or abilities have to be conducive to survival, but their accuracy needs to be important to our survival;
- there is some mechanism that explains how these beliefs could have been selected.

All three of these points seem to be satisfied by our logical beliefs and abilities. Having abilities to out-think rather than out-run or overpower our prey and predators has certainly helped humans to survive and breed. Deductive logical reasoning is important in this regard. Moreover, if our logical beliefs were *wildly* inaccurate, they could lead us to do things that would harm us. Finally, if our logical abilities are hard-wired into our brains, then clearly there is some mechanism that causes this to be so, and this could well have been selected in the evolutionary process. Thus, at the very least it would seem that an evolutionary argument could support the claim that our logical beliefs are generally accurate. With logic, however, we want an argument that our beliefs are perfectly accurate in the sense that the laws of logic are necessarily true and that the rules always preserve truth in all possible worlds. It is to this problem that we turn in the next section.

10.6 The necessity of logic

An evolutionary argument can show, at best, that certain beliefs accurately represent the actual world. For it is in this world that we have survived. What happens in other possible worlds is not treated by this sort of argument.

But we do have arguments that purport to show that logical systems – collections of laws and rules – preserve truth in all possible worlds. Here is one such argument. We use a set of primitive statements of a formal logical language to represent all the possible facts that could be true in a possible world. We take an arbitrary set of these primitive statements and then, for all the statements that are not in this set, we add the operator "not" on the front. For example, say that the primitive statement p is chosen and the primitive statement q is not. Then in our final set we have p and not-q.

This set of statements and negated statements together represents a possible world. We then can show, using standard logical methods, that if we apply all our laws and rules to this set we cannot derive any new primitive statements. The philosophical reading of this proof is that for any possible world, our logical system does not allow us to derive any fact in that world that is not already true in it. If we can actually prove this, it gives us good grounds to claim that our logical system preserves truth in all possible worlds.[6]

Arguments like this help to convince us that our logical systems do not contain tonk-like rules, that is, rules that allow us to derive falsehoods. Thus, they help to avoid the puzzle that Prior sets for conventionalism.

These arguments are also useful in convincing ourselves that our logical systems are not empirically defeasible. For Field, this sort of evidence is extremely important. It can legitimately convince us that we are entitled to adopt a logical system without any further argument (see Chapter 1).

It is clear, however, that this argument is circular. We have used logical means to justify that our logical system preserves truth in all possible worlds. We have already run into this sort of circularity with logic. As we have seen, coherentists and reliabilists allow this sort of circular justification.

There is something else, however, to be said in this case in favour of circularity. If we were to find a new fact that is entailed by a set of logical laws in a possible world of this sort, then that would refute the system. It would show us that the logical system is not really an appropriate logic. The fact that we use logic to prove this does not mean that it is impossible for a logical system to fail the test. We could invent such a system very easily.

There are some logicians who disagree with this sort of argument. They claim that logical systems do not need to be formal in the sense that they do not tell us about what sort of primitive statements are true in the world. For example, some philosophers think that statements such as "If a thing is red, then it is coloured" is a law of logic. If so, and if we have a possible world with the fact that a particular thing is red, then our logic will tell us that it is also coloured.[7] The sort of argument we have above treats the statement that a thing is coloured as a primitive statement. The argument will not work if we include laws like this.

If we do include statements such as "if a thing is red, then it is coloured" as laws of logic, then we say that the proof given above shows that a certain part (or "fragment", as logicians call it) of the logical system preserves truth in all possible worlds. It does not prove it for the entire system. But proving it for part gives us more confidence that it is true for the whole system.

10.7 The problem of alternative logics

There is another difficulty for the nativist view of logic. There are serious debates about which logical system is correct. Recall Locke's criticism of nativism. He argues that there can be no innate beliefs since there is no subject on which everyone agrees. Locke is right concerning logic. There is no absolute agreement about which logical system is correct.

Some nativists, such as Hanna and Maddy, claim that we do not have a full logical system innately within us. Only some logical principles are innate. Other logical principles are learned or invented by us. Thus, there may only be a small number of logical principles that we all agree on.

William Lycan (1993) argues that there are no such principles. He points out that even the principle of *modus ponens* is debated, and he holds that it is not a valid rule.[8] This is important to us, because this is the rule that it seems we need to have before we can understand the presentation of a logical system.

We do not need to go through Lycan's argument. What we need to note is that there are different forms of conditional statements.

In Chapter 6 we saw the distinction between counterfactual and indicative conditionals – Lycan's argument concerns indicative conditionals – but there are other sorts of conditionals. For example, there are strict conditionals. A strict conditional "S_1 strictly implies S_2" is true if in every possible world in which S_1 is true so is S_2. On occasion, we can express a strict conditional in English by an ordinary sounding "if … then" statement. We do so sometimes in talking mathematics or when we are giving definitions. In this book we have used the sentence "If John is a bachelor then he is unmarried". This statement can be taken in some circumstances to be a strict conditional (if, for example, the speaker is explaining to someone that being unmarried is a necessary part of being a bachelor).

Lycan may be right about certain sorts of conditionals, but not about all of them.[9] *Modus ponens* is valid for strict conditionals. It may be these that we are expressing when we explain the rules of logic and we have some innate rules governing strict implication.

The topic of the validity or invalidity of certain rules also raises the issue about the debate between logical systems. The problem is that of deciding which one is the right logic. Now, there are some philosophers – called "logical pluralists" – who think that there can be more than one right logical system. They hold that, in different circumstances, it is appropriate to reason using different logical systems.

Let us set aside the general issue of logical pluralism versus logical monism (the view that there is only one right logical system for all circumstances). Instead we shall discuss one particular use for a logical system and look at three logical systems that their supporters claim are right for that use.

The use is the theory of truth. It has long been a problem for logicians to deal with the so-called "liar paradox". Consider the statement "This statement is false". In the standard two-valued logic this sentence poses a serious problem. The statement must be either true or false. If it is true, then it must be false. But if it is false, then what it says is true; that is to say, if it is false then it is true. So, we have a contradiction.

Many logicians who adopt the standard logic claim that "this statement is false" is not a real statement. It does not express a proposition. It is not meaningful. They typically ban *self-reference*.

They set up their logical languages so that sentences are not allowed to refer to themselves.

One way of doing this is due to Alfred Tarski (1901–83). On Tarski's view, there is a hierarchy of logical languages. For each language, there is a *metalanguage*. A metalanguage is a language that talks about another language. The notion of truth (or falsity) is not one notion, but rather there is a separate concept of truth for each of these languages. The concept of truth for a language *L* is not expressed as a part of the vocabulary in *L*, but rather belongs to the metalanguage for *L*. Thus, we cannot have "This statement is false" because no language is allowed to talk about the truth or falsity of statements in that language.

According to Tarski's theory, there is an infinite hierarchy of languages. We start with a language. It has a metalanguage. That metalanguage has a metalanguage, and so on. There is no one logical language that we can use to talk about all the metalanguages.

Although Tarski's solution to the liar paradox is quite popular among logicians, it is not universally accepted. As Priest (2003) has pointed out, we do seem to be able to talk and reason about Tarski's whole hierarchy of languages. Tarski himself seems to do so. Moreover, as Kripke, Anil Gupta and others have pointed out, in ordinary speech we use "true" in ways that are not able to be stratified in Tarski's sense. Suppose that two people mutually admire one another and both think that everything the other person believes is true. There is nothing wrong with that, but it violates Tarski's principles.

There are many theories that are opposed to Tarski's, but we shall look at only two here. First, there is a theory of truth based on the three-valued logic that we discussed briefly in Chapter 5. According to this three-valued logic, some sentences are neither true nor false. We can use this logic as the basis of a theory of truth that says that the liar sentence ("This statement is false") is neither true nor false. This blocks the paradox. Let us call this the *gappy* solution to the liar paradox, because it allows there to be gaps in the truth-values of statements (i.e. some statements do not get a real truth-value).[10]

But this solution is not perfect. Consider now a statement known as the *strengthened liar*: "This statement fails to be true". If this statement is false, then it is true. If it is neither true nor false, it is also true. So it looks like the paradox returns. One solution to this is to ban the locution "fails to be true" from our logical language. But that is somewhat disappointing, since this phrase seems to make perfect sense and so should be expressed within a logical language.

Our third solution is what is known as the *dialethic* solution. According to one form of the philosophy of dialetheism, a statement can either be just true, just false, or both true and false. The liar statement and the strengthened liar statement, on this view, are both true and false. What they say is true but also false. In some ways, this is the most uniform and simplest solution to the paradoxes.

But dialetheism has difficulties too. The rule of disjunctive syllogism is the following:

S_1 or S_2
Not-S_1
_____

Therefore, S_2

We use this rule very often. When we reason about detective novels (or play the game *Cluedo*), we often eliminate suspects and then conclude that the one left is the murderer; when we search for our keys or wallet, we will often eliminate likely places where they might be and then conclude that they are in one of the remaining places; and so on. The problem is that this rule is not valid according to dialetheism.

According to dialetheism, a rule is valid if and only if in every case when all of its premises are true its conclusion is true. Suppose that S_1 is both true and false. Then "not-S_1" is also both true and false. Moreover, "S_1 or S_2" is also true if S_1 is true. Now suppose that S_2 is just false. Then the premises of a disjunctive syllogism are true, but its conclusion is just false. In other words, disjunctive syllogism is invalid according to dialetheism.

Looking at our solutions, all three are imperfect. The hierarchy solution saves traditional logic, including disjunctive syllogism, and it bars both the liar and strengthened liar paradoxes, but does not allow us to reason logically about some very normal ways of thinking and talking. The gappy solution does better in treating our talk about truth and falsity, but it bans other apparently meaningful discourse. The dialethic solution seems better with regard to its treatment of the paradoxes, but it loses disjunctive syllogism.

The argument between these views, then, is rather difficult. Proponents of each, of course, concentrate on the virtues of their own view and try to treat its vices either by arguing that they are unimportant or by adding more theory. For example, some dialetheists adopt theories that allow disjunctive syllogism to be used in particular cases. A choice between alternative logics can only be made holistically. That is, we have to consider the theories as wholes that are competing against one another. These choices are not easy.

10.8 Rationalism and Aristotelianism about logic

Rationalists about logic claim that we have rational insight into the laws and rules of logic. Rationalism about logic seems quite reasonable. As I argued in Chapter 3, our rational insight depends on our logical abilities. It seems reasonable that our logical abilities allow us, in at least some circumstances, to reliably recognize laws of logic and valid logical rules. But then the claim that we have rational insight into the laws and rules of logic is not very exciting or very helpful.

It would seem that we could say almost the same thing about Aristotelianism. Aristotelian justification depends on our logical abilities. But Aristotelian justification can be used to justify logical beliefs in a different way. We have different logical systems that represent different structures. Consider temporal logic. It represents time. One way of understanding the way in which this works is that we abstract some general features of the nature of time from our experience and then use these features to characterize a logical system. In temporal logic, we represent time using a set of points that are lined up one after another. Sentences are treated as being true or false at times. If a sentence S is true in a point of time t_2 and t_2 comes after t_1 in this order, then at t_1 "it will be the case that S" is true. Similarly, if S is true at t_1, then "it was the case that S" is true at t_2 and so on.

This logical model is a very abstract representation of time. On the Aristotelian view, we develop this representation by abstracting from our experience. There are, similarly, spatial logics that are used in robotics to teach machines to reason about space. An Aristotelian view of how these systems can be justified seems plausible.

10.9 Kant and logic

Kant's view of logic fits in with his view of other a priori knowledge. Like what we know about geometry or the law-likeness of the world, our logical knowledge does not extend beyond the world as constituted by our own minds. But our logical knowledge is more general in a sense than these other sorts of knowledge. Kant says that in order to determine the laws of logic:

> We abstract away from all empirical conditions under which our understanding is exercised, e.g. from the influences of the senses, from the play of imagination, the laws of memory, the power of habit, inclination, etc., hence also from the sources of prejudice. (*Critique* A52–3/B77)

The idea is that the laws of logic are conditions that make it possible for us to comprehend anything. This clearly includes both empirical objects and noumena. But Kant's epistemology remains consistent: although we have to use our logical categories, laws and inference rules to think about noumena, we cannot know that these really do apply to noumena.

Kant's claim is not that people actually do think logically all the time. Logic is not a theory of empirical psychology (*Critique* A54/B78). Rather, he claims that our minds construct the world in accordance with logic in the sense that we saw in Chapter 7. Thus, on Kant's view the normative force of logical laws is given by the fact that they constitute the basic structure of the world. Just as the fact that we construct a law-like world is supposed by Kant to give justification for the search for laws of nature on the part of scientists, the fact that the world is also constituted in accordance with laws of logic justifies a demand that people argue in accordance with those laws.

The laws of logic, for Kant, preserve truth in the sense that they preserve truth about the world as we understand it. Thus, we can see that Kant is giving us a transcendental argument for the apriority of logical principles. No world would be comprehensible to us if it did not incorporate some logical principles. And these must be the same as the principles that we use to comprehend things. Thus, we constitute the empirical world in accordance with our principles of logic.[11]

It seems plausible to say that we need some logic or logic-like structure to understand the world. But, given the fact that there are alternative logical systems now, it seems difficult to claim, as Kant does, that there is a specific system to which our thoughts have to conform in order to understand the world. It seems that Kant's view has the same problem with logic as it does with geometry. Perhaps a form of logical relativism, such as Friedman's scientific relativism, is the best option for Kantians.

Once again, when confronted with the choice of adopting a Kantian view – in this case with regard to the epistemology of logic – one needs to consider whether one wants to commit oneself to a very strong form of anti-realism. In this case, the Kantian view forces on us the view that our logical inferences may not be reliable concerning noumena.

10.10 Summary

It seems that some form of nativism about logic is unavoidable. It is not clear exactly how much we need. Moreover, it can only be determined empirically how much logic is hard-wired into our brains. Our inbuilt logical beliefs can be justified to some extent by an evolutionary argument, but we have seen that even where such arguments are successful, their conclusions are quite weak. Stronger, but circular, justification can be given by appeal to the logical laws and rules themselves; this is a form of analytic justification. This circularity does not seem vicious, and fits in with both reliabilist and coherentist theories of justification.

Rationalism and Aristotelianism were seen to be of limited use as epistemologies of logic. Both presuppose the use of logic, and appeals to them do not add any more than is already available in analytic justification. I suggested that an Aristotelian theory may be of use in understanding how we justify logical theories about specific structures, such as temporal logic, which is an abstract theory of time and tensed statements.

The chapter ends with a brief discussion of Kant's approach to logic. His view is that logic describes the most general preconditions of thought. Like all of Kant's theoretical views, his epistemology of logic limits the scope of logic to reasoning about things that are within experience. Even logic can tell us nothing about noumena.

Further reading

For a very clear and readable introduction to the issue of alternative logics, see Graham Priest's *An Introduction to Non-Classical Logics* (2001).

Harman's views on logic are in his *Change in View* (1986) and in a collection of his articles, *Reasoning, Meaning, and Mind* (1999).

Carnap's conventionalism is in his very difficult and strangely translated *Logical Syntax of Language* (1937). Quine's attacks on conventionalism are in his *Ways of Paradox and Other Essays* (1976a). Paul Syverson presents a defence of conventionalism in *Logic, Convention, and Common Knowledge* (2003).

Two classics by psychologists arguing for nativism about logic are John McNamara's *A Border Dispute* (1986) and Lance Rips's *The Psychology of Proof* (1994). Robert Hanna's view is in his *Rationality and Logic* (2006) and Penelope Maddy's is in her *Second Philosophy* (2007). Another interesting work attempting to argue that our innate logical skills are reliable is Georges Rey's "A Naturalistic A Priori" (1998).

On the circular justification problem, see Paul Boghossian's "Knowledge of Logic" (2000).

11 Mathematical knowledge

11.1 Introduction

As we have seen, Kant claims that we have innate intuitions of time and space, and that these produce in us knowledge about arithmetic and geometry. In Kant, there is no real distinction between geometry as a study of formal relations within a theory and the study of the structure of physical space. This distinction is more recent than Kant. It is, however, an important distinction. Pure mathematics is the study of abstract structures. The natural sciences apply mathematical theories to actual physical systems.

In this chapter I discuss the epistemology of pure mathematics. However, I also look briefly at the problem of applied mathematics. Mathematicians, scientists and philosophers have found it difficult to explain why mathematical theories are so easily applied to physical reality. One might think that the Aristotelian has an easy answer to this: mathematics is easily applied to physical reality because it is created through a process of abstraction from our experience of physical reality. This may be part of the answer, but it cannot be the whole answer to the problem. Modern physics, in particular, uses very difficult and abstract branches of mathematics (probability theory, vector space and so on). These are not related to experience in a straightforward way. Aristotelianism, even if we do accept it as part of our epistemology of mathematics, needs to be supplemented in some way.

We shall begin with pure mathematics and leave the problem of its application until later.

11.2 Platonism and rational insight

One of the most popular *metaphysical* theories of mathematics is Platonism. Recall from Chapters 3 and 4 Plato's view that there are Forms that exist outside time and space. Platonism about mathematics holds that there are mathematical objects that exist outside time and space. This view gives a tidy theory of truth for mathematics. It claims that mathematical statements, such as $2 + 2 = 4$, are true because of the properties of certain non-spatial and non-temporal objects, in this case 2 and 4.

This metaphysics has important epistemological difficulties. If we cannot experience these objects, how can we form reliable beliefs about them? This difficulty is known as Bennaceraf's problem, since Paul Bennaceraf is responsible for an early version of it. Bennaceraf's problem plagues both reliabilist and coherentist forms of rationalism when they are combined with Platonism. Both of those require that there is some way to explain our beliefs in terms of natural science or in terms of our other beliefs.

One sort of explanation is rather like Huemer's version of rational insight in moral epistemology. Some philosophers and mathematicians claim that we have some sort of direct insight into the mathematical objects. Two of these are the mathematician Kurt Gödel and the philosopher Mark Steiner. According to Gödel and Steiner, we have a form of rational insight into the Platonic realm that is rather like sense perception of physical things. Some philosophers have assumed that a Platonist metaphysics requires a foundationalist rationalist epistemology like Gödel's, but it is not clear that it does.

A somewhat more moderate view is due to Max Cresswell. According to Cresswell, we come to know about mathematical objects through their involvement in facts about physical things. For example, it may be that the average number of children in a New Zealand family is 2.3. From reflecting on facts like this, we can come to know things about the mathematical objects themselves. Bob Hale makes a point rather similar to Cresswell's. According to Hale, we think about abstract objects all the time. For example, we think about propositions. When we come to have a theory of these objects, we abstract from dealings with them and come to understand the features they have so that they can play the roles they do. I suppose that Cresswell's and Hale's views are versions of Aristotelianism, since they involve a form of abstraction and then reflection as the basis of mathematical knowledge. We shall look at Aristotelianism about mathematics in greater depth below.

11.3 Logicism

The doctrine of logicism states that mathematical truths are all logical laws. Thus, if logicism is correct, the problem of mathematical knowledge becomes just part of the problem of logical knowledge.

One logicist is Frege. However, Frege does not hold that every mathematical truth is a logical law; he only believes that every law of arithmetic is a logical law. Arithmetic, as you might recall from school, is the theory of the natural numbers (0, 1, 2, ...) together with certain operations (such as + and ×).

Frege's goal is to show that every arithmetical truth is analytic. His way of proving this is first to set out the laws of logic (axioms and rules), then define all the concepts of arithmetic, and then show that each truth of arithmetic can be reduced to a law of logic using these definitions.

The concept we shall be interested in here is that of number itself. Arithmetic treats numbers as *objects*. In equations such as $2 \times 3 = 6$, we have symbols that seem to refer to numbers: "2", "3", "6" and "2×3". We can have all sorts of different symbol systems – Arabic numerals, Roman numerals, Chinese numerals (一, 二, 三, ...), and so on – but the symbols in each seem to refer to the same numbers.

The axioms and rules for arithmetic are supposed to generate the truths about the natural numbers. One such truth is:

If $(x + 1) = (y + 1)$, then $x = y$.

This is clearly a truth about arithmetic as we know it. In order for this statement to be true, there must be infinitely many numbers. For suppose that there is a last number, n. Then we would have to set $(n+1) = n$. But consider the number that comes just before n. This is $n - 1$. We would have of course

$$(n - 1) + 1 = n$$

As we have said, we also have:

$$(n + 1) = n$$

From these two we can derive:

$$(n + 1) = (n - 1) + 1$$

But we have the rule that if $(x + 1) = (y + 1)$, then $x = y$, so we also obtain:

$$n = (n - 1)$$

This means that the number that comes before n is n itself. This is absurd.

Frege does not think that an axiom that states that there are infinitely many numbers is a good candidate for a basic law of logic. It is not self-evident. What he tries to do instead is to give self-evident laws and rules from which we can derive that there are infinitely many numbers.

At one point Frege considers adding what has come to be called Hume's law in order to derive the infinity of natural numbers. Frege rejects Hume's law, but certain contemporary logicists – Crispin Wright, Bob Hale and George Boolos – accept it. Hume's law is supposed to be a partial definition of the notion of number. On the modern definition of number, two collections of things can be said to have the same number if and only if there is a *one-to-one correspondence* between them. Consider, for example, the set $\{1, 2, 3\}$ and the set $\{5, 9, 13\}$. We can put these two sets into a one-to-one correspondence with one another by associating 1 with 5, 2 with 9 and 3 with 13. Clearly there are other one-to-one correspondences here as well, but I hope you can see what is going on from this one example. Given two predicates, F and G, Hume's law says:

> The number of Fs is identical to the number of Gs if and only if there is a one-to-one correspondence between the Fs and Gs.

Here is how Hume's law allows us to generate the infinity of numbers. Let us start with a predicate that is not true of anything, such as "x is not identical to itself". Let us call this predicate Px. As we have just said, there is nothing that *Px* characterizes. But, even though there are no such things, we can say that there is a one-to-one correspondence between the things characterized by *Px* and themselves. This one-to-one correspondence is sometimes called a vacuous correspondence because it does not really map things to things, but rather maps nothing to nothing.

Thus, by Hume's law, we can deduce that the number of things that are characterized by *Px* is identical with itself. If something is identical with itself, according to a belief commonly held among philosophers, then it exists. So the number of things that are characterized by *Px* exists. But what is this number? It is zero. Thus we have proved that 0 exists.

Now that we have the number 0, we can generate the number 1. We do the same derivation as before, but instead of using the predicate "*x* is not identical to *x*" we use "*x* is identical to the number 0". Similarly, we can derive the existence of the number 2, the number 3, and so on. Thus, Hume's law allows us to derive that infinitely many numbers exist.

If it is true, Hume's law is necessarily true. It may even be analytic in the metaphysical sense. But can we give an analytic justification of it? It seems not. The problem is that on the left-hand side of the "if and only if", Hume's law mentions entities: numbers (*the number* of *F*s and *the number* of *G*s). In order to justify this law, we really need first to justify that there are things such as the number of *F*s and the number of *G*s. That is to say, we need to justify that for any predicate there is a number associated with it. But the point of Hume's law is to justify the existence of numbers and to show that there are infinitely many of them. Thus, Hume's law is of limited epistemological use.[1]

Of course, showing that Hume's law is not a good basis for an epistemology of arithmetic does not condemn logicism as a whole. There are many other logicist projects. In the next few sections, we examine another form of logicism, one that might seem at first sight to be rather plausible.

11.4 Conditional axioms

Instead of asserting an axiom, we can use it *conditionally*. The axiom of infinity (an axiom that states that there are infinitely many numbers) is a case in point. Because of technical issues to do with his version of logicism, Bertrand Russell rejected Frege's attempt to prove that there are infinitely many numbers. Instead Russell proved theorems about arithmetic in the form "If there are infinitely many numbers then …". Russell cannot prove that, for example, if $(x + 1) = (y + 1)$, then $x = y$. Instead, he can only prove that if there are infinitely many numbers, if $(x + 1) = (y + 1)$, then $x = y$. Much of mathematics uses conditional axioms of this kind. In algebra, for instance, one studies all sorts of structures characterized by very different sets of axioms and the same is true of geometry. All the theorems about these structures are, in effect, conditional in this way ("if such and such axioms, then …").

If we treat axioms conditionally, then only the logical relationships between the axioms and the truths that they are supposed to entail are of interest to the pure mathematician. The epistemological burden of showing that the axioms are true is removed if we are only studying pure mathematics. If, however, we want to look at applied mathematics, then this burden returns. Applied mathematics, as the name suggests, is just the application of mathematics to the real world, for example in physics and the other sciences. In applied mathematics we do not want to know just what occurs in structures of certain sorts, but rather whether the things that we are dealing with are structures of these sorts.

The logical positivists, however, welcome this division between pure and applied mathematics. Pure mathematics, on their view, is about conditionals of the sort given above. These conditionals, moreover, are a priori. A claim by an applied mathematician that a real thing has the structure described by one of these conditionals is, in contrast, empirical.

This division of labour seems nice and tidy. It allows the reduction of mathematics to logic and it makes many of the epistemological difficulties concerning mathematics empirical (and so not of present concern). But there is a serious problem with the division of labour. In the next section, we describe this problem.

11.5 The limits of axiom systems

Consider again conditionals of the form "If such-and-such axiom, then …". Suppose that the axiom under consideration is false. Then, according to classical logic, the conditional is true. Most of the philosophers who have held an "if … then-ist" view of mathematics have also been classical logicians. They did not, however, want every such conditional to be true. What they really mean by a conditional of this form is "From such-and-such axiom, we can prove …". That is, from the axiom and the laws and rules of logic, we can prove whatever takes the place of the ellipsis.

There is, however, a problem with this picture of mathematics. Let us return to arithmetic. In his famous incompleteness theorem, Gödel proves that no finite set of axioms can prove all the truths of arithmetic. His proof is very complicated and cannot be presented in full here, but here is the flavour of it. He shows that given any finite axiomatization of certain important parts of arithmetic, we can produce a formula that intuitively says "This formula cannot be proved". Let us call this formula G. If our formalized system can prove G, then it is inconsistent (because G says that it cannot be proved, so we are proving that what we have proved cannot be proved!). But, intuitively, G is true. We just showed that it is true (because it cannot be proved in a consistent system). So no finite set of axioms will entail everything that we think is true about arithmetic.[2]

Now we have a paraphrase of "the sentence S is true in arithmetic" as "S follows from the axioms and rules of arithmetic". But the list of axioms and rules is infinitely long. The question now arises as to what determines what these axioms are. The usual answer, and I think a plausible one, is that we have in mind a particular structure: the *standard model of arithmetic*. This standard model consists of the natural numbers (0, 1, 2, 3, …) and the "standard" interpretations of +, ×, = and so on. When we claim that a statement S is a truth of arithmetic, what we are saying is that "S is true according to the standard model of arithmetic".

Much of the literature in the philosophy of mathematics deals with the assumption that the standard model exists and what it is. We shall deal with this problem to some extent later in this chapter. But we are more interested in an epistemological question. From Gödel's theorem we know that we cannot fully specify the standard model in English or any other language. But it seems that we have some way of knowing what it is like. The epistemological problem is just this: how do we grasp the standard model for arithmetic?

11.6 The Kantian solution

Kant claims that we know the truths of arithmetic through our innate intuition of time. We understand an infinite sequence of elements (such as the numbers) because we can reflect on this intuition and understand what it is for a discrete sequence of things to be placed in a temporal order going on forever. This intuition has structure; it allows us to understand the basic operations of arithmetic, such as multiplication and addition.

As we saw in Chapter 7, Kant also believes that we have an intuition of space that guarantees our ideas about geometry. On Kant's view, both time and space are mental projections: they are ways that we perceive the world to be, but not how it is in itself.

What is very nice about this view is that it also purports to solve the problem of the application of mathematics. As we have seen, this is the problem of explaining why our pure mathematics can be applied so well to the world. Mathematical theories have been very successful in providing parts of scientific theories that have themselves successfully explained an extremely wide range of phenomena.

As we saw in Chapter 7, Kant's theory of geometry may be too rigid. It may constrain science to using a single geometry. As we have seen, science sometimes progresses by changing even our most fundamental beliefs about the universe, including those about the geometry of space. The same complaint can be made about Kant's view of time. Our intuition of time, Kant claims, is of something with infinitely long duration and no start. It may be that, in fact, time had a starting-point in the Big Bang, and may well have an end in a big crunch.

What we need instead is a philosophy of mathematics that explains how mathematical theories of whatever sort, which are invented (or discovered) by mathematicians, can later be successfully applied to concrete objects. Moreover, not all of the theories that mathematicians develop need find real-world applications. A philosophy of mathematics should explain both the creativity of mathematicians in developing or discovering theories and why some (but not all) of them prove to be so useful.

We did see, however, how contemporary Kantians such as Friedman take mathematical theories to be conventions. This both explains how some of them are useful – some of them are used – and characterizes the creativity of mathematicians merely in terms of the construction of these theories. But conventionalism does not help us at all with the current problem. It cannot tell us how we can understand structures that cannot be characterized by a finite number of statements.

11.7 An Aristotelian solution (or is it nativist?)

Aristotelians treat mathematical facts as relations between properties. These properties, moreover, are abstracted from our experiences of things. In coming to understand arithmetic, we abstract properties from real discrete sequences of objects or events and then reflect on these properties.

This view finds a natural companion in *structuralism*, a view about the metaphysics of mathematics. According to structuralism, there is not a single standard model of arithmetic, but rather there are many different models that are structurally the same. This structure includes an infinite discrete ordering. Many different sorts of things can be ordered in this way. The study of arithmetic is concerned not with the objects that are ordered, but with the properties of the ordering and other relations that can be defined on the ordering.

On the Aristotelian view, we abstract a concept of an infinite discrete ordering from our experiences of orderings. Not every structuralist is an Aristotelian.[3] As we saw in Chapter 9, there is sometimes a thin line dividing the Aristotelian from the nativist who claims that we impose properties on experience. The property of being infinite is an interesting case in point.

Do we meet with infinities in experience? Consider your own experience of a continuous line or surface. On reflection, it seems that we experience a thing that can be divided up into infinitely many parts. It does not matter that it is physically impossible to divide anything into infinitely many parts. What matters is that we seem to confront the property of being infinitely divisible in our experience. But we do not ever see anything divided up into infinitely many parts. So, is this "experience" of infinite divisibility an actual experience or is it something we impose on our experience?

Although it is crucial to the distinction between Aristotelianism and various versions of nativism that we be able to answer this question, it may be that there is no clear-cut answer. It may be that our imaginations make it possible for us to "abstract" the property of infinite divisibility from our experiences of lines and surfaces. This ability may be innate. Does this mean that the idea of infinite divisibility is innate? As we saw in Chapter 4, there is no clear distinction to be made between innate ideas and innate dispositions of this sort.

11.8 Beyond arithmetic

Until now we have been discussing arithmetic. There is much mathematics beyond arithmetic: there is the theory of the real numbers (the natural numbers, negative numbers and decimals numbers), calculus, algebra, geometry and so on. Many philosophers and mathematicians who work on the foundations of mathematics attempt to find a single framework of entities in which all these different fields can be worked out.

This task is made more difficult by the way in which mathematicians work. Once mathematicians have found an interesting structure, they find an interesting generalization to a wider class of structures. This process of generalization is ubiquitous in mathematics. Mathematicians discovered non-Euclidean geometry through this process, many of the advances in algebra and logic have been discovered in this way and so on.

Many mathematicians and philosophers take *set theory* to be the foundation of mathematics. A set is a collection of objects. A set theory is a system of axioms and rules that allows us to derive the existence of setps of certain sorts. We can represent the number series (1, 2, 3, ...) as sets. The number 0 is just the empty set, $\varnothing$. The number 1 is $\{\varnothing\}$, the set that just has the empty set in it. The number 2 is $\{\varnothing, \{\varnothing\}\}$, the set that has the empty set and the number 1 in it. And so on. Note that each of these sets has the number of members corresponding to the number that it represents (the set representing 0 has zero members, the set representing 1 has one member, the set representing 2 has two members, ...).

The rational numbers – the fractions – are sets of "ordered pairs" of natural numbers. An ordered pair is a structure of two elements in a particular order. Thus the ordered pair of A and B – written (A, B) – is a set $\{\{A\}, \{A, B\}\}$. Thus the fraction 2/3 contains the ordered pair (2, 3). The construction of the real numbers is slightly more complicated. It is done using a technique known as Dedekind cuts. The square root of 2, for example, is represented by a pair of sets (A, B). In this pair, A is the set of rational numbers n such that n^2 is less than 2, and B is the set of rational numbers m such that m is greater than any number in A.[4] We can also represent other theories of mathematics, such as geometries, in set theory.

Here is an example of an axiom that was proposed for set theory. We start by assuming a formal language.

- For every predicate in our formal language, P, there is a set that contains exactly the objects that satisfy P.

For example, according to this axiom, there is a set that corresponds to the predicate "$x = x$"; this is the set of everything, since everything is identical to itself. But this axiom is not tenable, since it allows us to derive a contradiction.

Consider the predicate "is a set that does not belong to itself". Sets have members. These members are said to belong to the set. The set of all sets, if there is one, belongs to itself. The set of cats does not belong to itself because the set is not a cat. But what of the set of sets that do not belong to themselves? Let us call it R. Does R belong to itself? If R does belong to itself, then it does not belong to itself. But if R does not belong to itself, then the predicate fits it and so R does belong in that set. Given the law of excluded middle (see Chapter 10), either R does belong to itself or R does not belong to itself. But if R does belong to itself, R does not belong to itself, and if R does not belong to itself, R does belong to itself. So we have a contradiction. This is called *Russell's paradox*.[5]

Ernst Zermelo suggests replacing this axiom (called a "naive comprehension axiom") with the following axiom:

- Given a set of objects S and a predicate P of our formal language, there is a set that consists of all and only members of S that satisfy P.

This axiom demands that there be a pre-existing set before we can use our predicates to pick out sets. This prevents the derivation of Russell's paradox because we cannot assume that R is a subset of this pre-existing set. This axiom is called the "axiom of separation".

There are many other axioms in standard set theories. There is an axiom that says that any sets with the same members as one another are in fact identical to one another. There is often another axiom in theories of sets that tells us that there cannot be any "membership loops", that is, we cannot have a set *a* that is a member of a set *b* which is a member of a set *c* that is a member of *a*, or anything like this. There are other set theories that have different axioms than these.

Although set theory has traditionally been seen as the foundation for mathematics, there are now some mathematical theories that go beyond set theory. Perhaps the most important of these is category theory. Category theory is a general theory of mappings between mathematical structures. Among those structures that category theory studies is the entire universe of sets. So, category theory can be treated as a way of studying set theory, rather than as something that is represented within set theory. Work on category theory can be seen as an extreme example of the way in which mathematicians search for ever more general theories.

11.9 Top-down versus bottom-up epistemologies of mathematics

How do we know which mathematical objects exist? There are two approaches to this problem: a top-down approach and a bottom-up approach. A top-down approach starts with some general principle or principles and derives the existence of mathematical objects from them. One famous top-down approach is Frege's. He postulates general laws that are supposed to be self-evident and then derives the particular truths of arithmetic (not all of mathematics) from them. A bottom-up approach begins with some particular mathematical truths: truths that we are fairly certain about. Then general principles are postulated to explain these particular truths and relate them together. One famous bottom-up approach is Russell's regressive method. He uses the fact that we can derive particular truths from the axiom system of his and A. N. Whitehead's *Principia Mathematica* as a justification for that axiom system.

Top-down methods have a fine philosophical pedigree. We have seen in this book various attempts to derive a great deal of knowledge from a small number of self-evident principles. Apart from Frege's logicism, there is Descartes' project from his *Meditations*, the post-Kantian attempts to reconstruct Kant's theory from a single principle and so on.

Bottom-up methods may seem, on the other hand, quite out of place in a book on a priori reasoning. Russell refers to his method as the "empirical regressive method". Quine and Putnam also put forward a version of the regressive method, according to which a mathematical theory can be justified by virtue of the theories of natural science that employ it.

There does not seem to be anything about the regressive method that is necessarily empirical. The particular truths that a theory connects and explains may themselves be a priori. In fact, I think a good deal of mathematical thought is like this. When Georg Cantor first postulates the existence of sets, he does so in order to provide a treatment of mathematical objects like functions and to understand the continuum (the points in space) in an abstract way. On my view at least, the theory of the continuum and the theory of functions are not empirical.

The way in which bottom-up arguments proceed is first to show that the postulated theory does allow the derivation of the desired particular propositions, and second to argue that the theory is superior (in terms of the theoretical virtues) to its competitors. This latter stage takes the same form as the arguments that we discussed in Chapter 10 about choices between alternative logics.

It is not certain which of top-down or bottom-up methods are to be preferred. But it is also not clear that we have to choose one over the other. One could imagine a case in which some of the postulates of a theory are self-evident but others require bottom-up justifications. And there does not seem to be anything wrong with hybrid justifications of this sort.

11.10 Radical empiricism and mathematics

So far we have been discussing a priori interpretations of mathematics. There are also several radical empiricist interpretations. Mill, as always, describes mathematical methods in terms of empirical induction. His views are rather complicated, but we can get the gist of them quite easily. We do mathematical operations, such as adding or collecting things together. Our mathematical knowledge generalizes from these operations. Mill applied his view only to arithmetic and geometry, but there is a great deal of mathematics that is not arithmetic or geometry. It is an interesting question about how one could construct an inductive view of the more abstract-seeming branches of mathematics, especially algebra.

Kitcher thinks Mill's view is essentially right. He thinks that our mathematical knowledge is a series of generalizations from our actual empirical practices of adding, subtracting, collecting and so on. Although Kitcher claims to be a radical empiricist, on the taxonomy that I am using in this book, he looks more like an Aristotelian. Kitcher's generalizations are not inductive generalizations. He says that we can imagine a perfect mathematician who can collect together infinitely many objects, and do other things that no actual person can do.[6] Mathematics, then, is about this fictional perfect mathematician. This does not sound like radical empiricism.[7]

As we seen, some radical empiricists, such as Quine, say that the natural sciences justify statements about mathematics. Quine is a Platonist. He believes in the existence of mathematical entities and he thinks that they are not things we can experience directly. But we need them to make sense of many statements of the natural sciences. Although mathematicians may seem to use formal (a priori?) methods, what they say can be fully justified only once it is used in the natural sciences. The empirical success of scientific theories that employ mathematics justifies the mathematics.

Maddy argues that Quine's view is backwards. The natural sciences typically follow mathematics. In most cases, scientists use mathematical theories that were already discovered. Einstein used a geometrical theory, for example, that was discovered several decades earlier. If scientific applications were required to justify mathematical theories, then we need to explain why scientists rely on pre-existing mathematical theories and why mathematical theories are so well suited to being applied to nature.

Quine is mostly interested in justifying beliefs in the existence of particular mathematical objects, such as sets. Perhaps he is right that we need something like the successful application of theories about such objects to justify the belief that these objects exist. But Maddy has a good point. We still need to explain what it is that mathematicians are doing and why it works so well.

This discussion brings us to the problem of applied mathematics. Clearly this is a serious problem for the epistemology of mathematics. How can a priori reasoning, perhaps about objects outside time and space, tell us so much about objects in time and space? Steiner (1998) thinks this is one of the most serious problems in the philosophy of mathematics. It seems to me that part of the explanation has to do with the tendency for mathematicians to generalize. A more general theory will be applicable to more possible physical systems. Another part of the answer may be that scientists invent theories with mathematical theories in mind. But Steiner might be right that these explanations are not complete and that there is something more that needs explaining. To continue the discussion of the application of mathematics would require delving into technicalities that are well beyond the scope of this book. So I will end here.

11.11 Conclusion

There seem to be some live options for an aprioristic philosophy of mathematics. Clearly, coherence methods – both top-down and bottom-up – seem to be important for the way in which mathematicians know what they know. Aristotelian and nativist solutions to how we know about certain fundamental structures of mathematics both seem viable. But only serious empirical work on whether there are innate mathematical ideas or a good Aristotelian solution to the problem of why certain sequences seem natural to us can decide the issue between them.

Further reading

The best modern book about logicism is Crispin Wright's *Frege's Concept of Numbers as Objects* (1983).

Carrie Jenkins's *Grounding Concepts* (2008) defends a version of Aristotelianism with regard to arithmetic.

Penelope Maddy's *Naturalism in Mathematics* (1997) contains her reply to Quine and Putnam.

Mark Steiner's *Mathematical Knowledge* (1975) is a defence of Platonism and rationalism in the philosophy of mathematics. His *The Applicability of Mathematics as a Philosophical Problem* (1998) is an exploration of the problem of applying mathematics to the physical world.

12 Modality

12.1 The place of modality in a priori knowledge

The problem of justifying our beliefs about what is possible or necessary has been a recurring theme for us since Chapter 2. One of the central reasons why people have postulated a priori knowledge is in order to deal with modal knowledge. In this chapter we face this problem directly using the resources that we developed in earlier chapters.

12.2 Radical empiricism

We have already briefly discussed the radical empiricists' view about modal knowledge in Chapter 6. By and large, they reject modal knowledge. Mill, for example, says:

> Why are mathematics by almost all philosophers and, even those branches of natural philosophy which, through the medium of mathematics, have been converted into deductive sciences, considered to be independent of the evidence of experience and observation, and characterized as systems of Necessary Truth?
>
> The answer I conceive to be, that this character of necessity, ascribed these truths of mathematics … is an illusion.
>
> ([1843] 1974: ch. V, §1)

This is just a simple rejection of necessity. But in Quine the matter is somewhat more subtle than this.

Quine distinguishes between three ways to interpret modal statements. He calls these "three degrees of modal involvement" ([1953] 1976c). First, one might treat *necessity* as a predicate of sentences. This means we take the word "necessary" to indicate some property of a sentence. Quine thinks that this is legitimate. To say that a sentence is necessary is just to say that it can be derived in some theory that we accept. Second, one might treat a statement of the form "it is necessary that *A*" not as saying anything about the sentence *A*, but rather about what *A* says. In the terms of Chapter 2 (but with which Quine disagrees) we might think of necessity in this sense as saying something about propositions: that there is some special property of propositions. Quine does not think there is any such property (that does not reduce to his first degree of modal involvement). "The third and gravest degree" of modal involvement concerns statements of the form "it is necessary that *i* is *A*". To participate in this degree of modal involvement is to allow such statements to say that an object has a property necessarily. For Quine, to say that objects have properties necessarily is to commit to the doctrine of Aristotelian essentialism, which he thinks is disreputable (*ibid.*).

What is wrong with Aristotelian essentialism, according to Quine, is that it confuses objects with ways of describing them. For example, it is necessarily the case that every cyclist has two legs.[1] And it is necessarily the case that every mathematician is rational, but mathematicians are not necessarily two-legged. Now consider a mathematician who is also a cyclist. Is she necessarily two-legged or not? Quine says:

> An object, of itself and by whatever name or none, must be seen as having some of its traits necessarily and others contingently, despite the fact that the latter traits follow just as analytically from some ways of specifying the object as the former do from other ways of specifying it.   (1980a: 155)

It "follows analytically" from the fact that a person is a cyclist. This means, according to Quine, that if we say of someone that she is a cyclist then we are committed to holding that she is also bipedal. But we should not confuse the fact of this commitment (that we must attribute her being bipedal) with the claim that she is necessarily a cyclist. On Quine's view, then, attributions of essential properties are born of a confusion between what we must say and what properties a thing necessarily has.

Quine has in mind philosophers such as C. I. Lewis and Carnap, who do not accept metaphysically loaded notions of necessity. Lewis and Carnap both hold that what is necessarily true is determined by the way in which we use language. Lewis holds a stipulational view of analyticity. As we shall see in the next section, Carnap's view is more complicated, but given either Lewis's or Carnap's views, it seems there is only one sense in which we can reasonably talk about essential properties. The essential properties of an object are those that we can derive from the ways in which we characterize those objects. We can derive the feature of being bipedal from the meaning of "cyclist".

More modern essentialist theories, such as those put forward by Kripke and David Wiggins, however, hold that statements such as "Sue is necessarily human" are true. This is true not because of meanings of the words "Sue" and "human", but rather because of the *metaphysical fact* that there could be no entity Sue without her humanity. She could not exist without being human. As Quine points out, if we even accept that it *makes sense* to attribute essences to things, we have to admit that every object has at least one essential property, that is, it is necessary of each thing that it is identical to itself.[2]

Quine rejects this more metaphysically loaded notion of essence out of hand. He says that "such a philosophy is as unreasonable by my lights as it is by Carnap's or Lewis's" (1980a: 156). The acceptance of the third degree of modal involvement does commit one to a metaphysics of essences: that some properties of things are necessarily had by those things and some of them are not; and that the attribution of these properties does not depend on how we describe those things. Quine's real objection to essentialism is that he does not want to accept the metaphysics behind it.

Quine's objections to the metaphysics of necessity do not stop with essentialism. He also rejects the view that there are other possible worlds. In order to make statements about the modal characteristics a thing has, it would seem that the thing has to be in more than one possible world. For example, the statement "I could have had a sister" is true if in some other possible world I have a sister (see Chapter 2). Thus, it would seem that I exist not only in this world but in other possible worlds as well. Quine doubts that we can meaningfully talk about a thing's being in more than one world. In different worlds, a thing would have different properties. We can talk about things changing through time because changes tend to be continuous. But we cannot talk about continuous changes through possible words (Quine 1981: 126–7).

There are various solutions to this problem. David Kaplan, Alvin Plantinga and others have postulated *haecceities*. My haecceity is my Edness: it is what makes me me. It might be a property, or it might be what is known as a "bare particular": that which I am after all my properties have been removed. This solves the problem because it allows a thing to be identified through possible worlds. A thing is me in another possible world if and only if it has my haecceity.

Another solution is to adopt *counterpart theory*. This theory – developed originally by David Lewis – holds that no object really exists in more than one possible world. When we ask whether a thing necessarily or possibly has a particular property, we are really asking whether its counterparts in other possible worlds have that property. An object's counterparts in another world are those things that are most similar to it.

As we saw in Chapter 6, we also use possible worlds to evaluate counterfactual conditionals. For example, to evaluate the conditional "if I were to go to Brussels, I would eat too much chocolate", we consider what happens in the closest possible worlds to our own in which I go to Brussels. If in those worlds I also eat too much chocolate, then the conditional is true. Thus, the rejection of the metaphysics of modality and with it the rejection of possible worlds leads to difficulties in understanding counterfactual conditionals as well.

Quine thinks, however, that there is something suspect about counterfactuals, and that perhaps we should not attempt to give them a semantics. He asks us to consider these two counterfactuals:

> If Julius Caesar were in charge during the Korean War he would have used nuclear weapons.

> If Julius Caesar were in charge during the Korean War he would have used catapults.

Intuitively, only one of these counterfactuals can be true. But which one? If we pick worlds to evaluate the conditional that are like our own, in which Caesar lived in the first century BCE, then the second conditional is true. If we pick worlds in which Caesar lived during the 1950s when the Korean War actually took place, then we would pick the first conditional. If we get to choose, however, it seems that it is our choice rather than possible worlds that makes them true. So, why do we need possible worlds? And, Quine concludes, why do we need counterfactuals (if they can be made true or false on a whim)?

Defenders of counterfactual conditionals, such as David Lewis, have answered that the context in which we utter the conditionals can decide which worlds we should look at. If, for example, you are a soldier during the war and you would like a more proactive commander, you might utter the first conditional and mean that there should be a commander now (not in the first century BCE) like Caesar. If, on the other hand, you want to illustrate what would have happened if the war were fought during Caesar's time, then you might utter the second conditional, in which case it is appropriate to look at worlds in which the war was fought in the first century BCE.

We use counterfactuals all the time. We often ask "what if?" questions when we study history, when we do thought experiments in science, when we mourn a defeat by our favourite sporting team, after almost any tragedy and so on. To accept that there are no specific answers to these questions is a very high price to pay.

12.3 Modality and ontology

Quine rejects talk of necessity because it comes with metaphysical baggage. But how heavy is this baggage? There are various theories about the nature of possible worlds that attempt to answer this question. It would take us too far afield from the main purpose of this book to survey them all here,[3] but I will present a few different theories to give the reader a flavour of the debate, and to introduce the specific issues regarding knowledge of what is necessary and what is possible.

Let us begin with *modalism*. Modalism holds that there are primitive modal truths about the world or about individual objects. This theory is committed to primitive modal truths and primitive modal properties. Although these commitments might seem less onerous than the commitment to other possible worlds,[4] modalism has serious problems of its own.

Modalism does not, in any straightforward way, give us a compositional semantics for our modal language. (The notion of a compositional semantics is covered in Chapter 2.) Possible-worlds semantics does give us a compositional semantics. Suppose that we say that a particular thing has the property of being necessarily such that if it is dropped on a hard surface it will shatter. According to possible-worlds semantics, this is analysed as saying that in every possible world in which the object is dropped, it shatters. But how do we analyse the claim in modalist terms? We might say that the object just has the property of being such that necessarily if it is dropped on to a hard surface it shatters. Although this may be an analysis in metaphysical terms, it is not an analysis in semantical terms. The demand of a compositional semantics is that a complex claim can be understood in terms of its semantical parts. Treating modal claims in terms of primitive truths or primitive properties does not provide us (by itself) with an analysis of the truth conditions of complex claims in terms of the truth conditions of the sentences that they contain.

I take it that one of the central reasons for coming up with a metaphysics of modality is to provide us with a semantics for our modal discourse. It seems that the theory of possible worlds does a better job of this than does modalism.

This book is about epistemology. In order to know modal truths, on the theory of possible worlds, we must know at least some facts about the contents of other possible worlds. Our view about access to other possible worlds in some ways depends on what we take these worlds to be.

Following David Lewis (1986), most philosophers now separate theories of possible worlds into extreme realist theories, which hold that other possible worlds are quite a bit like our own universe, and ersatz theories, which hold that possible worlds are abstract constructs of some sort. Ersatzist views seems at first glance to make the epistemological problem easier, so let us look at them first.

One of the original ersatz theories is Carnap's theory of state descriptions. In his book *Meaning and Necessity* (1947), Carnap presents a view that attempts to tie together modality, modal knowledge and analyticity in a very tidy way. Carnap's central idea is that possible worlds are constructions from a logical language. He calls these worlds "state descriptions". In a logical language, there are atomic sentences. Out of these atomic sentences, other sentences are created. Atomic sentences themselves are made up of constituents, but none of these constituents are themselves sentences.

The language that we shall use to illustrate Carnap's method will have two names of individuals: *s* (Susan) and *j* (Jesse). It will also have two basic predicates: *M* (married) and *A* (male). These predicates and names are used to construct atomic sentences, such as *Aj* (Jesse is male), *Ms* (Susan is married), and so on. We also need negation ("not"). This will help us recreate Carnap's construction.

The atomic formulas from our language and their negations can be put into the following possible combinations to form possible worlds:

- World 1: *Ms, Mj, As, Aj*
- World 2: *Ms*, not-*Mj, As, Aj*
- World 3: not-*Ms, Mj, As, Aj*
- World 4: not-*Ms*, not-*Mj, As, Aj*
- World 5: *Ms, Mj, As*, not-*Aj*
- and so on

There are sixteen such combinations, so there are sixteen possible worlds for this language. In each world, an atomic sentence appears either negated or un-negated, but not both.

Carnap's view provides us with an easy solution to the problem of knowing what is in other possible worlds. Our knowledge of what is an atomic sentence together with a simple understanding of how to combine such sentences or their negations allows us to find out what is possible or necessary. But the view has extremely serious difficulties.

In this example, all the worlds that we construct are internally consistent. But consider what would happen if we have a language with the same names and the following two predicates: *M* (married) and *S* (single). Then we could have in a world in which a thing is both *M* and *S*. What we need is a constraint on worlds that says that in no world can the same thing be both married and single. But, as

Quine points out in response to Carnap, to add such a constraint is circular. It makes the construction of possible worlds – which are supposed to analyse the notion of modality – presuppose facts about modality such as the fact that no one can be both married and single. Carnap's worlds can be used to give a semantics for our statements about what is necessary and what is possible. But they cannot be taken to give a complete theory of what makes certain truths necessarily true.[5] Thus Carnap's view fails to deliver what is intended.

The problem is even worse if we consider a posteriori analytic statements such as "Water is H_2O". As we saw in Chapter 2, this is necessarily true. But how could we reasonably constrain Carnap's possible worlds all to contain this sentence? The idea that it is true by stipulation violates the claim that it is a posteriori. It is very difficult to think how Carnap's theory could be modified to incorporate necessities such as this.

Some other ersatz theories of possible worlds take worlds to be sets of propositions or of states of affairs (fact-like entities). These theories might have some of the same difficulties as Carnap's theory has. These theories need to give us some reason why the state of affairs or proposition that all bachelors are unmarried and the state of affairs or proposition that water is H_2O are in every possible world. If we say merely that these states of affairs or propositions are necessary, then the theory fails to give us an analysis of necessity.

There may be a way that these ersatz theories can avoid this problem. We might say, for example, that a possible world need not *contain* the state of affairs that water is H_2O in order to make the sentence "Water is H_2O" true. Let us say that the meaning of "water" is such that, in our context of utterance, it refers in every possible world to H_2O. Then, from the perspective of our context of utterance, the sentence "Water is H_2O" is true in every possible world because "water" and "H_2O" refer to the same substance in every possible world. This solution is intuitive because it makes analytic statements true, not because of the contents of the various possible worlds, but because of the way we use our language.

Ersatz theories, however, have other difficulties. Consider the statements:

The Taj Mahal is white all over.
The Taj Mahal is black all over.

These statements cannot both be true at the same time in the same world. It seems, moreover, that, if one of them is true in a world, then it is made true not by the way we use language but because of specific states of affairs in that world. Ersatz theories, thus, have to give us a reason why we cannot have the states of affairs that make the Taj Mahal black together with those that make it white in the same world.

Against all varieties of ersatzism, there is David Lewis's extreme realism. According to extreme realism, possible worlds are real universes in the same sense that our world is a real universe. My world, according to Lewis, consists of me and my surroundings (which includes everything in all of our space–time). So, other universes consist in concrete things in their own space–times. This theory has the advantage of providing a simple and non-ad hoc theory of the truth or falsity of modal statements. A statement such as "There could be talking donkeys" is true if and only if there happens to be another world in which there are talking donkeys. One problem with this view is that it makes it very difficult to know whether there could be talking donkeys.

There are also theories of possible worlds that are opposed to any sort of realism. One radical proposal in this regard is the doctrine of fictionalism, originally suggested by Gideon Rosen (1990). According to fictionalism about possible worlds, our modal claims are true if and only if they accord with what is true in some particular fictional story about possible worlds. This fictional story may be just one of the current theories of possible worlds, or it may be some other story.

Fictionalism has the virtue of making the epistemology of modality seem somewhat easier. We do not need to understand what really is in other universes to know what is actual or possible. We only need to know what some fiction says is in other universes. And, I assume, this fiction is something we create. But it might be very difficult to specify the right fiction regarding our modal notions.

In sum, it seems that there is a trade-off between how well a theory does in providing us with a straightforward semantics for our modal statements and how much modal knowledge it seems to allow us. Extreme modal realism gives us a good straightforward theory of the truth or falsity of statements about necessity and possibility, but it makes it hard to know the content of other possible worlds. Ersatz theories may allow us access to other worlds, but they may also presuppose notions of possibility and necessity rather than explain them. Fictionalism might be a way out of the difficulty, but it also faces important difficulties.

12.4 Analyticity and necessity

As we have already seen in Chapter 5, there are certain strong connections between analyticity and necessity. There is a very simple sense in which analytic justifications help us to understand certain things about other possible worlds. Suppose that the sentence S_1 is true in some world w. Then we know that the sentence "Either S_1 or S_2" is true in w. Taking this point further, we know that in all possible worlds the sentence "If S_1, then either S_1 or S_2" is true.

We can know necessary truths such as "if S_1, then either S_1 or S_2" without knowing anything substantive about other possible worlds. All we need to know is that there are possible worlds and the truth conditions for "if … then" and "or". When we do logical semantics, of the sort we discussed in Chapters 2, 5 and 10, we treat worlds like "black boxes". It does not matter what really happens in them. It only matters that they are there and that we can apply the truth conditions for the logical operators to them.

Thus, we can derive many necessary truths using analytic justifications. But we cannot find out anything about the real goings on in other worlds that way. We cannot discover by analytic justification whether it is possible that there are talking donkeys or whether disembodied spirits could exist.

12.5 Coherence methods and empirical methods

The use of coherence methods in the sense of Chapter 1 is rather common in modal epistemology. The most striking example is perhaps in the first chapters of David Lewis's *On the Plurality of Worlds* (1986). There Lewis argues that accepting possible worlds can give us a unified theory of modality, counterfactuals, propositions and properties. Thus, Lewis contends, we should accept that there are worlds other than our own.

But this is not the most interesting part of the argument, from our point of view. Lewis is not only arguing for the existence of other possible worlds. He is arguing for us to accept that there is a variety of other worlds. According to Lewis, there are worlds in which there are talking donkeys, ghosts and all sorts of wonderful or horrible (or neutral) objects. Only if we have such a variety of worlds can the class of worlds act as a basis for a theory of possibility and necessity. If, for example, there were no possible world in which I have a sister, then we would say that the set of worlds is deficient and does not exhaust all the possibilities. In this case, we would search for another theory of possibility and necessity.

Lewis's argument claims that a theory of worlds can provide one basis for several different theories. The theory of possible worlds is like the theory of sets in mathematics. It provides us with one sort of entity that can be used in many other theories.

Lewis's argument for the existence of worlds is a priori. It does not appeal to any empirical evidence, but rather it appeals only to the ability of the theory of worlds to provide a unified ontology for certain other theories. Although the argument for the existence of worlds is a priori, he provides us with empirical methods for finding out what is in other possible worlds.

According to Lewis, one of the central ways we have of determining what is in other possible worlds is by using the *principle of recombination*. This principle says that any way of recombining parts of worlds will constitute a part of a possible world. For example, consider the part of this world that consists of my dog's standing in my lounge. This is part of the actual world at this moment. My kitchen now is empty, but let us imagine that there is a person in it, say my partner Sue. This is a part of another possible world. But we can combine my lounge with Zermela in it with my kitchen with Sue in it.[6]

Williamson (2005, 2007) claims that much of our modal knowledge is empirical. This seems reasonable. We find out what are bits of this world empirically and, given our knowledge of this world, we can argue for the existence of similar bits of other worlds. But it seems an a priori principle that we can argue on the basis of what this world is like to what other worlds are like, and it is an a priori belief that there are other possible worlds. Williamson thinks that it is unimportant to distinguish these a priori elements of our modal thinking. It is difficult to argue with people about what is important unless you have some common ground. It may be that Williamson's view of epistemology is different enough from the one I present in this book that no such common ground exists.

12.6 Rationalism and rational insight

At the other end of the spectrum from the radical empiricist, with regard to modal knowledge, is the pure rationalist. The rationalist about modality holds that we can use what we can conceive of as a guide to what is possible without further justification.

The notion of conceivability includes what we can imagine, but it is not limited to that. As David Chalmers (2002) points out, there are two senses in which we find a statement to be conceivable. It is *positively conceivable* if we can imagine or otherwise find a way of understanding what it would be like for that statement to be true. A statement is *negatively conceivable* if we cannot rule out that it is possible. I can imagine a pig flying, so "pigs can fly" is positively conceivable by me. I cannot imagine or otherwise get a real grip on the idea that matter is made out of waves and nothing else, but I cannot rule it out, so I find it negatively conceivable. The use of positive conceivability often feels like much stronger justification than negative conceivability. Often it seems that when we cannot rule something out it is because we just do not know enough.

I might not have a great understanding of the notion of a wave, say, and so what I can or cannot conceive of with regard to waves may not be a reliable guide to what is possible with regard to them. But the question is whether under any circumstances we should accept conceivability in either of its forms as a guide to what is possible.

Chalmers claims that we should, with some reservations. Chalmers holds a position with regard to conceivability rather like the view of self-evidence that I outlined in Chapter 3. What is conceivable should be understood against a background of one's reasoning abilities (in this case, including imagination). If one has a perfect understanding of the concepts involved and is a perfect reasoner (and perfect imaginer), then whatever she conceives of will be possible, at least according to the theory of possible worlds that was argued for in the previous section. Of course, all those perfections are hard to come by.

But we do on certain occasions approximate perfect reasoners (when the reasoning required is not too difficult) and we do on some occasions know all that we need to know about the concepts involved. So, as Chalmers argues, if we are confident about our reasoning and grasp of the concepts involved, it is not irrational for us to take what we can conceive of as a reliable guide to what is possible.

Consider an easy case. It is possible for there to be a ball one mile in diameter that is half red and half blue. You and I can reason about this and see that the conception of such a ball contains no contradiction. We can imagine such a ball, if we have visual imaginations. And we know a lot about balls, red and blue. Surely our judgement is reasonable and we should accept that it is possible for such a thing to exist. As cases get harder, when our grip on the concepts becomes looser, and the reasoning becomes more complicated, we should become less and less confident about our pronouncements about what is possible.

This defence of rationalism with regard to modality is most convincing in its coherentist and reliabilist forms. Given a Lewis-style argument for the existence and diversity of other possible worlds, we should be confident that we can trust rational insight in cases such as these. But without an argument for the existence and diversity of other possible worlds, it is hard to see why rational insight should be compelling. As usual, one could be a foundationalist and claim that our beliefs about what is possible are basic, but this should be a last resort.

12.7 Aristotelianism

In §12.5 we saw that Williamson claims that empirical methods are needed to discover what is in other possible worlds. It may be, however, that what Williamson claims to be empirical methods can be construed as a form of Aristotelian justification. Let us consider an Aristotelian version of the principle of recombination: what seems on reflection to us to be a coherent combination of properties is a *reliable indication that this combination is instantiated in some possible world.*

Here is a simple example. You look around your kitchen and you do not like the colour of the walls. You imagine your walls different colours and different shades. The different combinations of these colours with the other properties of your walls are coherent: you can easily imagine them and you can tell there is nothing impossible about, say, painting the walls yellow or painting them green. According to the Aristotelian version of the principle of recombination, then, what we can conceive of is a reliable guide to what is possible.

The question, of course, is whether reflection on properties is a reliable guide to whether they can be coherently combined. Chalmers's justification of rationalism can also be used to support Aristotelianism (which is a form of rationalism, as we construe those theories). But there may be additional support for Aristotelian justification of beliefs about what is possible. We might once again employ an evolutionary argument. That we are able to plan and construct things, using our empirical concepts, has helped our communities and our species to survive. This ability requires an understanding of what properties can be coherently combined. Clearly, this is not a very convincing argument as it stands. It requires real empirical support and the hypothesis needs to be properly formulated as a scientific hypothesis. But for the purposes of this book, we can leave the issue at this point.

Note that I am not claiming that we can know the entire range of possibilities through Aristotelian reflection. There is no reason to think that we can.

12.8 Kantianism

According to Kant, what is possible is dictated by what we can experience. He says that what is possible is what satisfies the "formal conditions of experience" (*Critique* A218/B265). By this he means that only things that cohere with our intuitions of space and time, as well as with the laws of logic, can exist. Correspondingly, what is necessary is what must exist or occur according to our intuitions of space and time and the other conditions of experience. There must, for example, be permanent matter, according to Kant. Similarly, there must be laws of nature. And so on.

Unfortunately, Kant does not stick with this analysis of necessity. Each category – possibility and necessity are categories – has a form that connects it with the intuition of time. One might think that the notion of possibility as described above is already connected with time, but the temporal (or "schematized") form of a category tells us how to apply the category within our experience. The schematized form of the category of possibility tells us that an event is possible if and only if it occurs at some time. Correspondingly, an event is necessary if it occurs at all times.

These notions of possibility and necessity are known sometimes as Diodorian possibility and necessity, after the Greek philosopher Diodorus Cronus (3rd–4th centuries BCE). As notions of possibility and necessity they are extremely limited. And they do not come close to capturing what is meant in the description of the categories. Usually the temporal forms of the categories are treated as empirical counterparts of the categories themselves. But in this case, they seem like quite distant relatives. Our notion of possibility is of what could happen, not what will happen.

In Friedman's relativist Kantianism, the notions of necessity and possibility can be liberated from Kant's specific formal conditions for experience. Instead the theories that we adopt would dictate what we could call possible or necessary. The scientific and mathematical theories that we adopt that are a priori – that dictate the framework for the interpretation and testing of empirical theories – would tell us what is physically possible. If we were to adopt relativism about logic, which I suggested for Kantians in Chapter 10, then the specific logic that we adopt would dictate what we could call possible and what we could say is necessary in the metaphysical sense.

12.9 Conclusion

As has been the case with moral knowledge, logical knowledge and mathematical knowledge, coherence methods play a large role in reasoning about modality. It seems that the case for possible worlds and our understanding of the relationship between them and what we can conceive is supported largely by a coherence-style argument. But when that argument is in place, rational insight seems a reasonable guide to what is possible. Although we can make a case, as Williamson does, that some of our knowledge about what is possible is empirical, we may also be able to think of the same reasoning processes in Aristotelian terms. Once again, Kantianism delivers either a very rigid theory or a form of relativism.

Further reading

Despite its age, the most important work on the philosophical aspects of modality is still David Lewis's *On the Plurality of Worlds* (1986). Another classic is Alvin Plantinga's *The Nature of Necessity* (1974). An excellent collection of papers on the epistemology of modality is Tamar Gendler and John Hawthorne's *Conceivability and Possibility* (2002).

13 Scorecard

13.1 Taking stock

Now that we have finished our glimpse into applications of a priori reasoning, it is useful to look back and think about which theories of a priori belief are best combined with which fields of enquiry. Clearly, one of the big winners of this investigation is the use of coherence methods. We use such methods to reason about every one of the fields that we have discussed. In what follows, we look at the other theories of a priori belief and summarize their successes and failures.

13.2 Rationalism

Rationalism is the doctrine that rational insight can give us true beliefs about the world. In its analytic and Aristotelian forms we deal with it under "analytic justification" and "Aristotelianism". Rationalism has coherentist, foundationalist and reliabilist forms.

- *Ethics*: It seems implausible that we have rational insight about moral truths that are not analytic. There is a serious danger of dogmatism with this view.
- *Logic*: Rationalism seems to be of little help since rational insight requires, perhaps among other reasoning abilities, logical abilities.
- *Mathematics*: linked historically with Platonism. A foundationalist rationalist might accept some mathematical beliefs as basic.

- *Modality*: Given an argument for the existence and diversity of possible worlds, it seems reasonable to accept what rational insight tells us about the contents of other worlds.

13.3 Nativism

Nativism is the doctrine that we have innate ideas, beliefs or abilities. On the surface, it looks like a thesis of psychology or cognitive science rather than an epistemological view. But combined with an argument that, say, these innate beliefs are reliable, it can be used in a theory of a priori justification.

- *Ethics*: Although it may be true that we have some innate ethical beliefs, nativism about morality does not seem to be much use in helping us justify our moral beliefs.
- *Logic*: Some degree of nativism about logic seems to be unavoidable. Evolutionary arguments and fairly circular justifications of our innate logical principles seem available and promising.
- *Mathematics*: We may have some innate mathematical beliefs. This might explain how we can grasp certain infinite sequences given a finite amount of evidence.
- *Modality*: It is not clear how nativism can help with regard to modal epistemology.

13.4 Analytic justification

The analytic–synthetic distinction is a distinction about how certain sentences are made true or false. It does, however, give rise to a sort of justification that appeals to the meanings of the words or phrases in a sentence to justify its truth.

- *Ethics*: Jackson's treatment of moral terms as defined within "mature folk morality" seems reasonable. It promises us access to moral principles through analytic justification.
- *Logic*: Analytic justification is the only available form of justification for most principles of logic. This form of justification is circular, but does not seem to be viciously so.
- *Mathematics*: Mathematical axioms, if correct, are perhaps

also analytic. But it seems that analytic justifications are not available for many mathematical axioms.

- *Modality*: Analytic justification is useful in telling us about certain necessary truths, such as logical truths.

13.5 Radical empiricism

Radical empiricism is the doctrine that there are no a priori truths. Admittedly, it is the "enemy" in this book. Perhaps I have not been fair to it. It is a good essay topic for a student to defend radical empiricism against one or more of my sneers against it.

- *Ethics*: Radical empiricists have to buy into relativism, non-cognitivism or error theory. If you can live with those choices, then perhaps a radical empiricist moral epistemology is for you.
- *Logic*: Radical empiricism treats logic as a set of general truths about the actual world. Standard notions of validity and logical truth are lost.
- *Mathematics*: It is difficult to see how a radical empiricist philosophy of mathematics really works.
- *Modality*: Radical empiricists typically reject the idea that there is anything like metaphysical necessity.

13.6 Kantianism

Kant's view is that thought has a fairly rigid structure, and this structure gives rise to a priori beliefs about science, mathematics and logic. We can know about the world a priori because the world that we know about is a construction of our minds. The structure of cognition is also the structure of the world. More recent versions of Kantianism remove this rigidity and adopt a form of relativism instead. These still claim that the world is a construct, but there are no innate rules about how to construct the world.

- *Ethics*: Perhaps Kantianism gives us a way of getting objective moral principles without assuming non-natural moral facts. If this can be made to work without appeal to Kant's theoretical philosophy, then this may be the way to go.

- *Logic*: Kant's own view seems implausible. Perhaps the only way to save it is to adopt some form of relativism about logic.
- *Mathematics*: Kant's view is extremely rigid. Once again, the only Kantian alternative seems to be relativism.
- *Modality*: It seems that the only Kantian choices are to hold that possibility is determined by what we can experience or to hold the relativistic view that what is possible is determined by the theories we adopt.

13.7 Aristotelianism

Aristotelianism is the view that we abstract concepts from experience and then reflect on them to produce beliefs. This reflection is a form of a priori justification.

- *Ethics*: Aristotelianism is probably not much use here. Aristotelianism seems committed to non-naturalism.
- *Logic*: Aristotelianism is some use in explaining our deductive reasoning about time and space, and perhaps other structures.
- *Mathematics*: Aristotelianism comes into its own here: an epistemology for a structuralist philosophy of mathematics.
- *Modality*: Thinking about which empirical concepts can be combined together (and so describe some possible world) seems to be a form of Aristotelian justification. And it seems to be what we often do in determining what is possible.

■ Notes

1. Introduction

1. I follow the tradition in thinking that belief is an element of knowledge: that when we know something we also believe it. Timothy Williamson (2000) has criticized this view and claimed that knowledge is a more basic notion than belief. It would be interesting to discuss whether the view that knowledge does not involve belief has any consequences for the topic of a priori knowledge, but it is not a topic that I discuss in this book.

2. Of course, one could have an empirical belief that this sentence is true. One could believe that all people called bachelors are unmarried on the basis of an empirical induction.

3. To see why certain innate beliefs might be considered to be justified, see Chapter 4.

4. Although, as Max Cresswell (2010) argues, it would seem that facts that include abstract objects can play causal roles. For example, the fact that the average height of New Zealand men is 69.7 inches has caused clothing shops in that country to carry many pairs of trousers with a long inseam. It seems that the number 69.7, which is supposed to be an abstract object (see Ch. 11), is also supposed to play a role in causing shops to stock long trousers.

5. We shall look at a "holistic" argument like this against the existence of a priori beliefs in Chapter 6.

6. David Brink (1989) adopts this line.

7. Two that we shall mention again in Chapter 10 are Peter Lipton and David Papineau.

8. Note that Field does not think that we have to be certain that a given belief is empirically indefeasible. Field is a fallibilist: there may always be an epistemic possibility that our beliefs can be empirically refuted. This means that as far as we know there may be possible empirical evidence that can undermine our beliefs (Field 1998). See Chapter 2.

9. At various points in this book, I represent justifications in terms of arguments. I do not claim that all forms of justification (especially reliabilist justification) should be represented in this way, but many can be and it can be illuminating to do so.

10. Here I am equating the rejection of p with the acceptance of not-p. This is a view I have explicitly argued against in Mares (2000, 2002, 2004). The equation of the denial of a proposition with the acceptance of its negation presupposes the

use of classical negation (see Chapter 10). I reject classical logic and classical negation, and so I also must distinguish between denial and the acceptance of a negation. Making this distinction also makes the representation of these arguments much more complicated. This complication, moreover, does not really add to our understanding of the epistemological point involved here, which, after all, is our main concern in this book.

11. See Casullo (2003: ch. 2) for a lengthy criticism of this hybrid conception.

2. Necessity and certainty

1. This is an extremely interesting topic and I would love to have something to say about it. Unfortunately, I do not.
2. "Tui" is a Maori word. It is a name for a bird, but it is also used as a proper name for people.
3. The theory of infinitesimals is known to be consistent relative to a modern mathematical theory, Zermelo–Fraenkel set theory (see Chapter 11). This was shown by Abraham Robinson in the 1960s. Newton's use of the theory of infinitesimals, however, was inconsistent in a sense. He would make calculations using infinitesimals in crucial ways – acting as though they had tiny but positive length – but then at the end of a proof he would remove them if they showed up in the result, acting as though they had no length at all. Newton was taken to task for doing this by, among others, the idealist philosopher George Berkeley.
4. This is not contextualism in the sense that philosophers of language use the word. That notion was covered in §2.4 in the discussion of two-dimensionalism.

3. Rationalism and self-evidence

1. Perhaps not *so* clearly. As all commentators point out, few, if any, of these derivations actually work. If Spinoza knows this, then he may have another epistemology at work behind the façade of foundationalism.
2. This criticism is in Hegel ([1830] 1975: ch. III).
3. See Casullo (2003: 105) for a similar distinction.
4. Descartes' works are included in the *Oeuvres de Descartes* (Descartes 1964–76), cited hereafter as AT, and *The Philosophical Writings of Descartes* (Descartes 1984).
5. Descartes is usually taken to be the paradigm foundationalist. I think that is his line in the *Meditations*, but I am not sure this was his view in his earlier *Discourse*.
6. To be fair to BonJour, he puts forward the empirical defeasibility claim very tentatively (see BonJour 1998: §4.6).
7. For example, the belief that any predicate of a mathematical language determines a set of objects (the objects that it is true of) seems obvious. But this leads to a contradiction, as Bertrand Russell showed.
8. BonJour's view is a form of Aristotelianism (see Chapter 8). According to BonJour, we abstract properties such as the colours from experience, and then in reflecting on them come to realize various facts about them, such as that they cannot be made to overlap.
9. With regard to Audi's view, I am treating the process of finding a proposition to be self-evident as a form of rational insight. Audi, as far as I know, does not use the term "rational insight".
10. Audi puts forward these two conditions only to give a rough characterization of self-evidence, but I think they can be developed into quite a useful conception.

11. We also use what logicians call the "deduction theorem", which says that if "*A*, therefore *B*" is a valid inference then the proposition "if *A*, then *B*" is a law of logic.
12. Note that I am using "see" here in a fairly weak sense. Just because we see that something is true does not mean that it is. BonJour thinks that we can be wrong about propositions we think are self-evident.
13. For an overview of theories of concepts, see Margolis and Laurence (2011).
14. Not everyone believes that Descartes' cogito argument is a deductive inference. Famously, Jaakko Hintikka (1962) holds that it is another form of argument.
15. It is somewhat harder to see that this view is compatible with Descartes' position, though. He thinks that if one follows a particular method in using rational insight, one will reach the truth. There does not seem to be any possibility of error in the use of this method, except perhaps in our use of memory.

4. Nativism

1. A good secondary source on Locke's criticism of nativism is Atherton (1998).
2. This belief is not one that tiny babies have, but one that they develop at a certain stage of development. Thus, we are not using "innate" here as indicating of a belief that we have it from birth but rather that it is not learned.
3. See Pullum & Scholz (2002) for a survey of criticisms of poverty of stimulus arguments.

5. Analyticity

1. Quine presents many arguments against the analytic–synthetic distinction, but unfortunately considerations of space have prevented me from discussing all of them. In particular, Quine uses his famous argument for the indeterminacy of translation to attack analyticity in his *Word and Object* (1980c). Although this is an interesting argument, it would take a great deal of space to deal with it properly, so I have omitted it.
2. This section and the next two owe a great deal to Russell (2008).
3. This argument is an adaptation of an argument in Lycan (1994: 204–5).
4. Zermela is not a trifactored sable merle. She is a tricolour.
5. This problem becomes even more interesting if we also adopt logical pluralism (see Chapter 10). According to logical pluralism, no one logical system is correct. Then there is no fact of the matter about whether this sentence is analytic. On the version of logical pluralism that is currently being developed by Stewart Shapiro, whether one logical system is correct depends on the context we are in. Then we could say that, on his view, a sentence might be analytic in one context but not in another.
6. My dog Lola is a chewerrier.
7. Except some common logical notions. On the impossibility of stating all the rules of reasoning, see Chapter 10.
8. Apparently, C. I. Lewis allows imagination to play exactly this role in analytic justifications. On this point in Lewis, Sandra Rosenthal says: "It is true that we must get behind the words red and green to understand the proposition ['nothing that is red all over can be green all over'] at all. And it is further true that the meaning of red does not include the meaning of green. Yet, an 'experiment in imagination' is sufficient to reveal that the absence of green is essential to apply the expression 'red all over'" (Rosenthal 2007: 38–9).

6. Radical empiricism

1. I shall discuss Harman's metaethical views in Chapter 9.
2. This criticism of the inductive view is due to Field (1998: 12–13).
3. I take this from Wilson (2007).
4. There are problems with Mill's position even if we weaken it in this way. Mill claims that we cannot know whether anything is necessary, even the law of non-contradiction. But he also claims that we *must* use induction. It seems that, on his own view, he cannot know that we must do anything. This seems to be a serious tension. But it might be that Mill holds that we can know what is nomically necessary (that is, necessary by virtue of laws of nature) but not metaphysically necessary (see Chapter 2). It may be that we are nomically forced to use induction and that this is all we need to use the "might implies ought" principle.
5. Peirce argues for his view of reasoning in "The Fixation of Belief " and "How to Make our Ideas Clear" (in Peirce 1958). These arguments attempt to show that the scientific method is the only reliable means for settling our doubts in a way that will satisfy us. The argument is empirical, although not rigorously so.
6. As far as I know, Quine does not use this term, but it is standard in the literature on belief revision.
7. In Quine's later work, especially in his and Joseph Ullian's *Web of Belief* (1978), Quine's view comes very close to Harman's. Quine talks of the use of theoretical virtues, such as simplicity, to judge which way to revise our beliefs.
8. This might sound like a radical conclusion, but it is rather common for epistemologies to hold that there are certain propositions that it is incoherent to reject. For example, Bayesian theory holds that we must accept any proposition that always gets the probability 1. This includes all the logical laws.
9. If the renormalization theory is inconsistent, then according to classical logic it entails every proposition. Thus it predicts that every proposition is true. I do not believe that this is right and it is one of the reasons why I adopt relevant logic over classical logic. See Mares (2004).
10. This is essentially an argument that Michael Friedman puts forward against Quine. See Friedman (2001).
11. Although not in those words. He talks about science sometimes, instead, as a "language game" (1990: 21).
12. For Quine, it is not important (or possible) to justify all our beliefs. We begin with a belief system and then modify it as we accumulate new information. It is never the case that all the beliefs in the system are justified. In this sense, Quine's epistemology is very different from that of coherentists, who claim that there should be relations of mutual justification connecting all of our beliefs to other beliefs.
13. In some of these theories, the norms support the belief in the validity of certain logical rules rather than logical truths. For the difference, see Chapter 10. This difference is not really important here.

7. Kantianism

1. References to the *Critique of Pure Reason* are of the form of a number prefixed A or B. These letters indicate page numbers in the first or second edition of the *Critique* as they appear in the Prussian Academy edition of his works. So, for example, "A182/B224" refers to page 182 of the first edition and page 224 of the second. These page numbers appear in the margins of every translation of the *Critique*.

2. The way things appear in space is a construct, but Kant thinks the things that appear are not constructs. These are given to us in sensation. Thus, there is a sense in which we are not inventing what we perceive.
3. Kant often uses the term "objective knowledge" to make this point.
4. This argument is quite famous and is due to C. I. Lewis ([1929] 1956: 221).
5. It has the *feel* of Moore's paradoxical assertion "It is raining, but I don't believe it", but it is not quite a pragmatic contradiction either.

8. Aristotelianism

1. This interpretation of Locke is heavily influenced by Peter Alexander (1985).
2. She calls herself a "conceptualist". This is a reasonable title, but all the forms of a priori justification that we discuss in this book use concepts in an important way. Moreover, other philosophers use "conceptualist" in other ways (see e.g. Kitcher 1985). So we do not use this label.
3. One might object that the dependence of Aristotelian justification on the reliability of an empirical learning process makes this form of justification empirical. Once again I point to a parallel with analytic justification. One's intuition that one understands a sentence (especially one said by someone else) on the basis of one's understanding of the words involved can be justified on the basis that one's learning of language was reliable. That too was an empirical process. Once again, I claim that the empirical process enables justification to take place, but is not part of that justification.
4. Interestingly, Kitcher can be classified as an Aristotelian, even though he denies the existence of a priori justification. He holds that mathematicians idealize from their experiences of collecting together objects to form the concept of a set. On his view, mathematicians in effect think about an ideal mathematician, one who can, for example, collect together infinitely many objects. This sounds like a form of Aristotelianism rather than a radical empiricism.
5. See also the discussion of Goodman's "grue paradox" in Chapter 4.

9. Moral knowledge

1. One philosopher who thinks that this method is "dubious" is Peter Singer (see Singer 2005).
2. Ayer is not a radical empiricist overall. He merely takes a radical-empiricist line on moral knowledge.
3. As my colleague Nick Agar pointed out to me, the claim that moral principles help us to survive is ambiguous. Overall, the adoption of moral principles has helped humanity and individual human societies to survive. It has even helped some individual people to survive. But there are cases in which adopting moral principles has had the opposite effect. For example, one might sacrifice one's life for others because of a moral belief. Despite this sort of example, it seems that overall there are good evolutionary arguments for the adoption of moral principles.
4. Mackie (1977), Ruse and Joyce (2001, 2006) argue that our moral beliefs are a product of natural selection, but none of them commit themselves to nativism about moral principles. There are other methods of transmission that can be used in theories based on natural selection. For example, moral beliefs may be transmitted from people in a society to others in that society (e.g. from parents to children). This is called "cultural transmission".

5. Some might claim that this is a principle of political theory, not moral theory. Rawls (1985) claims that it is both. Unfortunately, Rawls is very keen to avoid commitments to any metaphysical or epistemological theories, so he does not claim that the principle is analytic.

6. Boyd claims that "good" acts like a natural-kind term (see Chapter 2). His evidence for this may be empirical (e.g. studies of how people use "good"). We can reconstruct his argument as follows. Let the cluster of properties that "good" refers to in this world be C. And let C refer to this cluster in every possible world. Because "good" is a natural-kind term (or is natural-kind-like) it refers to the same thing in every possible world. Therefore, "an action is good if and only if it has C" is necessarily true. The last premise is a priori.

7. For an explanation of what an implicit definition is, see Chapter 4.

8. Huemer believes that this is a necessary cost of accepting moral realism; Mackie thinks that this cost is too high. There are other moral rationalists who do not hold views as extreme as those of Huemer. Robert Audi thinks that some moral truths are self-evident in the sense of Chapter 3. His view is, in my opinion, very close to the thesis that some important moral truths are analytic.

9. Frank Jackson claims this as well, but we did not examine that aspect of his view.

10. This is a very Kantian view. In the *Prolegomena*, Kant characterizes experience as something we can relate to others. Korsgaard's view of reasons appears to be the moral counterpart of that.

10. Logical knowledge

1. Foundationalism's view of circular arguments of this sort is rather complicated. It does not accept the use of a belief to justify itself, but the use of a rule to justify the belief in that rule is not obviously banned. But foundationalists tend to be nervous about circularity of any sort.

2. This point comes from Dummett (1991) and Boghossian (1996). They both (tentatively) advocate circular justifications as justifications to oneself for the rules or laws that one adopts, but they both claim that such circular justifications are useless in debate.

3. Not all philosophers agree with Prior's conclusions. Michael Dummett has argued that the relationship between the tonk introduction and elimination rules is the problem: they are "out of harmony" with one another and with the rest of the logic. Dummett's views on harmony and logic are in Dummett (1991).

4. There are logical systems with infinitely many axioms. One such is something called full second-order logic and is used a lot in the philosophy of mathematics. This topic is too technical to go into here, but the interested reader can consult Shapiro (1991).

5. Quine puts it very nicely this way: "In a word, the difficulty is that if logic is to proceed *mediately* [that is, inferentially] from conventions, logic is needed for inferring logic from the conventions" ([1936] 1976b: 105). And, he says, logic, considered as a convention, "is incapable of being communicated until after its adoption" (*ibid.*: 106).

6. This is oversimplifying. We usually show that the truths in a "possible world" of this form correspond to the truth conditions for the operators. Also, if we are dealing with non-classical logics, then the construction we describe may be modified slightly.

7. The philosopher G. E. Moore gives this as an example of a logical law.

8. Lycan's argument is based largely on McGee (1985).

9. I have argued against Lycan's and McGee's arguments in Mares (2004).
10. Kripke has developed the three-valued approach into a rigorous theory of truth.
11. One Kantian with regard to logic is the American idealist philosopher Josiah Royce. He says that in doing the philosophy of logic we ask: *"What are the necessary 'logical entities,' and what are their necessary laws? What objects must the logician's world contain? What order-systems must he conceive, not as contingent or arbitrary, but as so implied in the nature of our rational activity that the effort to remove them from our world would inevitably imply their reinstatement,* just as the effort to remove relations and classes from the world would involve recognizing both relations and classes as, in some new way, present" (Royce 1961: 67).

11. Mathematical knowledge
1. I am grateful to Alasdair Urquhart for convincing me of this point and for discussing with me at some length. But see Wright (1983) for an excellent defence.
2. One might think that we can just add G as an axiom. But then another "Gödel sentence", G^*, can be formulated such that neither G^* nor not-G^* can be proved. And so on.
3. John Bigelow (1988) is a structuralist but is undecided whether he is an Aristotelian or a nativist.
4. This is the lower Dedekind cut. The upper cut is the set of rational numbers whose square is greater than or equal to 2.
5. It should be called the Russell–Zermelo paradox because Zermelo derived it at about the same time.
6. In fact, Kitcher wants us to postulate that the perfect mathematician can collect together transfinitely many objects, for any transfinite number. The transfinite numbers are different sizes of infinity. They get very large indeed.
7. Kitcher thinks that statements about the fictional mathematician are not, strictly speaking, true. Thus, in a sense, most of what we think of as mathematical knowledge is not knowledge at all. What he should say is that these statements are about a fiction; what he does say is that they are false (see Kitcher 1985).

12. Modality
1. This is Quine's example. There are now hand-powered bicycles for people who cannot use a foot-powered bicycle. I leave it to the imaginative reader to think up an alternative example.
2. In one of Quine's discussions of quantified modal logic, he says that Necessarily $(x = x)$ must be satisfied by everything but Necessarily $(p \ \& \ x = x)$ must not be satisfied by anything where p is a contingent truth (Quine 1980c: 155).
3. For a survey, see Melia (2003).
4. M. J. Cresswell (2006) argues that even if we adopt modalism, we can think of it as giving us a theory of possible worlds. So it might be that modalism is not really an alternative to possible-worlds semantics.
5. Carnap's response is to claim that the statement "if someone is married, then they are not single" is a *meaning postulate*. A meaning postulate is supposed to be analytic. Quine's response to this is to say that the theory of possible worlds is supposed to explain what analyticity is. As we saw in Chapter 5, we do need possible worlds to define analyticity in the metaphysical sense. Carnap's meaning postulates, however, are analytic in the stipulational sense. Whether this saves Carnap's view, I leave to the reader to decide.

6. To be more exact, for Lewis there is another possible world with a dog just like Zermela in it and a kitchen with a person just like Sue in it.

Bibliography

Aaron, R. I. 1971. *John Locke*. Oxford: Oxford University Press.

Alexander, P. 1985. *Ideas, Qualities, and Corpuscles: Locke and Boyle on the External World*. Cambridge: Cambridge University Press.

Allison, H. E. 1983. *Kant's Transcendental Idealism: An Interpretation and Defense*. New Haven, CT: Yale University Press.

Atherton, M. 1998. "Locke and the Issue over Innateness". In *Locke*, V. Chappell (ed.), 48–59. Oxford: Oxford University Press.

Audi, R. 1986. *Belief, Justification, and Knowledge*. Belmont, CA: Wadsworth.

Audi, R. 1996. "Intuitionism, Pluralism, and the Foundation of Ethics". In *Moral Knowledge? New Readings*, W. Sinnott-Armstrong & M. Timmons (eds), 101–36. Oxford: Oxford University Press.

Bigelow, J. 1988. *The Reality of Numbers: A Physicalist's Philosophy of Mathematics*. Oxford: Oxford University Press.

Boghossian, P. 1996. "Analyticity Regained". *Noûs* 30: 360–91.

Boghossian, P. 1997. "What the Externalist Can Know A Priori". *Proceedings of the Aristotelian Society* 97: 161–75.

Boghossian, P. 2000. "Knowledge of Logic". In *New Essays on the A Priori*, P. Boghossian & C. Peacocke (eds), 229–54. Oxford: Oxford University Press.

BonJour, L. 1998. *In Defense of Pure Reason: A Rationalist Account of A Priori Justification*. Cambridge: Cambridge University Press.

BonJour, L. 2002. *Epistemology: Classic Problems and Contemporary Responses*. Lanham, MD: Rowman & Littlefield.

BonJour, L. & E. Sosa 2003. *Epistemic Justification: Internalism vs. Externalism, Foundations vs. Virtues*. Oxford: Blackwell.

Boyd, R. 1988. "How to be a Moral Realist". In *Essays on Moral Realism*, G. Sayre-McCord (ed.), 181–228. Ithaca, NY: Cornell University Press.

Bridgman, P. W. 1927. *The Logic of Modern Physics*. Cambridge: Cambridge University Press.

Brink, D. O. 1989. *Moral Realism and the Foundations of Ethics*. Cambridge: Cambridge University Press.

Brock, S. & E. Mares 2007. *Realism and Anti-Realism*. Stocksfield: Acumen.

Brown, J. R. 1991. *The Laboratory of the Mind: Thought Experiments in the Natural Sciences*. London: Routledge.

Brown, J. R. 2010. "Thought Experiments". In *Stanford Encyclopedia of Philosophy*,

E. Zalta (ed.). http://plato.stanford.edu/entries/thought-experiment/ (accessed July 2011).

Carnap. R. 1937. *Logical Syntax of Language*, A. Smeaton (trans.). London: Kegan Paul, Trench Trubner.

Carnap, R. 1947. *Meaning and Necessity: A Study in Semantics and Modal Logic*. Chicago, IL: University of Chicago Press.

Carnap, R. [1952] 1990. "Quine on Analyticity". In *Dear Carnap, Dear Van: The Quine–Carnap Correspondence and Related Work*, 427–32. Berkeley, CA: University of California Press.

Carnap, R. & W. V. Quine 1990. *Dear Carnap, Dear Van: The Quine–Carnap Correspondence and Related Work*. Berkeley, CA: University of California Press.

Carroll, L. 1895. "What the Tortoise Said to Achilles". *Mind* 4: 278–80.

Carruthers, P., S. Laurence & S. Stitch (eds) 2005. *The Innate Mind: Structure and Content*. Oxford: Oxford University Press.

Cartwright, N. 1992. "Aristotelian Natures and the Modern Experimental Method". In *Inference, Explanation, and Other Frustrations: Essays in the Philosophy of Science*, J. Earman (ed.), 44–71. Berkeley, CA: University of California Press.

Cassirer, E. 1923. *Einstein's Theory of Relativity*. Chicago, IL: Open Court.

Casullo, A. 2003. *A Priori Justification*. Oxford: Oxford University Press.

Chalmers, D. 2002. "Does Conceivability Entail Possibility?" In *Conceivability and Possibility*, T. Gendler & J. Hawthorne (eds), 145–200. Oxford: Oxford University Press.

Chappell, V. (ed.) 1998. *Locke*. Oxford: Oxford University Press.

Chase, J. & J. Reynolds 2010. "The Fate of Transcendental Reasoning in Contemporary Philosophy". In *Postanalytic and Metacontinental: Crossing Philosophical Divides*, J. Reynolds, J. Chase, J. Williams & E. Mares (eds), 27–52. London: Continuum.

Cottingham, J. (ed.) 1992. *The Cambridge Companion to Descartes*. Cambridge: Cambridge University Press.

Cowie, F. 1998. *What's Within: Nativism Reconsidered*. New York: Oxford University Press.

Cresswell, M. J. 1985. *Structured Meanings: The Semantics of Propositional Attitudes*. Cambridge, MA: MIT Press.

Cresswell, M. J. 2006. "From Modal Discourse to Possible Worlds". *Studia Logica* 82: 307–27.

Cresswell, M. J. 2010. "Abstract Entities in the Causal Order". *Theoria* 76: 249–65.

Daniels, N. 1996. *Justice and Justification: Reflective Equilibrium in Theory and Practice*. Cambridge: Cambridge University Press.

Descartes, R. 1964–76. *Oeuvres de Descartes*, C. Adam & P. Tannery (eds). Paris: Vrin. [AT]

Descartes, R. 1984. *The Philosophical Writings of Descartes*, J. Cottingham, R. Stoothoff, & D. Murdoch (trans.). Cambridge: Cambridge University Press.

Dummett, M. 1991. *The Logical Basis of Metaphysics*. Cambridge, MA: Harvard University Press.

Etchemendy, J. 1999. *The Concept of Logical Consequence*. Stanford, CA: CSLI Publications.

Evans, J. D. G. 1987. *Aristotle*. New York: St Martin's Press.

Feynman, R. 1967. *The Character of Physical Law*. Cambridge, MA: MIT Press.

Feynman, R. 1990. *QED: The Strange Theory of Light and Matter*. Harmondsworth: Penguin.

Field, H. 1998. "Epistemological Nonfactualism and the A Priority of Logic". *Philosophical Studies* 92: 1–24.

Field, H. 2005. "Recent Debates about the A Priori". In *Oxford Studies in Epistemology*, T. Gendler & J. Hawthorne (eds), 69–88. Oxford: Oxford University Press.

Fodor, J. 2001. "Doing Without What's Within: Fiona Cowie's Critique of Nativism". *Mind* 110: 99–148.

Friedman, M. 1995. *Kant and the Exact Sciences*. Cambridge, MA: Harvard University Press.

Friedman, M. 2001. *Dynamics of Reason*. Stanford, CA: CSLI Publications.

Friend, M. 2007. *The Philosophy of Mathematics*. Stocksfield: Acumen.

Gärdenfors, P. 1988. *Knowledge in Flux: Modeling the Dynamics of Epistemic States*. Cambridge, MA: MIT Press.

Gendler, T. & J. Hawthorne (eds) 2002. *Conceivability and Possibility*. Oxford: Oxford University Press.

Goodman, N. 1983. *Fact, Fiction, and Forecast*, 4th edn. Cambridge, MA: Harvard University Press.

Gould, S. J. & R. C. Lewontin 1979. "The Spandrels of San Marco and the Panglossian Paradigm: A Critique of the Adaptationist Programme". *Proceedings of the Royal Society of London* 205: 581–98.

Hahn, L. E. & P. A. Schilpp (eds) 1986. *The Philosophy of W. V. Quine*. La Salle, IL: Open Court.

Hanna, R. 2006. *Rationality and Logic*. Cambridge, MA: MIT Press.

Harman, G. 1973. *Thought*. Princeton, NJ: Princeton University Press.

Harman, G. 1977. *The Nature of Morality: An Introduction to Ethics*. Oxford: Oxford University Press.

Harman, G. 1986. *Change in View: Principles of Reasoning*. Cambridge, MA: MIT Press.

Harman, G. 1996. "Analyticity Regained?" *Noûs* 30(3): 392–400.

Harman, G. 1999. *Reasoning, Meaning, and Mind*. Oxford: Oxford University Press.

Hegel, G. W. F. [1830] 1975. *Hegel's Logic, Being Part One of the Encyclopedia of the Philosophical Sciences (1830)*, W. Wallace (trans.). Oxford: Oxford University Press.

Hintikka, J. 1962. "Cogito, Ergo Sum: Inference or Performance?" *Philosophical Review* 71: 3–32.

Hudson, W. D. 1967. *Ethical Intuitionism*. London: Macmillan.

Huemer, M. 2006. *Ethical Intuitionism*. London: Palgrave Macmillan.

Huenemann, C. 2008. *Understanding Rationalism*. Stocksfield: Acumen.

Hume, D. [1739–40] 1975. *A Treatise of Human Nature*, 2nd edn, L. A. Selby-Bigge & P. H. Nidditch (eds). Oxford: Clarendon Press.

Hume, D. [1748–51] 1979. *Enquiry Concerning Human Understanding*, 3rd edn, L. A. Selby-Bigge & P. H. Nidditch (eds). Oxford: Clarendon Press.

Husserl, E. [1913] 1982. *Ideas Pertaining to a Pure Phenomenology and to a Phenomenological Philosophy – First Book: General Introduction to a Pure Phenomenology*, F. Kersten (trans.). The Hague: Nijhoff.

Hylton, P. 2007. *Quine*. Abingdon: Routledge.

Illies, C. (ed.) 2003. *The Grounds of Ethical Judgment: New Transcendental Arguments in Moral Philosophy*. Oxford: Oxford University Press.

Jackson, F. 1998. *From Metaphysics to Ethics: A Defence of Conceptual Analysis*. Oxford: Oxford University Press.

Jenkins, C. 2008. *Grounding Concepts: An Empirical Basis for Arithmetical Knowledge*. Oxford: Oxford University Press.

Jenkins, C. forthcoming. "A Priori Knowledge: The Conceptual Approach". Online draft of paper to appear in *The Continuum Companion to Epistemology*, A.

Cullison (ed.). London: Continuum. http://carriejenkins.co.uk/Documents/APrioriConceptualApproachDraftForComments.pdf (accessed August 2011).

Joyce, R. 2001. *The Myth of Morality*. Cambridge: Cambridge University Press.

Joyce, R. 2006. *On the Evolution of Morality*. Cambridge, MA: MIT Press.

Kant, I. [1781/1788] 1929. *Critique of Practical Reason*, N. Kemp Smith (trans.). New York: St Martin's Press.

Kant, I. [1785] 1964. *Groundwork of the Metaphysic of Morals*, H. J. Paton (trans.). New York: Harper & Row.

Kant, I. [1781/87] 1965. *Critique of Pure Reason*, N. Kemp Smith (trans.). New York: St Martin's Press.

Kant, I. [1783] 1977. *Prolegomena to Any Future Metaphysics*, P. Carus & J. W. Ellington (trans.). Indianapolis, IN: Hackett.

Kaplan, D. 1989. "Demonstratives". In *Themes from Kaplan*, J. Almog, J. Perry & H. Wettstein (eds), 481–564. Oxford: Oxford University Press.

Kitcher, P. 1985. *The Nature of Mathematical Knowledge*. Oxford: Oxford University Press.

Korsgaard, C. M. 1998. *The Sources of Normativity*. Cambridge: Cambridge University Press.

Kripke, S. 1980. *Naming and Necessity*. Oxford: Blackwell.

Lakatos, I. 1978. *The Methodology of Scientific Research Programmes: Philosophical Papers Volume 1*. Cambridge: Cambridge University Press.

Leibniz, G. W. 1981. *New Essays on the Understanding*, P. Remnant & J. Bennett (trans.). Cambridge: Cambridge University Press.

Lewis, C. I. [1929] 1956. *Mind and the World Order*. New York: Dover.

Lewis, C. I. 1946. *An Analysis of Knowledge and Valuation*. La Salle, IL: Open Court.

Lewis, D. 1986. *On the Plurality of Worlds*. Oxford: Blackwell.

Lipton, P. 2004. *Inference to the Best Explanation*, 2nd edn. London: Routledge.

Locke, J. [1690] 1959. *An Essay Concerning Human Understanding*. New York: Dover.

Loeb, L. E. 1992. "The Cartesian Circle". In *The Cambridge Companion to Descartes*, J. Cottingham (ed.), 200–235. Cambridge: Cambridge University Press.

Lycan, W. G. 1993. "MPP RIP". *Philosophical Perspectives* 7: 411–28.

Lycan, W. G. 1994. *Modality and Meaning*. Dordrecht: Kluwer.

Mackie, J. L. 1977. *Ethics: Inventing Right and Wrong*. Harmondsworth: Pelican.

Maddy, P. 1997. *Naturalism in Mathematics*. Oxford: Oxford University Press.

Maddy, P. 2007. *Second Philosophy: A Naturalistic Method*. Oxford: Oxford University Press.

Mares, E. D. 2000. "Even Dialetheists Should Hate Contradictions". *Australasian Journal of Philosophy* 78: 503–16.

Mares, E. D. 2002. "A Paraconsistent Theory of Belief Revision". *Erkenntnis* 56: 228–46.

Mares, E. D. 2004. *Relevant Logic: A Philosophical Interpretation*. Cambridge: Cambridge University Press.

Margolis, E. & S. Laurence 2011. "Concepts". In *Stanford Encyclopedia of Philosophy*, E. Zalta (ed.). http://plato.stanford.edu/entries/concepts/ (accessed July 2011).

Markie, P. 1992. "The Cogito and its Importance". In *The Cambridge Companion to Descartes*, J. Cottingham (ed.), 140–73. Cambridge: Cambridge University Press.

McGee, V. 1985. "A Counterexample to Modus Ponens". *Journal of Philosophy* 82: 462–71.

McNamara, J. 1986. *A Border Dispute: The Place of Logic in Psychology*. Cambridge, MA: MIT Press.

Timmons, M. 1999. *Morality without Foundations: A Defense of Ethical Contextualism*. Oxford: Oxford University Press.

Urmson, J. O. 1950. "On Grading". *Mind* 59: 145–69.

Welbourne, M. 2001. *Knowledge*. Chesham: Acumen.

White, R. 2005. "Epistemic Permissiveness". *Philosophical Perspectives* 19: 445–59.

Williams, B. 1978. *Descartes: The Project of Pure Enquiry*. Harmondsworth: Penguin.

Williamson, T. 2000. *Knowledge and its Limits*. Oxford: Oxford University Press.

Williamson, T. 2005. "Metaphysical Modality and Counterfactual Thinking". *Proceedings of the Aristotelian Society* 105: 1–23.

Williamson, T. 2007. *The Philosophy of Philosophy*. Oxford: Blackwell.

Wilson, F. 2007. "John Stuart Mill". In *Stanford Encyclopedia of Philosophy*, E. Zalta (ed.). http://plato.stanford.edu/entries/mill/ (accessed July 2011).

Wright, C. 1983. *Frege's Conception of Numbers as Objects*. Aberdeen: Aberdeen University Press.

Melia, J. 2003. *Modality*. Stocksfield: Acumen.

Meyer, R. G. 2006. *Understanding Empiricism*. Chesham: Acumen.

Mill, J. S. [1843] 1974. *A System of Logic, Ratiocinative and Inductive*. In *The Collected Works of John Stuart Mill*, volumes VII and VIII. Toronto: University of Toronto Press.

Mill, J. S. [1861] 1969. *Utilitarianism*. In *Collected Works of John Stuart Mill*, volume X, 203–60. Toronto: University of Toronto Press.

Moore, G. E. 1903. *Principia Ethica*. Cambridge: Cambridge University Press.

Moravcsik, J. 1978. "Learning as Recollection". In *Plato I: Metaphysics and Epistemology*, G. Vlastos (ed.), 53–69. Notre Dame, IN: University of Notre Dame Press.

Newman, L. 2010. "Descartes' Epistemology". In *Stanford Encyclopedia of Philosophy*, E. Zalta (ed.). http://plato.stanford.edu/entries/descartes-epistemology/ (accessed July 2011).

Nichols, S. 2005. "Innateness and Moral Psychology". In *The Innate Mind: Structure and Content*, P. Carruthers, S. Laurence & S. Stitch (eds), 353–69. Oxford: Oxford University Press.

Norton, J. 2004. "Why Thought Experiments Do Not Transcend Empiricism". In *Contemporary Debates in the Philosophy of Science*, C. Hitchcock (ed.), 44–66. Oxford: Blackwell.

Norton, D. & J. Taylor (eds) 1993. *The Cambridge Companion to Hume*. Cambridge: Cambridge University Press.

O'Neill, O, 1975. *Acting on Principle*. New York: Columbia University Press.

O'Neill, O. 1989. *Constructions of Reason*. Cambridge: Cambridge University Press.

Papineau, D. 1993. *Philosophical Naturalism*. Oxford: Blackwell.

Patton, H. J. 1948. *The Categorical Imperative*. Chicago, IL: University of Chicago Press.

Peirce, C. S. 1958. *Selected Writings: Values in a Universe of Chance*, P. P. Wiener (ed.). New York: Dover.

Piattelli-Palmarini, M. (ed.) 1980. *Language and Learning: The Debate Between Jean Piaget and Noam Chomsky*. Cambridge, MA: Harvard University Press.

Pigden, C. (ed.) 2010. *Hume on Is and Ought*. London: Palgrave Macmillan.

Pinker, S. 1994. *The Language Instinct: How the Mind Creates Language*. New York: Harper.

Plantinga, A. 1974. *The Nature of Necessity*. Oxford: Oxford University Press.

Priest, G. 2001. *An Introduction to Non-Classical Logic: From If to Is*. Cambridge: Cambridge University Press.

Priest, G. 2003. *Beyond the Limits of Thought*, 2nd edn. Oxford: Oxford University Press.

Priest, G. 2005. *Doubt Truth to be a Liar*. Oxford: Oxford University Press.

Priest, G. 2006. *In Contradiction*. Oxford: Oxford University Press.

Prior, A. 1960. "The Runabout Inference-Ticket". *Analysis* 21: 38–9.

Pullum, G. K. & B. C. Scholz 2002. "Empirical Assessment of Poverty of Stimulus Arguments". *Linguistics Review* 19: 9–50.

Putnam, H. 1979. "Philosophy of Physics". In *Philosophical Papers, Volume 1: Mathematics, Matter, and Method*, 2nd edn, 79–92. Cambridge: Cambridge University Press.

Quine, W. V. 1969. "Epistemology Naturalized". In *Ontological Relativity and Other Essays*, 69–90. New York: Columbia University Press.

Quine, W. V. 1976a. *Ways of Paradox and Other Essays*. Cambridge, MA: Harvard University Press.

Quine, W. V. [1936] 1976b. "Truth by Convention". In *Ways of Paradox and Other Essays*, 77–106. Cambridge, MA: Harvard University Press.

Quine, W. V. [1953] 1976c. "Three Grades of Modal Involvement". In *Ways of Paradox and Other Essays*, 158–76. Cambridge, MA: Harvard University Press.

Quine, W. V. 1980a. *From a Logical Point of View*. Cambridge, MA: Harvard University Press.

Quine, W. V. [1951] 1980b. "Two Dogmas of Empiricism". In *From a Logical Point of View*, 20–46. Cambridge, MA: Harvard University Press.

Quine, W. V. 1980c. *Word and Object*. Cambridge, MA: MIT Press.

Quine, W. V. 1981. *Theories and Things*. Cambridge, MA: Harvard University Press.

Quine, W. V. 1990. *Pursuit of Truth*. Cambridge, MA: Harvard University Press.

Quine, W. V. & J. S. Ullian 1978. *The Web of Belief*. New York: McGraw-Hill.

Rawls, J. 1985. "Justice as Fairness: Political, Not Metaphysical". *Philosophy and Public Affairs* 14: 223–51.

Resnik, M. 1985. "Logic: Normative or Descriptive? The Ethics of Belief or a Branch of Psychology?" *Philosophy of Science* 52: 221–38.

Rey, G. 1998. "A Naturalistic A Priori". *Philosophical Studies* 92: 25–43.

Rips, L. J. 1994. *The Psychology of Proof*. Cambridge, MA: MIT Press.

Rosen, G. 1990. "Modal Fictionalism". *Mind* 99: 327–54.

Rosenthal, S. B. 2007. *C. I. Lewis in Focus: The Pulse of Pragmatism*. Bloomington, IN: Indiana University Press.

Ross, W. D. 1930. *The Right and the Good*. Oxford: Oxford University Press.

Routley, R. 1973. "Is There a Need For a New, an Environmental Ethic?" *Proceedings of the 15th World congress of Philosophy*, vol. 1, 205–10.

Royce, J. 1961. *Principles of Logic*. New York: Philosophical Library.

Russell, B. [1912] 1959. *The Problems of Philosophy*. Oxford: Oxford University Press.

Russell, B. [1918] 1986. "The Philosophy of Logical Atomism". In *The Collected Papers of Bertrand Russell*, vol. 8, 157–244. London: George Allen & Unwin.

Russell, B. 1919. *Introduction to Mathematical Philosophy*. New York: Simon & Schuster.

Russell, G. 2008. *Truth by Virtue of Meaning*. Oxford: Oxford University Press.

Russell, M. 2006. *Husserl: A Guide for the Perplexed*. London: Continuum.

Searle, J. 1969. *Speech Acts*. Cambridge: Cambridge University Press.

Sedlar, I. 2009. "C. I. Lewis on Possible Worlds". *History and Philosophy of Logic* 30: 283–291.

Shapiro, S. 1991. *Foundations Without Foundationalism: A Case for Second-Order Logic*. Oxford: Oxford University Press.

Sider, T. 2010. *Logic for Philosophy*. New York: Oxford University Press.

Singer, P. 2005. "Ethics and Intuition". *Journal of Ethics* 9: 331–52.

Sinnott-Armstrong, W. & M. Timmons (eds) 1996. *Moral Knowledge? New Readings*. Oxford: Oxford University Press.

Steiner, M. 1975. *Mathematical Knowledge*. Ithaca, NY: Cornell University Press.

Steiner, M. 1998. *The Applicability of Mathematics as a Philosophical Problem*. Cambridge, MA: Harvard University Press.

Stroud, B. 1968. "Transcendental Arguments". *Journal of Philosophy* 65: 241–56.

Stroud, B. 1977. *Hume*. London: Routledge.

Stroud, B. 1984. *The Significance of Philosophical Scepticism*. Oxford: Oxford University Press.

Syverson, P. 2003. *Logic, Convention, and Common Knowledge*. Stanford, CA: CSLI Press.

WITHDRAWN
from
STIRLING UNIVERSITY LIBRARY